The VROOMS of the FOOTHILLS

COWBOYS & HOMESTEADERS

Other titles in the series
The VROOMS of the FOOTHILLS:

Volume 1 Adventures of My Childhood

The VROOMS of the FOOTHILLS

Volume 2

COWBOYS & HOMESTEADERS

Bessie Vroom Ellis

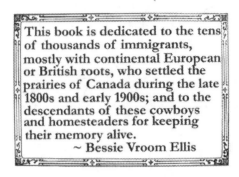

This book is dedicated to the tens of thousands of immigrants, mostly with continental European or British roots, who settled the prairies of Canada during the late 1800s and early 1900s; and to the descendants of these cowboys and homesteaders for keeping their memory alive.
~ Bessie Vroom Ellis

Front cover: Emery LaGrandeur on "Fox", Calgary Stampede, 1919, Glenbow Archives NA-217-50
Title page: Ralph E. Vroom & Alice Velma Truitt, circa 1909, Author's collection
Contents page: Marion Vroom Cyr & children, 1918, courtesy Adeline Cyr Robbins
Back cover: Pete LaGrandeur on "Funeral Wagon", Calgary Stampede, 1924, Glenbow Archives NA-3164-74; Bessie, Belle and Ruby Mitchell, 1906, courtesy Ruby Peters Jaggernath; Marion Vroom Cyr & children, 1918, courtesy Adeline Cyr Robbins
Front and back cover design; editing; photographic restoration and layout: Edi-May Annand Smithies
Map cartography: Shelley McConnell   Map illustrations: Edi-May Annand Smithies

Order this book online at www.trafford.com
or email orders@trafford.com

Most Trafford titles are also available at major online book retailers.

Print information available on the last page.

ISBN: 978-1-4251-8269-4 (sc)

Trafford rev. 05/01/2019

 www.trafford.com

North America & international
toll-free: 1 888 232 4444 (USA & Canada)
fax: 812 355 4082

*1918 Marion Vroom (Mrs. Dominic) Cyr with Adeline, Eugene and Alberta
on their homestead northwest of Twin Butte, AB*

CONTENTS

Acknowledgements		iv
Prologue		1
1	**Old Time Cowboys & Pioneers**	5
2	**Ribbon of Steel**	23
3	**Ralph Vroom: "I Want to be a Cowboy"**	47
4	**Homesteads Become Homes**	65
5	**Ralph Becomes a Cowboy**	87
6	**Klondikers**	105
7	**W.J.A. "Wash" Mitchell: Overland by Covered Wagon**	117
8	**T. B. Tyson: Scion of an Adventurous Family**	135
9	**Mollie Tyson: "I'm Going to Marry a Cowboy"**	151
Epilogue		165
Maps		167
References and Sources of Information		169
Index		171
About the Author		179

Acknowledgements

With the encouragement and co-operation of my children and the descendants of pioneers who settled in the Northwest Territories (NWT) and in Alberta after it became a province in 1905, I have looked at thousands of photographs showing the everyday lives of people of that era. From these, I have selected more than 220 photos for this book. Looking at and thinking about these photos enabled me to create what I hope will be a valuable addition to the fabric of the social history of western Canada.

With great gratitude I acknowledge the gracious help and support of those who assisted me in this work, especially my children, Edi-May Annand Smithies, my main researcher and editor, Evelyn Annand Lailey, David Annand and Jim Annand, and their spouses; my brother, Donald Vroom and his wife, Doreen Lund Vroom, my sister-in-law Moe Swainger Vroom (Mrs. Bill), my sister Marion Vroom Grechman, and my good friend Joe Meade for their ongoing encouragement and support. I especially thank Shelley McConnell, wife of Jim Annand, for helping by using her expertise in map-making, and Shirley Tyson and her friend Dalcy D. (Tootie) Gripich for crucial research findings. Special thanks as well go to Jim Bowman, Archivist, & Lindsay Moir, Senior Librarian, Glenbow Museum, Calgary, for their very capable research assistance, so willingly given.

I also thank people who described family pictures and told related stories to me. They made invaluable contributions to this book, and so to Canadian history. These include Dorothy Archibald, Archives of the Pincher Creek & District Historical Society, Marguerite Link Bennett, Mary Brandes, Alessina Bruce-Brooks, Katherine Bruce, Doris and Larry Bruder, Jean McEwan Burns, City of Surrey (BC) Museum and Archives, Mildred Hole Clark, Alvina Bond Clavel, Hector Cote, Essie McWhirter Cox, Marion Vroom Cyr, Ken and Jessie Gamache, Vera Cyr Gingras, Anna de Geest Gladstone, Frank and Linnea Hagglund Goble, Kevin and Heather Bruce Grace, Edith Jack Hochstein, Jack Holroyd, Ruby Peters Jaggernath, Bud Jenkins, Tom and Frances "Frankie" Jenkins, Alma "Jo" Ballantyne Johnson, Robin LaGrandeur, Robert Lang, Kathleen "Kay" McRae Leigh, Bert Link, Bill Link, May Mann, Elva Ballantyne McClelland, Ina Kokkila McDowall and Mary Lou McDowall, Frances Riviere McWhirter, Frances Dennis McWhirter, His Grace Archbishop Michael O'Neill, Bertie Jenkins Patriquin, Lorraine Riviere Pommier, Elmer Randle, Adeline Cyr Robbins, Ted and Emma Satterthwaite, Bob Thomas, Burns Thomas, Adam and Hazel Anderson Truitt, George Tyson, Ralph and Linda Tyson, Bob and Isabel Vroom, David and Ans Vroom and Peter Vroom, and Farley Wuth, Kootenai Brown Pioneer Village.

Some people, for example, my great-grandmother Sara Ann Woodman Vroom, my grandmother Elizabeth Mary Brotherston Tyson (Mrs. George W.), my mother, Mollie Tyson Vroom (Mrs. Ralph), and my mother's cousin Ruth Tyson Brandes (Mrs. Elmer) of Cedar Falls, Iowa, were prolific letter writers. Their letters, both business and personal, over the years gave valuable insights and information used in this book.

If there are other people I have missed with my thanks, I apologize for the omission. Readers who would like to contact me are invited to do so in care of Trafford Publishing.

PROLOGUE

U sing photos taken in the later 1880s and the 1890s, *Cowboys & Homesteaders*, Volume 2 in a series titled *The VROOMS of the FOOTHILLS*, tells about various elements that affected the settlement and development of southwestern Alberta.

Ralph Vroom

It emphasizes the cowboy aspect of the era I am writing about, starting at roughly 1885, with some people's stories going into the 1930s. Volume 2 is research-based and contains more than 200 pictures from the collections of a number of families other than the Vrooms who settled in the area surrounding Pincher Creek in the late 1800s and early 1900s.

I have always been interested in history, particularly the history of Canada. But I did not realize until I wrote this book how much of Canada's history I have learned first hand. I lived during a good part of the history of the twentieth century, and heard from my parents and various relatives and friends about life in southwestern Alberta during the early years of Canada's nationhood.

In researching material for this book the richness of Canada's history impacted me to the point where I can confidently say that the people who currently live in Canada owe a debt of gratitude to Canada's pioneers for their contributions. These led to the shaping of Canada into a great nation.

In the early part of the 20th century, tens of thousands of people from England, Scotland and Ireland, and from many countries in continental Europe, left comfortable, but ordinary lives, to seek freedom, fortune and adventure in the exciting young country of Canada.

Alluring advertisements in British and European newspapers, and colourful descriptive articles written from Canada to loved ones left behind, made a compelling argument for the choice of coming to Canada.

1

Mollie Tyson Vroom

These advertisements and letters had the desired effect, especially on adventurous young men, particularly those other than the eldest son, in a social system where the eldest son inherited the estate of the parents and the younger sons were left to scramble for themselves. The needs of daughters weren't even considered. They were expected to make a good marriage, obey their husbands, raise a big family, and forget any grandiose schemes about personal freedom that might come into their heads.

Key to the settlement of western Canada was the building of a transcontinental railway across Canada. In fact, after the first all-Canada rail link with the west coast was in operation, the need for another route across the southern prairies and through the Crowsnest Pass in the Rocky Mountains was abundantly clear. As funds for the construction of this railway became available, the laying of the railway tracks across Manitoba, Saskatchewan and Alberta and into British Columbia continued apace.

My interest in history was piqued anew when I realized my great-uncle T. B. Tyson came very early to Canada in 1885, and that my grandfather Oscar Vroom was one of the men who helped to lay this "ribbon of steel", as the Candian Pacific Railway is sometimes called, across the western prairies and through the Rocky Mountains to BC.

Chapter 1, **Old Time Cowboys & Pioneers,** tells how tales of the exploits of the tough and daring young cowboys of the day helped to cast a spell on newcomers in the late 19th and early 20th centuries. The tales influenced most particularly my grandfather, Oscar Vroom, who helped build the Canadian Pacific Railway (CPR) across the southern prairies of western Canada from Medicine Hat, NWT, to Macleod, NWT, and subsequently through the Rockies to Cranbrook, BC.

Oscar made a number of trips back and forth across Canada before settling on Crown land in the Beaver Mines Creek Valley, NWT, in 1902. Initially, in 1886-87, Oscar came west by train on a pre-marital adventure. The end of steel in 1886 was Medicine Hat, NWT.

That summer and over the winter Oscar worked on a track laying crew helping to build the CPR from Medicine Hat to Lethbridge. He took the stagecoach to Macleod and then rode by horseback to investigate homesteading possibilities in the Pincher Creek area. He talked with oldtimers, scouted out the countryside, and chose his dream ranch on Crown land in the Beaver Mines Creek Valley southwest of Pincher Creek. Oscar returned to Nova Scotia in the fall of 1897 to marry Alena Blanche Munro.

Oscar came west a second time in 1897-1898, again to work on track laying crews. The crews were by then building the CPR through the Crowsnest Pass to Cranbrook, BC. In 1902, after a trip to Mexico to visit his brother Herbert, Oscar returned to Alberta and settled on "Sunny Vale Ranche," the land that he chose during his 1886-1887 trip.

Oscar made three more trips from southwestern Alberta to Clementsport, NS, by train. In 1905 his mother-in-law, Elizabeth Munro Dodge, became ill. Oscar went back to Nova Scotia to bring her to live with him, Alena and their family in Alberta. Oscar went back again in 1906 when Elizabeth Munro Dodge died. He and Alena took her body back to Nova Scotia for burial.

Oscar's fifth and final trip to Nova Scotia was for the 50th wedding anniversary of his parents, Wm. Voorhees and Sara Ann Vroom in Clementsport, NS, on January 2, 1909.

Oscar met W. D. McDowall while returning from his 1909 trip, starting a friendship that lasted a lifetime.

During the times he was back in Nova Scotia, Oscar was able to visit with his parents, who both lived long lives. Sara Ann especially welcomed him on his trips home to Nova Scotia. Oscar was her favourite son.

Sara Ann Vroom died in March 1909. Saddened almost beyond endurance by his mother's death, Oscar did not attend her funeral.

Alena Munro Vroom

Chapter 2, **Ribbon of Steel**, tells about my grandfather Vroom's second trip, along with four other young men—three brothers and a brother-in-law—to the Northwest Territories in 1897-98. They were part of the crews laying CPR track from Macleod, NWT, through the Crowsnest Pass in the Rocky Mountains to Cranbrook, BC.

Chapter 3, **Ralph Vroom: "I Want to be a Cowboy"** tells how my dad eagerly awaited moving to their homestead in southwest Alberta so he could fulfil his dream of becoming a cowboy. It also tells how the Vroom family and other homesteader families in the Beaver Mines district adapted and changed over the next 10 years.

Chapter 4, **Homesteads Become Homes**, tells how my paternal grandparents and their neighbours and children adapted to homestead life in southwestern Alberta in the early 1900s.

Chapter 5, **Ralph Becomes a Cowboy**, tells how my dad learned the lore of the West and became almost a legend as a "working cowboy" amongst people who knew him.

Chapter 6, **Klondikers** tells about my great-uncle Herbert Vroom taking cattle to the Yukon in the 1890s and about Edward Bruce, one of our neighbours during the 1930s, going to Dawson City in 1894 and of Edward's subsequent immigration to Canada with his wife and family in 1911.

Chapter 7, **W.J.A. "Wash" Mitchell: Overland by Covered Wagon**, by using a number of early 1900 photographs, tells how W.J.A. "Wash" Mitchell and his family travelled from Meridian, Idaho, to a homestead in Gladstone Valley, AB, in 1906.

Chapter 8, *T. B. Tyson: **Scion of an Adventurous Family***, tells some of the experiences of my much-travelled maternal Tyson family relatives, who originated in the Lake District of northwestern England.

My great-uncle T. B. Tyson, affectionately called "T. B." by his friends and neighbours, came to Canada in 1855. "T.B." worked first as a farmhand in Ontario, then travelled westward by train and Red River Cart (from Winnipeg). He arrive in the Fishburn district in southwestern Alberta in 1889, finally homesteading there in 1892. Others of "T.B.'s" family moved to Australia, New Zealand, and South Africa.

Elizabeth Mary and George Tyson

Oscar Vroom

Chapter 9, **Mollie Tyson: "*I'm Going to Marry a Cowboy*,"** talks briefly about my mother's life as a young girl in England. But quick changes to circumstances led my grandparents, George W. and E. Mary Brotherston Tyson to immigrate to Canada in 1914, bringing their children, Tommy and Mollie, with them.

The story then moves on to tell about the life of the Tyson family, and that of their neighbours, living in the farming district of Fishburn, AB, in the period just previous to and during WWI.

With regard to the photos, I realize that some of them are of poor quality. Nevertheless, I have included even those pictures, some of which are more than 140 years old, because they represent the era I write about in this book, and to preserve them for posterity.

OLD TIME COWBOYS & PIONEERS

M y grandfather Oscar Vroom was a romantic, a dreamer, a roamer and an adventurer. His first great love was western Canada, particularly southwest Alberta and his "Sunny Vale Ranche," which was south of Beaver Mines. Oscar's love for his land was closely followed by his love of his family - his parents and siblings, and later his wife and children.

The foundations of Oscar's family life were laid long before any of the Vrooms came west. At least four generations of my Vroom family female ancestors were born in Nova Scotia. John Vroom (1756-1833), and his wife, Jane Ditmars Vroom (1753-1830) fled from the United States to Nova Scotia as United Empire Loyalists in 1783, following the American Revolution.

Both John and Jane were born in New Jersey, one of the Thirteen Colonies. In Canada, the family settled in the Annapolis Valley in Nova Scotia. Without the courageous people who came to Canada at that time the Vroom story in Canada would be drastically different.

Two women who were destined to play large roles in my grandfather Oscar Vroom's life were born in Nova Scotia in the mid 1800s. One was Oscar's mother, Sara Ann Woodman Vroom. The other was his mother-in-law, Elizabeth Pierce Munro Dodge.

Elizabeth, married to Alfred Munro, was the mother of my grandmother Alena Munro Vroom (1863-1927) and of Alena's brother, Brent Munro (1836-1874) of Amherst, NS.

My great-grandmother Elizabeth Pierce Munro Dodge, widowed about 1873, was left to raise her two children, Alena and Brent, on her own. Brent was about sixteen years old and Alena only about 10 years when their father died.

In 1874, Elizabeth became the second wife of Cromwell Charles C. C. "Crummy" Dodge (1825-1899), a well-to-do hotelier in Middleton, NS. He was able to help her care for her children, and Alena was sent to boarding school in Halifax.

Shown here in Middleton, NS, about 1890, Elizabeth is a mature, but still very attractive, woman. Courtesy Ruby Jaggernath

Unlike my grandmother Alena, my grandfather William Oscar Vroom (1858-1933) came from a large and loving family.

In 1877, Sara Ann Woodman Vroom realized that her beloved oldest son, Oscar, was growing up and would soon want to leave home to seek his fortune.

Sara Ann gathered the whole family together for this family photograph, taken about seven years before Oscar's first trip west. She wanted to have it as a keepsake so she could remember their happy times together once her sons became widely scattered, as she suspected they would be.

Here Sara Ann and William sit in the midst of their large and loving family. Sara has a patient, kindly face. William, who according to my dad's remembrances was somewhat stern, wore a full, neatly trimmed, beard.

Ten of the 12 children borne by Sara Ann Woodman Vroom are seen here. Back row (l to r): Minnie, Oscar; Jennie Louise, Herbert Lockhart; Middle row (l to r): Maude Ellen, Ralph Voorhees, Sara Ann, William, Sarah; Front row (l to r): Archibald Tuttle, Ross and Claude, and Anna May. A son Isaac, twin of Maude, died young.

William is holding the twins, Ross and Claude, on his knee. Jennie Louise was a cousin of the other children. Sara Ann and William raised Jennie Louise, who was the daughter of their deceased daughter, Jennie.

My dad's paternal grandmother, Sara Ann Woodman (1838-1909), was the daughter of A. Woodman of Clementsport, NS. Sara Ann married William Voorhees Vroom (1833-1920) on January 2, 1859. Sara Ann was the second of the two women who played a pivotal role in the Vroom family. Courtesy Archbishop Michael O'Neill, Author's collection

This circa 1867 tintype shows Alena Blanche Munro, as a young girl about four years of age. She was born December 13, 1863 and became a schoolteacher in Nova Scotia.

When Alena and my grandfather Wm. Oscar Vroom met, fell in love and decided to get married, Alena's mother, Elizabeth Munro Dodge, was not anxious that Alena marry my grandfather. Elizabeth did not want Alena to face hardship nor an uncertain future.

But Alena had a mind of her own. On November 7, 1887, at twenty-four years of age, she married William Oscar Vroom.

By the time they died, Alena, at age 64, in Pincher Creek, AB, in December 1927 and Oscar, at age 74, at the home of his son and daughter-in-law Harold and Ruby Mitchell Vroom on June 12, 1933, they had lived in southwestern Alberta for many years. Oscar first came west in 1886 and settled on land in the Beaver Mines Creek Valley. Alena and their children joined Oscar on his homestead in 1904.
Courtesy Ruby Jaggernath

By 1877, Oscar was 18 years old and ready to leave home. He spent the next nine years working at various jobs in Annapolis, NS, where the family lived, and on sailing vessels up and down the Atlantic seaboard. Then he headed for the West.

The late 1800s were restless times in Canada. People who lived in Nova Scotia kept hearing stories of adventure and wonderful riches in the West and longed to have adventures, too. My grandfather Oscar Vroom was one of these people. The idea really took hold of him when he became betrothed.

En route to the West from Nova Scotia Oscar talked with fellow travellers. "You can get a whole quarter section of land for next to nothing in the West," they told him.

"Sounds too good to be true," observed Oscar, but in his heart he determined to investigate the prospects of homesteading in southwest Alberta

Oscar was adventurous, but he also needed work so that he could build up a stake to get married the following year. Just as when he had gone out to sea as a younger man Oscar was unfazed by the thought of hardship and danger.

With his eyes aglow from the excitement of the thought of this last big adventure before settling down to married life, Oscar said "Good-bye" to his beloved Alena, his family and buddies. Undeterred by the prospect of an arduous five-day trip by train 4000 miles across Canada to Alberta, he set out in the spring of 1886.

In 1886 Medicine Hat was the end of steel for the CPR. There was a shortage of men to work building the railway. Oscar, a blacksmith by trade, had no trouble getting a job with the CPR. As related by Ken Liddell (Calgary Herald 1952), Oscar went to work immediately, helping lay tracks from Medicine Hat to Lethbridge, AB.

The new standard-width C. P. R. rail line replaced the original narrow gauge "Turkey Train" tracks that Margaret Skiffington (Mrs. W.M.R.) Dobbie and Johanna (Mrs. C.C.) Schoening, among others, traversed when travelling to the Northwest Territories before 1890 to join their husbands in the Pincher Creek area (Friesen 1974).

Oscar returned to Nova Scotia in the fall of 1887. He married his long-time sweetheart, Alena Blanche Munro, on his 29th birthday.

Here Alena Munro Vroom, in a picture taken about the time that she and Oscar were married, is a beautiful, high-spirited young woman. When Oscar left his family home in 1877, Alena of neighbouring Middleton, NS, was 14 years old.

The idea of seeking adventures in western Canada fired the imagination of young Oscar Vroom, who had already had his share of adventure. Though she loved Oscar dearly, Alena did not want to marry a sailor and Oscar--not quite ready to settle into married life--decided to travel to western Canada looking for job prospects. He saw this as an opportunity to have some more adventures.

Alena was not too keen on the idea, but in the end, wisely keeping her misgivings to herself, she accepted the fact that she really could not do much about the situation. Courtesy Ruby Jaggernath

MAP 1 Trails/Creeks/Rivers of Extreme Southwest Corner Alberta circa 1910

Accurate as to scale and locations this map was developed over many years thanks to the help of many old-timers, such as Betty Annand Baker, George R. "Geordie" Annand, Bud Jenkins and Tom and Frankie Jenkins. It is believed to be a one-of-a-kind map. It shows the creeks and rivers that defined an area of the Northwest Territories that was used by the indigenous people for thousands of years and by the early cowboys who came there in the late 1800s looking for adventure and a new life.

The number of creeks and rivers as shown by this map helps explain the natural beauty of the area. Some years ago Robert Collins, a staff writer for McLean's magazine, described the view looking westward to the mountains from about the location of the Dobbie Iron Mine as "the most beautiful view in the world." That description still holds true.

This map also shows the route of the Canadian Pacific Railway through southwest Alberta, as well as some of the old-time roads and trails that were used by the early cowboys and homesteaders and by people who came to the area seeking wealth at Oil City, the original oil find in the area and the site of the first producing oil well in western Canada.

In 1902, Oscar settled on Crown land in the foothills south of Beaver Mines, NWT at that time, southwest of Pincher Creek (Friesen 1974). In 1904 Alena and their four children joined him on "Sunny Vale Ranche." Oscar proved up on his homestead in 1909 and lived on or near that land for the rest of his life.
Illustration by Edi-May Smithies, Cartography by Shelley McConnell

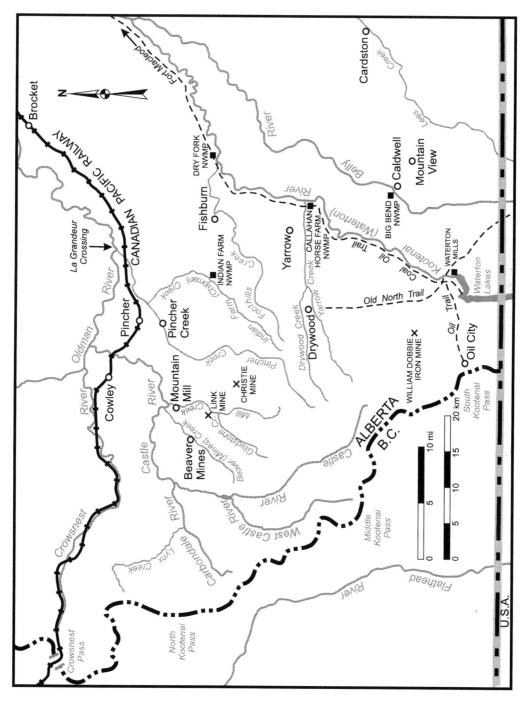

MAP 1 TRAILS/CREEKS/RIVERS OF EXTREME SOUTHWEST CORNER OF ALBERTA, circa 1910

The work crews encountered no major obstacles as they laid new tracks across the relatively flat land west of Medicine Hat as far as Lethbridge. As he and his workmates progressed westward Oscar saw grass-covered land that stretched as far as the eye could see. Occasionally he saw Indian villages with the white teepees arranged in a neat campsite gleaming in the sun.

By the time the CPR reached Fort Whoop-Up on the St. Mary's River southwest of Lethbridge in the fall of 1886 Oscar had heard more exciting tales about the beauty of the mountains and the frequency of Chinooks in the area. He decided to find out more about this wonderful part of the country first hand so he quit the CPR track laying crew at Whoop-Up and travelled to Macleod by stagecoach.

Upon arriving in Macleod, Oscar spent some time talking with the local ranchers and other people who came into town for supplies. Then he bought a saddle horse and headed west towards Pincher Creek to explore the homestead situation for himself. Oscar spent the next year in the Pincher Creek area of the Northwest Territories getting to know the people and the geography of the countryside before retuning to Nova Scotia to get married.

Shown here is a Sun Dance lodge on the Siksika reservation near Cluny and Gleichen. Cluny is northeast of Medicine Hat, while Macleod is straight west. Though Oscar did not pass through Cluny on his way to MacLeod, sundances were held each summer in various locations in southwestern Alberta.

Anthony Bruce, in his memories, "Nigel & Carolyn," wrote: "I remember Mother telling me that when they first went to Cluny (in 1909), the country was so unsettled that one could have ridden in 3 directions from the farm for 150 miles, and not met a fence. Directly across from the farm house (that is, across the road allowance), was the Blackfeet Indian Reserve, with the Indians still living in their teepees."

The difference between the simple designs used to decorate ordinary tribe members' teepees and the elaborate designs used to decorate the medicine man's tip is striking.

Teams of horses pulling democrats are drawn up beside the teepees. These outfits may be those of nearby ranchers who, like the Bruces, were invited by the local Indian chief to visit the camp during the Sun Dance festivities.
Courtesy Katherine Bruce

Looking southwest, Beaver Mines Creek Valley is bounded on the west by the main range of the Rocky Mountains opening out to the prairies on the east. The land showing in the foreground was a part of Oscar's homestead. When Oscar first viewed this land it was covered with brush and poplar trees, which he had to clear before breaking the land for cultivation.

With his heart brimming over with the romance of the west, Oscar gloried in the wide-open spaces of the prairies and the great blue dome that is the prairie sky. He even loved the wild winds that swept across the wide-open prairie, in the summertime drying out the grassland, in mid-winter bringing blinding blizzards, and often in mid-January bringing a snow-melting Chinook to southern Alberta. He kept a keen eye out for a suitable place to homestead.

Riding southwest from Pincher Creek Oscar came closer and closer to the main range of the Rockies Mountains, eventually coming to this view of the Beaver Mines Creek Valley. Here he stopped to gaze at the enthralling scene before him. "This is where I want to live for the rest of my life," he thought resolutely to himself.

Oscar settled on this land, described as NE ¼ -29-5-2-W5th, *in 1902. He led a bachelor's life until his wife and family joined him in 1904. Oscar filed for a homestead July 21, 1908, receiving his homestead patent December 16, 1909. He had resided on his homestead for the required three years and had made certain improvements.*

Oscar and Alena's house was on the east side of Beaver Mines Creek, where Ruby Creek, a tributary from the east, empties into Beaver Mines Creek. Some of Alena's collected receipts for dry goods bought in Pincher Creek show her address as "Beaver Creek."

The Beaver Mines Post Office did not open until December 15, 1911. A long-time family friend of the Vrooms, George Ballantyne, came west in 1902 and homesteaded at Beaver Mines, NWT. When coal was discovered on his quarter, George sold his homestead to a mining company and "bought another quarter section, being S.W. ¼ of Section 14, two miles east of Beaver Mines, AB". George took over the Beaver Mines Post Office in 1919 (Friesen 1974). Courtesy Edi-May Smithies

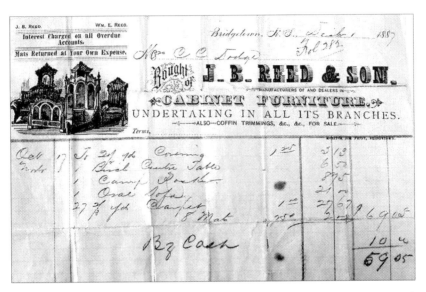

Alena's mother, Elizabeth (Mrs. C. C.) Dodge, expected that the home of her daughter and son-in-law would be the centre for lively social gatherings. Consequently, she wanted Alena to have fine furnishings to grace her home in Clementsport, where Mrs. Dodge believed that Oscar and Alena would live for many years. To help Alena get started on her collection of fine furnishings she bought several rather fine wedding gifts for the young couple from a Clementsport merchant, J.B. Reed & Son, Bridgetown, NS.

The newlyweds settled in Clementsport, NS, living near Oscar's parents. Oscar stayed in Clementsport for the next ten years (Ellis, 1996). During that time the young couple had four children--Harold Palmer, born October 5, 1888, died February 26, 1974; Ralph Ernst, born May 16, 1891, died 1969; Marion Munro Vroom, born October 14, 1893, died 1984; and Alfred Stanley Vroom, born October 27, 1895, died 1963. Author's collection

Oscar returned to the West again in 1897, this time accompanied by three of his brothers and a brother-in-law. The Vroom family men worked 1897-98 building the CPR from Macleod, NWT, through the Crowsnest Pass to Cranbrook, BC. They played key roles in this epic construction project.

Immediately west of Lethbridge the railway builders were confronted by the wide and deep Old Man River Valley. Construction of a railway bridge across that yawning chasm was the first of many stiff challenges the railway builders faced on the southern route of the CPR.

An article in Internet Explorer, "The St. Mary's River Crossing and the High Level Bridge at Lethbridge, Alberta," in the file Crowsnest Railway Construction 12/15, states that the High Level Bridge west of Lethbridge built of all-steel construction in 1907-1909 "is one of the largest railway structures in Canada." The article states further that before 1909 the CPR through the Crowsnest Pass bypassed Lethbridge, which was reached by a one and one-half mile long spur. At that time the railway crossed the St. Mary's River at Whoop-Up, and the Old Man River at Monarch, on wooden trestles. These were two of the many coulees on the prairies that were crossed on wooden trestles, which were designed to last only 10 years. Before constructing the

High Level Bridge at Lethbridge, engineers did careful planning, which included careful studies and reports and a throrough assessment of the area.

There is no record of the workers' reaction to the task presented by the spanning of that wide river valley, but the reactions of some of the thousands of settlers who travelled west on the completed railway line fortunately were recorded by some of their descendants. For instance, Mrs. C. G. (Charles) Thomas, when coming west to join her husband who homesteaded in the Robert Kerr – Fishburn - Utopia district east of Pincher Creek in 1900, was so frightened going across the trestle over the St. Mary's River at Whoop-Up that she made her four children stand in the aisle in the centre of the car to keep it balanced so that the railway car would not tip off the rails (Bob Thomas, August 2005).

Here, circa 1870, Kootenai Brown holds his little white dog, a constant companion for many years. At this time he worked as a mail carrier (pony express rider) for the United States Army.

At one point, notes William Rodney in his book Kootenai Brown: his life and times *(1969), Brown and his companion "a Santee Sioux half-breed," narrowly escaped death when the Sioux chief Sitting Bull and a band of young warriors captured the two mail carriers while they were en route from Fort Stevenson to Fort Totten in Dakota Territory in 1868.*

Kootenai Brown gave this photo to Phil and Mary "Dot" Lucas Upton of Twin Butte (Children: Charlie and Phyllis). Kootenai was a frequent visitor to the Upton ranch in the early 1900s, stopping there en route to and from Macleod when he rode from Waterton Park for mail and supplies.

In Macleod, Oscar talked with men who had arrived in the west before he did and whose talk of tall grass and warm winter winds whetted Oscar's interest in the West.

One of the men Oscar talked with was Fred Kanouse, a cattle rancher from near Macleod. It wasn't long before Kanouse introduced Oscar to his friend John George "Kootenai" Brown and, eventually, to his friends Bill Damon and Henri "Frenchy" Riviere. Courtesy Essie McWhirter Cox

The *Macleod Gazette* (September 10, 1897) described the track laying operation of a second crew working eastward from Macleod as being "toward Whoop-Up on the St. Mary's River just west of Lethbridge," and saying further, "When the Belly River, ten miles out (eastward from Macleod), is reached, ...the bridge will have to be put in and then there should be no delay until they reach the St. Mary's River near Whoop-Up, some 30 miles from Macleod. The track should reach the far east by the end of the present month." The *Macleod Gazette* also remarked on how efficient the trackmen were at laying each section of rail.

H. A. "Frenchy" Riviere came to the Pincher Creek area about one year after my grandfather Oscar Vroom first visited there.

In Macleod Oscar also met cowboys from the Jughandle Ranch, a big spread southeast of Pincher Creek in the Fishburn disttrct. The ranch received its moniker "from the way the skin at the animal's neck was slit (for identification) so that in healing there was left a hole, thus the name 'Jughandle'" (Friesen 1974).

Bill Damon is astride his favourite saddlehorse at the south side of the Stockade at Macleod, AB, in 1884. Bill signed on as a night herder on November 1, 1882, and drove a herd of cattle owned by Robert S. Ford from Montana up to Canada to provide food for the Indians. Robert Ford, an early Montana rancher, later moved to Spring Coulee, AB.

Bill was hired as stock rider for the Blood Indian Reserve near Cardston, AB. He killed beef once a week for the Indians living on the Blood Reserve. After some time Bill Damon moved to the Stewart ranch, which was also known as the Pincher Creek Ranch. Still later he drove a herd of cattle to the Gleichan (Blackfeet) Reserve southeast of Calgary. This herd also was to serve as food for the near-starving Indians. Bill Damon had no connection with the Pablo herd.

Bill had a brother, Ed. They were not related to the Art Damon, who worked as a mechanic in Waterton Lakes Park for a number of years. Bill also had a cousin, or a nephew, Willy Damon from Michigan, who came to visit him. Willy stayed on for several seasons, working as a cook for some the roundups.

Though western Canada never did experience the Wild West syndrome, there were times when tension between two or more cowboys resulted in short gunfights. The Macleod Gazette chronicled several such incidents reporting in the March 18, 1898, edition on "a shooting scrape at the Loop in the Crow's (sic) Nest Pass the other day" during which Hugh O'Neill grabbed the gun from one of the combatants and pounded him over the head with it. The Macleod Gazette of July 21, 1885, reported a gunfight between two cowboys on the Waldron Ranche that ended with one cowboy being hit in the shoulder resulting in his being taken to the Macleod hospital for treatment. Courtesy Bob Thomas

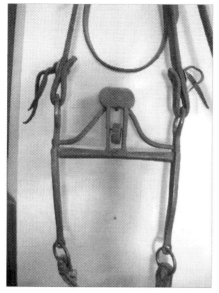

Bob Thomas explained that Bill Damon once owned this spade bit. A man known to Bob and his children as "Grandpa Athol Hovis" had this bit in his possession for a number of years before giving it to Bob. Bob also possessed Bill Damon's diaries, and read them from beginning to end.

Athol Hovis, at 18 years of age, had a chance to play major league baseball, but instead chose to go homesteading with Bill Damon. The two men became close friends and worked together for years. Bill raised purebred Clydesdale horses and had a lease on the Peigan Reserve.

Athol was a good friend to the Indians. Athol's homestead was near Glenwood and close to both the Peigan and Blood Indian Reserves. Bill Damon married Athol's aunt Fern.

Shirley Hovis, Athol's daughter and Bob's first wife, used to go with "Grandaddy" Damon to visit the Indians. She said that she was always scared when they went.

Shirley was the executor of Fern Hovis's estate. On Fern's death, she found Bill Damon's diaries amongst Fern's possessions. The diaries were transferred to microfilm and are now are held by the Glenbow Museum in Calgary. Courtesy Bob Thomas

As early as 1885 Crown land was opening up for settlement in the West. In Macleod Oscar quit his job on the CPR and bought a saddle horse. Riding westward toward the foothills, Oscar was greeted by an unrolling panorama of ever more beautiful scenery.

When he reached Pincher Station he got his first really clear view of the Rocky Mountains. He wanted to feast his eyes on the scenery, but hurried on so that he would reach the settlement of Pincher Creek before dark.

Less than one-half hour later he dropped down over the gently sloping hill on the north side of Pincher Creek Valley into the small village of Pincher Creek. Even by 1902, fewer than 200 people lived in Pincher Creek, their dwellings being an assortment of tents and small log cabins (Lang, Ellis, 1961 interview). But, several businesses were established.

Other men that Oscar met, who were pioneers or colourful homesteaders, included Wm. Shanks "Old Glad" Gladstone and Lionel Brooke. "Old Glad" (1853-1912) married and raised a family in southwest Alberta. Lionel Brooke remained a bachelor. .

Fascinated by the beautiful landscape, and in spite of the obviously rustic living conditions, Oscar decided to make Pincher Creek his home base while he explored the countryside. As he rode from ranch to ranch in the areas to the south and west of Pincher Creek, magnificent views of the Rocky Mountains, which filled the entire length of the western sky, greeted him.

Oscar became more and more interested in the area south west of Pincher Creek.

Here, in 1912, Henri Arnous "Frenchy" Riviere, stands with his family on the Whipple Ranch southwest of Pincher Creek a few years after dad first met the Riviere family. Frenchy and Nellie willingly provided overnight lodging for people who arrived late in the day. Frenchy first came to the Pincher Creek area in 1886 as a relatively young man. In a letter to the editor of the Pincher Creek Echo, March 25, 1954, *Frenchy told about one of his early jobs in the west as a packer and wrangler for Colonel Marshall. Marshall was a British Army officer from England who accompanied Lionel Brooke on a big game hunting and salmon fishing expedition in the Columbia country, around the source of the Columbia River.*

Shown, left to right, are: An unknown child who was staying with the Rivieres; George Riviere, ten years old; Bob Riviere three years old; an unknown child; Mrs. Nellie Gladstone Riviere, 33 years old holding baby James; unknown child; Mary "Girlie" Riviere, eight years old; John "Charlie" Riviere, two years old; Henry Riviere, 13 years old; Frenchy Riviere, 45 years old. Courtesy Frances Riviere McWhirter

Robert Lang (Lang, Ellis, 1961 interview), who came to Pincher Creek in 1902 and homesteaded west of Pincher Creek, but east of Mountain Mill, entered the town from the west, as did the Vrooms and all other homesteaders from the Beaver Mines-Gladstone Valley area.

In describing his first impression of the upstart foothills town Mr. Lang, naming the buildings and businesses from west to east along Main Street, stated: "In 1902 there were three stores in Pincher Creek. Jim Scofield had a general store, which is the Odd Fellows building now...C. Kettles had a store and a butcher shop east of the Veterans' Club. Then Tim Lebel, a French Jew from Montreal, came and went in partners with C. Kettles. They built a stone store on the corner. The rock was dug in the Pincher Creek Canyon.

The corner stones were from Nelson, BC...The Hudson's Bay Company had a store near where the Chinese restaurant is now, there was a general store and a lean-to on the east side for a liquor store...Then they built the store where the Co-op Hardware and Men's Furnishings is now."

Lionel Brooke, variously described as "a graduate of Oxford…a "descendant of the (British) aristocracy"… a "'Remittance Man'" …"a gentleman rancher"… and "an accomplished raconteur," arrived in the Pincher Creek district about 1886. Mr Brooke first worked along with his partner Herbert H. Hatfield on the Butte Ranch, which was "north by northwest of Pincher Creek."

In 1889, after dissolving his partnership with Hatfield, Mr. Brooke worked alongside Billy Huddlestun on the Garnett Brothers ranch, probably helping with the haying. Unsatisfied with the amount of grub the Garnett Brothers put on the table for the hungry ranch hands, Mr. Huddlestun went into the pantry and brought out all the food he could find telling "the rest of the boys to help themselves." Reminiscing about the incident with Billy in later years, Lionel Brooke, one of the crew at the time, stated, "If you hadn't been there we'd have starved to death."
(Friesen 1974)

The Western Canada Land Grants, 1870-1930, *documents show that Lionel Brooke homesteaded on and received his letters patent for the western half of Section 25 Township 6 Range 2 West of the 5th Meridian.*

As related by Lynch-Staunton (circa 1920), after proving up on his homestead, which became known as the Butte Ranch, Mr. Brooke sold his land to Martin Conrad. Among others, A. N. Mowat owned this land at a later time.

Here Lionel Brooke sits in a comfortable wicker armchair in his luxurious ranch house on his homestead west of Twin Butte in the 1890s. He is smoking his trademark pipe and gazing at the head and antlers of a 7-point bull elk, which he shot on one of his hunting expeditions into the mountains. His faithful dog lies at his feet.

On the wall behind the elk head are scenes from Nature, which Mr. Brooke, who possessed considerable artistic ability, painted in his leisure time. Mr. Brooke painted similar scenes on the walls of the homes of a number of his neighbours, where he stayed, being forced to work off his board and room, when he ran out of money while waiting for his next quarterly remittance cheque to arrive.

In a letter to the Pincher Creek Echo *Henri Riviere praised Lionel Brooke for his many kindnesses to the Riviere family—which were reciprocated—and for his generosity and unselfishness in dealing with people of the area.* Glenbow Archives NA-1403-1

Here in circa 1898, a young Billie Gladstone, William III, grandson of William I "Old Glad" Gladstone, poses in his cowboy clothes. William Gladstone III, who was the same age as my dad, was born in Macleod, NWT, in 1891.

Ralph Vroom knew William III from the time they were young cowboys riding the range together. Dad also knew Louise Spence Gladstone, Mrs. William Gladstone III. William Gladstone III's father, William II, was an interpreter for the RNWMP.

William Gladstone III homesteaded near Twin Butte next to Mrs. Margarette Louise Spence. He married Mrs. Spence's daughter Louise. William III and Louise Spence Gladstone were the parents of Leonard Gladstone, a long-time park warden in Waterton Lakes National Park.

William III was a good neighbour. When Nichemoos, second wife of Kootenai Brown, died on April 1, 1935, Billie III hitched up his team and sleigh and drove Nichemoos's body out to the highway through deep snow. A hearse took her remains into Waterton Lakes Park for the funeral service.

William Gladstone IV, son of Leonard and Anna de Geest Gladstone, is now retired and lives in Pincher Creek. Courtesy Anna de Geest Gladstone

Taken from near the present site of Coalfields School, this view shows the beautiful, almost symmetrical, foothills just to the west of Beaver Mines at the north end of Beaver Mines Creek Valley.

A few of the buildings that comprise the hamlet of Beaver Mines show up as small white marks at the base of foothills in the right centre of the above photo.

Oscar Vroom's homestead, which for many years was owned and lived on by his son Harold and daughter-in-law Ruby Mitchell Vroom and their family, was only a few miles north of Table Mountain.

My dad once told me that when he was young he and a friend raced their saddle horses along the top of Table Mountain. Courtesy Edi-May Smithies

Mrs. H.P. Vroom (Ruby Mitchell Vroom) sent this picture showing a picnic group at Beaver Mines Lake in 1917 to her husband, Harold, who at the time was serving Overseas with the Canadian Expeditionary Force (CEF) in France.

There are very few men in this picture. The fathers, sons, brothers, and husbands of most the women and/or children shown here were in the army or were away working elsewhere.

Left to right, 1917: Archie McDowall, "Father" (W. J. A. "Wash" Mitchell), Lawrence Truitt, Charlie Mitchell (holding watermelon), Oscar Vroom Jr. (kneeling), Charlie's wife ("Sis" Mitchell), Elsie McDowall (standing behind Marjorie), Marjorie McDowall holding Sissie (Mae) Vroom, Bessie Mitchell Truitt (seated), Glendora "Glenn" Mitchell (standing behind Bessie, holding ham), Leslie McDowall (holding pie), Mrs H.P. Vroom "your wife" Additional inscription: "Just before lunch. Good of Sissie & Daddy Mitchell"

Harold enlisted in the CEF at Pincher Creek (#898208, 192 Battalion) on March 1, 1916. Ruby was left to run the ranch. By August 1917 their children, Oscar and Mae "Sissie" were six years old and one year old, respectively.

Harold and his younger brother Alfred, who also served Overseas in WWI, returned home safely, but World War I tragically changed the lives of many of the people seen above. Courtesy Ruby Jaggernath

After a few months of working on ranches around Pincher Creek Oscar decided that he wanted to spend the rest of his life living in the shadow of the Rockies. The fall weather was getting cool so Oscar took a final ride out to the Beaver Mines district determined to file on his own homestead.

Nearing Beaver Mines Oscar's gaze fell upon ever more thrilling sweeps of landscape. In the Beaver Mines Creek Valley, Oscar found the location he wanted, but he did not file for a homestead just yet.

(Above left) *As the fall passed there was often a bank of clouds or thick fog hanging along the bottom of the mountains obscuring the beauty of the Rockies and reminding settlers of the fact that winter was just around the corner. A spectacular cloud formation hangs along the foothills, a scene often viewed by Oscar during the fall of 1886 while he was exploring the countryside southwest of Pincher Creek.* Courtesy Katherine Bruce

(Above right) *Oscar Vroom and other travellers to western Canada heard stories of hunting trips where a wide variety of wild game of all kinds was killed, both for sport and for food. When fall came Oscar realized that the stories he heard were indeed true. In addition to the scenery, wildlife abounded in the hills south and west of Beaver Mines. This is Ronald Bruce with a four-point buck deer that he shot for food for the family, circa 1933. Snow on ground indicates fall or early winter hunting.* Courtesy Katherine Bruce

Looking southeast from the hill behind Bruces' house at Beaver Mines the view toward Gladstone Valley spreads out before the viewer.

If Oscar had climbed to the top of the some of the high hills to the south and southwest of Beaver Mines he would have seen splendid views, such as this one, of the hills and mountains to the east, south and west.

The large open field is Ralph Vroom's west quarter section. The hill that as a child I called the "big hill," which was north of our ranch buildings, shows on the left.

In "Dad's Memories" Anthony Bruce wrote: "Where we were it was 4700 feet altitude and from the front door we could see the real Rockies. To the south and southeast we could see "Table Mountain," "Round Mountain," "Castle Mountain," "Mount McAlpine," and others further away. All these went up far beyond what is known as the "timber-line," meaning that above that line no trees could grow. To the northwest we could see another long line of mountains; this was the "Livingstone Range" and as far as one could see there was not a break in it for many miles. Courtesy Katherine Bruce

Anthony Bruce in the booklet,"Dad's Memories—Happy 80th Birthday, Dad" by Allesina Bruce Brooks describes the wildlife on those hills when the family moved there in the late 1920s:

"On the hills behind the house one might meet up with various wild animals. I have seen timber wolves (they will weigh up to around 70 kg), but they are not dangerous. Also, coyotes (prairie wolves) – they will seldom weigh more than about 15 kg--also deer, elk (wapiti) and bears, black and brown. I have shot them and they are good eating, but will seldom weigh more than about 100 kg. However, I have seen cattle with one side torn open where some bear has slashed at them with its claws, but luckily the cuts were not very deep so the animal did not need to be destroyed. It had probably come between the mother bear and her cubs."

Bert Riggall, in a handwritten description of this breathtaking view of the Rocky Mountains, states: "Looking Westward from (the) summit of Clarke Range near Hawk's Nest," the Riggall ranch south of Twin Butte. Shown here are the head of Castle River, the Great Divide and southeast British Columbia (BC). This is terrain with which my dad became very familiar over the years.

In the early 1900s Bert and Dora Riggall became friends with the Vroom family and other families in the Beaver Mines area. Bert Riggall, who became a well-known mountain guide and raconteur, became a role model for my dad, inspiring Dad to qualify for a Class A Alberta Guide licence. This license enabled my dad to take hunting, fishing and sightseeing parties out in the mountains for weeks at a time. Courtesy Katherine Bruce

When Oscar was in the west in 1886-87 he got a job working for a rancher in the Pincher Creek district. Board and room were part of his monthly pay. Oscar awoke one mid-October morning to find thick, white hoarfrost coating the bare branches of poplar trees and and willows. Hoarfrost and a few inches of wet snow covering the dry grass of autumn were the first signs that winter was just around the corner in the foothills of southwestern Alberta.

(Above left) Hoarfrost-coverered willows and poplars in Beaver Mines Creek Valley were a familiar scene to me in the early fall during my childhood. For dramatic effect, the photographer used two blades of grass to frame the "big hill," here girdled with a thick bank of low-lying, autumn fog. Courtesy Katherine Bruce

(Above right) As the months passed, winter came with a vengeance to southwestern Alberta. Here, Fluffy, but heavy and wet, fall snow weights down a shrub making the shrub, which is still shrouded in its dense summer foliage, look like a heap of woolly sheep stacked on top of one another. Courtesy Katherine Bruce

Young men who came west in the early days liked to impress their friends back east, and even back in England, with tales of their dramatic deeds. Here, in this circa 1927 picture, Tom Selby, nicknamed "Canada," appears to be standing neck deep in snow. Often the snow in the foothills was deep enough that this could be a true picture. Tom Selby was one of the many men who travelled from place to place during the Great Depression looking for work and a place to lay their heads.

Springtime came at last and Oscar was glad to see the several beautiful lakes located along the eastern edge of the main range of the Rockies in the Beaver Mines area free of ice and the streams, swollen by the melting of the winter's snows, rushing and roaring through the woods of the foothills. Courtesy Kathrine Bruce

RIBBON OF STEEL

Like a ribbon of steel, the Crowsnest route of the Canadian Pacific Railway (CPR) girds southern Canada. How many of us as passengers on that magnificent Canadian accomplishment ever thought of the men who laid the iron tracks over which lumbered massive steam locomotives through the challenging terrain on the southern route?

Constructed more than 100 years ago and following the southern route, the CPR crosses deep river valleys and traverses the main range of the Canadian Rockies. I must admit I never thought much about the building of the CPR anywhere in Canada during my several trips across Canada, going as far north as Churchill on Hudson Bay and crossing the Rockies, travelling westward and eastward, through the three main Canadian passes—the Yellowhead, the Kicking Horse, and the Crowsnest.

My grandfather Vroom was one of the hundreds of men who laboured to make the dream of the southern route of a railway line across Canada from the Atlantic Ocean to the Pacific Ocean, a distance of more than 5000 miles, a reality. This fact is very gratifying to me.

Oscar's first stint at railway building was while he was in the West in 1886 when he worked with construction crews building the section of the CPR from Medicine Hat to Lethbridge. Then true to his word, and after nearly two exciting years in the West, William Oscar Vroom returned to Clementsport, NS, to marry his betrothed, Alena Munro.

But ten years of married life did not dull Oscar's love of and longing for the west. By 1897, he again had itchy feet. This time, however, Oscar did not come west alone. He persuaded three of his brothers—Ralph Voorhees, Archie and Claude—and a brother-in-law, Peter O'Neill (husband of Maude Vroom) to go along with him.

Together, the five young men travelled west to Macleod, at that time the end of steel for the CPR. There, the Vroom brothers joined other railway construction workers and laboured from November 1897 to August 1898 punching the CPR through the Crowsnest Pass from Fort MacLeod, NWT, to Cranbrook, BC.

Robert Lang(1961) stated: "…by the winter of 1896-97 CPR construction crew camps were being built on the east side of the Oldman River northwest of Pincher Creek."

Oscar, Archie and Claude were blacksmiths and worked as such on the Macleod to Cranbrook leg of the CPR. Upon reaching Cranbrook Archie opened his own blacksmith business. Oscar and Claude took their blacksmithing tools to their homesteads at Beaver Mines. Claude proved up on his homestead, then sold his land and moved elsewhere. He gave his blacksmith outfit to my dad, who also was a blacksmith.

Oscar was the oldest of the 12 children born to William Voorhees Vroom and Sara Ann Woodman. William and Sara Ann also raised a thirteenth child, Jennie Louise, who was a cousin of the other children. All of William and Sara Ann's children were born in Clementsport, NS. William Oscar Vroom was born November 7, 1859 and died June 12, 1933, in his 74th year

Ralph Voorhees was born June 10, 1869, and died May 3, 1931. Archie Tuttle was born January 17, 1876, and died September 14, 1959. Ross and Claude (twins and the two youngest children) were born April 3, 1877. Ross died in September 1945. Claude died on June 5, 1945, in New Westminster, BC at 68 years.

Their brother-in-law Peter O'Neill, husband of Maude, who was born September 11, 1872 in Clementsport, NS, died May 4, 1966, in Timmins, ON. Another brother, Ross (1877-1945), twin of Claude, did not come west. Ross went to school in Boston, Massachucetts, trained to be a dentist and settled there. A fifth brother, Isaac, twin of Maude, died young (Obituary of Sara Ann Vroom, *Digby Courier* of March 12, 1909).

Archibald Tuttle "Archie" Vroom, taken in 1897 before Oscar, Ralph Voorhees, Archie and Claude and their brother-in-law Peter O'Neill went to the West to work on the railway. Sara Ann Vroom knew that four of her sons were soon to leave their home in Nova Scotia with the intention of perhaps settling in the West.

"We'll take the train to the end of steel at Macleod. Then we'll work on the building of the CPR through the Crowsnest Pass to Cranbrook." Oscar enthused to his younger relatives. "We'll go as far as Cranbrook, BC, and then we'll decide what to do from there. I already have plans for a life in the west."

First they would work on completing the stretch of Canadian Pacific Railway track through the southern Canadian Rocky Mountains from the current end of steel at MacLeod, NWT, on through the Crowsnest Pass to Cranbrook, BC. Once in Cranbrook the young men would enjoy some socializing with local families, and then decide what they would do with their futures.
Courtesy Peter Vroom

While he was railway building in the West, Archie Vroom kept his eyes open for interesting items that would be representative of the times.

This is a powder horn made from a buffalo horn by a nineteenth century hunter of wild bison on the great Canadian western plains. It was among the collection of "Old West" memorabilia that Archie acquired when he came west in 1897, laying tracks through the Crowsnest Pass to Cranbrook, BC. Courtesy Peter Vroom

When the Vroom men--Oscar, Archie, and Claude and their brother-in-law Peter O'Neill--left Clementsport for railway work in the West, their sister Maude, wife of Peter O'Neill, was left behind. At the time, "the Crowsnest Pass" sounded very remote and adventurous to Maude who, like countless other women, was left to manage on her own while her husband was far away trying to get a financial start for his family.

Maude's older son, Michael, my dad's first cousin, was ordained as a priest and eventurally became the Archbishop of Regina. When Michael was ordained my dad and mother and my Aunt Marion Cyr and my cousin Vera Gingras travelled to Regina for the ordination ceremony.

Archbishop O'Neill was delighted to see Ralph and Mollie about whom he had heard so many exciting tales from his mother and father. They were, perhaps, his favourite relatives. While I lived in Regina during the last quarter of the 20th century His Grace Archbishop O'Neill invited me for tea at his residence. I talked with the Bishop recording key points in my notes to use in the book I intended to write some day. Author's collection

Rodney (1969) states that Kootenai Brown wrote in his diary: "By mid-July 1897 contracts were let for the laying down of 50 miles of track west of MacLeod, and the town began to fill up with rough strangers of the labouring class." Obviously Kootenai Brown was impressed neither by the building of the railway nor by the workingmen involved in its construction.

At that time Kootenai Brown, along with his wife Olive and their two children, was squatting on a piece of land beside the Waterton River a short distance below the Middle Waterton Lake. Brown looked upon the railway workers and construction people who followed the railway as intruders and their coming as a threat to his idyllic way of life.

Kootenai Brown, an early adventurer in western North America, was a colouful character and was known to many people in the early days of western Canada. Rodney (1969) noted that Brown had worked as a mail carrier (pony express rider for the US Army) in 1868. Nothwithstanding Kootenai's objections to its presence, the railway building continued relentlessly.

Here, the twin Vroom brothers, Claude (right) and Ross (left), are seated in a photographer's studio. From this time onward their paths diverged. Of the twin boys, Claude and Ross, Claude was the more adventurous.

Claude travelled to the West in 1897 and worked on the construction of the Canadian Pacific Railway through the Crowsnest Pass, along with three of his other brothers and a brother-in-law. Upon reaching Cranbrook, BC, Oscar quit the railway.

Claude engaged in a period of socializing in the Cranbrook area, eventually marrying a Cranbrook woman. He then tried his hand at homesteading in the Beaver Mines area of southwestern Alberta, eventually proving up on NE ¼-34-5-2-W5th.

Ross, on the other hand, chose to go into the dentistry profession after attending university in Boston,

Mass. There he married and had a family. Ross spent the rest of his life in Boston. Courtesy Peter Vroom

Of the Vroom brothers who left home in Nova Scotia for distant parts of Canada (Oscar Archie, and Claude) or the United States (Ralph Voorhees and Ross) or Mexico (Herbert), only two of them—Oscar and Herbert-- did not have a departing portrait taken. Perhaps they made up their minds in a hurry and did not want to "waste time" on photo taking. Isaac, twin of Maude, died young.

The only photo of Herbert in the whole Vroom collection was taken in 1877 and titled "Old family group 1877" when the entire family was together.

Of the Vroom daughters, a portrait of Maude is the only one in the family memorabilia.

The family group photo on page 27 was taken in 1909 at the 50th wedding anniversary celebration of William Voorhees Vroom, born February 17, 1833 and Sara Ann Woodman Vroom, born February 17, 1838; Married 1859, are: Left to right, Back row: Oscar, William V., Sara Ann; Middle row: Maude, Sadie; Front row: Ralph V., Claude, Ross, Arch, Jennie (1st cousin), Amanda "Minnie"

Not present at their parents' 50th wedding anniversary celebrations: Herbert (born 1865), who by then was ranching in Mexico; Issac (born 1861), who was perhaps dead by then, having died young; and Annie (born 1879).

Amanda "Minnie" and Issac were twins. Minnie retired to San Diego. Jennie was a first cousin raised by Sara Ann and William Voorhees Vroom. Author's collection

Above, unidentified workmen, who were building the railway by the sweat of their brow, stand atop the partially completed CPR bridge being built across Pincher Creek. This is where it runs north to join the Old Man River a few miles west of Brocket, AB, and several miles east of the town of Pincher Creek between Brocket and Pincher Station. The picture was taken November 23, 1897, looking in a northwesterly direction.

This relatively small railway trestle over Pincher Creek west of Macleod gives some idea of how high above the ground the Lethbridge High Level Bridge would seem to a passenger travelling westward from Ontario across the southern prairies of Canada.

At the time, Oscar, Claude, Ralph Voorhees and Archie Vroom and their brother-in-law Peter O'Neill, were working on the building of the CPR from Macleod, NWT, through the Crowsnest Pass to Cranbrook, BC, during the period from November 1897 to August 1898.

A 1977 letter from the Corporation Archivist of the Canadian Pacific Railway notes that CPR employee record keeping was spotty until 1910; and that some men working on tracklaying crews were employed by private contractors, not the CPR.

The further description from National Archives website SHOULD READ: "Here, workmen stand atop the partially completed railway bridge being built to cross over Pincher Creek where it runs north to join the Old Man River between Brocket and Pincher Station, AB (NOT "between Cowley and Lundbreck").

Pincher Creek runs eastward through the town of Pincher Creek and joins the Oldman River between Pincher Station and Brocket. On some maps, Pincher Station is referred to simply as Pincher. The CPR crosses the Crowsnest River west of Lundbreck. The Crowsnest River flows into the Oldman River, north-northeast of Cowley.

My brother Don's conversation with our dad, Ralph Ernst Vroom, also confirms that this picture was taken looking northwest at the bridge across Pincher Creek, AB, between Brocket and Pincher Station, during construction of that leg of the CPR Crowsnest Pass route on November 23, 1897

This bridge crossing Pincher Creek just south of the Mose and Julia LaGrandeur homestead is located at the confluence of the Pincher Creek and the Old Man River a few miles west of MacLeod. The Crowsnest Route highway, number 3, running through the Crow Nest Pass to British Columbia at this time is north of this bridge.

Photo: National Archives Reproduction No. PA-021796, November 23, 1897, identified as "Pincher Creek, AB, bridge looking northwest, station 3090. Construction took place Nov 1897 - Aug 1898." LIBRARY AND ARCHIVES CANADA/ *PA-021796,* H. Travers, Coleman, Photographer

The first travellers to stay at LaGrandeur Crossing arrived by bumpy stagecoach from Lethbridge or Great Falls, Montana, via Macleod. The construction of the Canadian Pacific Railway through the Crowsnest Pass to Cranbrook brought new sights and sounds shattering the total stillness of the prairies forever.

As stagecoach after stagecoach and wagon after wagon passed over the same trail, the wagon-wheel ruts became deeper and wider. In rainy weather the ruts turned into thick, slimy "goo" and the heavy prairie clay clung to the wagon wheels in great chunks

.

There were no grades. The roads, following the natural contours of the land, wound along the shallow valleys of southern Saskatchewan and southern Alberta, switchbacking up, or down, steep valley sides when necessary.

There were no bridges, either. Streams—and rivers—were crossed at shallower places, called "fords" or "crossings."

In a November 23, 1886, article the Macleod Gazette gave a graphic description of the hardships of being a stagecoach driver, especially in the wintertime.

Flooding rivers presented a grave danger to travellers. Sometimes horses and/or people were drowned as riders and drivers tried to swim their horses across an unforgiving river.

While working on the section of the CPR Crowsnest Pass route just west of Macleod, the Vroom brothers met Julia and Mose LaGrandeur. The LaGrandeurs were widely known oldtimers who were famous for their hospitality. Unlike Kootenai Brown, Mose and Julia LaGrandeur embraced the changes occurring in western Canada and adapted to the times.

Their homestead house at LaGrandeurs Crossing was a stagecoach stop more than 10 years before the CPR was built and for about 20 years after the railway came through. Their homestead was located on the wide, flat river bottom at the confluence of Pincher Creek and the Oldman River just west of the Peigan Indian Reserve (Piikani Nation) at Brocket, AB.

Mose was originally from Montreal, Quebec. Julia was born in Nebraska. She married Mose in Oregon in 1874. When they first came to southern Alberta, they bought the Alberta Ranch, southwest of Pincher Creek in 1882. A few years later in about 1886 Mose and Julia LaGrandeur homesteaded at LaGrandeurs Crossing located at the confluence of the Pincher Creek and the Old Man River a few miles west of Brocket, AB.

Julia LaGrandeur's life in this seemingly idyllic spot was not without drama, said her grandson Robin. One day when Julia had just turned out a freshly baked batch of her famous homemade bread on the counter, she glanced up to see a desperate-looking man staring at her through the cabin's small window. Julia quickly hid her three young children, Pete, Emma and Albert, in a nearby clothes closet, completing the maneuver only moments before the stranger entered the room uninvited. It turned out that the man was "Charcoal," a notorious fugitive from the Blood Indian Reserve south west of Lethbridge, who was being chased by the RCMP as a suspect in a recent murder on the reserve.

In a handwritten description of his grandparents' homestead days, Robin LaGrandeur wrote: "House built ca 1886 by Mose and Julia LaGrandeur at (the) confluence where Pincher Creek runs into the 'Old Man' River. Just west is (the) creek. Used as a Road House or stopover for stages from Calgary, north, and Lethbridge, east. Known as 'LaGrandeurs Crossing' for 30 years. The house where "Charcoal"—fugitive from the Blood Reserve— stopped and got fresh-baked bread during his flight from justice."

On the back of another picture Robin wrote: "Pete, Emma and Albert were born in above house. All three were hidden in closet while 'Charcoal' made his visit of need for loaves of bread." Courtesy Robin LaGrandeur

The accident shown here was taken on the day before a previous picture in this chapter that has the description "unidentified workmen stand atop the partially completed Canadian Pacific Railway bridge being built across Pincher Creek where it runs north to join the Old Man River a few miles west of Brocket, AB." This accident occurred very near LaGrandeurs Crossing. LIBRARY AND ARCHIVES CANADA/C00763

Mose and Julia LaGrandeur were the patriarch and matriarch of a family of six children. Two of their four sons—Pete and Emery—were rodeo champions.

In 1913, Emery LaGrandeur won the title of World Champion Bronco Rider at the Calgray Stampede. Emery LaGrandeur was so highly regarded by Guy Weadick, long time manager of the Calgary Stampede and Rodeo, that Mr. Weadick wrote an 8-page article entitled "Emery LaGrandeur: World's Champion Rider," which was published in the December 1919 issue of the Canadian Cattleman, as a tribute to Emery following his death in 1919.

Pete LaGrandeur, born April 1, 1890, in Pincher Creek, Alberta, married Edith Vliet of Gem, Alberta, in 1925 (LaGrandeur, 2005). Pete and Edith had seven children—Esther (1926-1990), Raymond and Robin (1928-   ), Mary (1930-1995), Doris May "Chick" (1932-2002), Ivan (John) (1935-   ) and Dan (1937-   )

It was said that Pete had a special way with horses. No matter how rank the bronc or saddle horse was, Pete would have the patience to tame the animal and ride them as if he were a "Sunday pleasure horse." The animals seemed to sense that Pete had no fear of any horse. Furthermore, Pete never asked any man to do what he wasn't willing to do himself, said his son Robin (LaGrandeur, December 2007).

In an article headlined, "Pincher Creek Native Son Becomes Hall of Famer," the Pincher Creek Echo (December 1991) reported that Pete LaGrandeur was recognized "as one of the best ever cowboys in the country (Canada)…At a ceremony on November 16 during the National Finale Rodeo in Edmonton, Pete LaGrandeur was inducted into the Canadian Rodeo (Association) Hall of Fame (CRHA)…was born November 10, 1890, in Pincher Creek … (he) died in 1957 at the age of 67 years."

As told in the chapter titled "Killing a Grizzly Bear" in Volume 1, *The VROOMS of the FOOTHILLS: Adventures of My Childhood*, 2003 and 2006, Pete was employed as stock rider in the Castle River Forsest Reserve. Pete was with my dad and me when Dad shot the big grizzly bear he had trapped behind Castle Mountain in the main range of the Rockies in southwest Alberta in the fall of 1936.

My dad and Pete LaGrandeur, both of whom had a passion for the life and work of a cowboy, were lifelong friends. Coincidentally, they both died in 1967, my dad being 10 years older than Pete.

Renowned rodeo rider Emery LaGrandeur is seen above making a championship ride atop a snakey bucking bronco named "Fox" at the Calgary Stampede in 1919. Emery displays his skills as a bucking bronco rider by holding his right hand high above his head while clasping the bronco's halter shank in his left hand.

Emery rakes the bronco from its shoulders to its flanks using his rowelled spurs to make the specially bred and trained bronco do his worst. An enthusiastic crowd in the stampede arena cheers on their native son.

A few years prior to this Emery won the title of "World Champion Bronco Rider along with a gold medal and $1000 as first final money" in the giant amphitheatre at the Rodeo Grounds in Winnipeg, MN.

Robin LaGrandeur (October 15, 2006) said his uncle Emery LaGrandeur was to be inducted into the Rodeo Hall of Fame posthumously on October 28, 2006. Glenbow Archives NA-217-50

Pete LaGrandeur's championship ride on a bucking bronco named "Funeral Wagon" at Calgary Stampede 1924. On this bronc, Pete won the Canadian Bucking Horse Championship. He also won the Canadian All Around at the Calgary Exhibition and Stampede.

He used his knowledge of the sport of rodeo and judged at the Calgary Stampede for approximately ten years. Pete participated in various rodeos throughout Western Canada for many years as a contestant in a number of events as well as an arena director.

Pete worked as the foreman for various cow and horse outfits for many years. Among others, he worked for Jack Morton and J. J. Bowlen, both of Southern Alberta. From 1933 to 1943 Pete was the stockman for the Castle River Cattle Association after which he was the stockman for the Peigan Indian Reserve at Brocket from 1943 until his death in 1957. Glenbow Archives NA-3164-74

Gerry Hoff Annand (Mrs. David) sits atop Avion Ridge in Waterton Lakes National Park in southwest Alberta in August 2007. Gerry, an avid trekker, climbed Mount Kilimanjaro in Kenya, Africa, in July 2007.

Here Gerry is facing northward gazing down into the South Fork of the Castle River Valley.

Seeing "the other side of the mountains" from high up is very interesting to me. The valley that Gerry views is where I went with my dad, accompanied by stock rider Pete LaGrandeur, when Dad went to get the grizzly bear out of the trap in 1936. This is an adventure I described in Volume 1, Adventures of My Childhood.

The South Fork Valley is much more beautiful here, with the foliage of the trees and of various shrubs and bushes grown back than it was in 1936, the summer that a raging forest fire ravaged thousands of acres of prime forest land in the South Fork valley. The fire burned up the grizzly bears' natural food supply and caused the grizzlies to go outside the forest reserve to get food in the form of nearby ranchers' cattle. Courtesy David & Geraldine Hoff Annand

Working with the railway construction crews and nearing Pincher Station, located some two and one-half miles north of Pincher Creek, the Vroom brothers saw this sweeping view of the majestic Canadain Rocky Mountains. Deep valleys and wide ledges along the mountains are punctuated with remains of winter snows.

As they slowly proceeded westward, Oscar frequently gazed at the mountains he loved. Sometimes, unable to contain the thrill of seeing the Rockies again, Oscar excitedly pointed out the various mountains that he remembered from his 1886-87 sojourns in southwestern Alberta.

Pausing from their construction work for a few minutes Oscar's brothers gazed at their first close-up view of the Rockies. In this view, taken from Pincher Station looking southwest toward Beaver Mines, Victoria Peak shows on the right hand side of the picture. Massive Castle Mountain is in the centre. Spread Eagle Mountain is on the left. Courtesy Edi-May Smithies

As told by my brother Donald, at one point, as the Vroom brothers continued working westward through the Rockies during the winter of 1897-1898, Oscar's blacksmithing skills were put to a critical test. The locomotive of their work train broke down and needed a new part.

The closest railway yards where a replacement could be secured was at least Medicine Hat, perhaps even as far as Winnipeg. Something had to be done and quickly.

Luckily, Oscar was able to use his ingenuity and skill to hand-manufacture a new part using his on-site smithy's forge. After a minimum time's delay, the locomotive was repaired. Very little railway construction time was lost and construction proceeded apace through the southern Canadian Rockies.

Years later my dad inherited my great-uncle Claude's smithy's outfit and with practice also became skilled at blacksmithing. Dad repaired our farming equipment and shod our horses for as long as we lived on the ranch. Often he shod a horse, or mended some equipment, for a neighbour, perhaps trading his blacksmith's time and skill for the neighbour's work in the hay field.

Barely 15 miles west of Pincher Station another challenge greeted the railway builders. They had to build another wooden trestle, this time so they could lay tracks across the Crowsnest River just west of Lundbreck. This bridge was "duck soup," as the saying goes, the land at that point being relatively level so there is no deep river valley to cross at Lundbreck Falls.

It is now a provincial park and a favourite camping spot for tourists to southern Alberta. The falls eres another wonder of Nature as seen by the Vroom brothers early in the 20th century when they traversed that area while working on a crew laying CPR tracks through the Crowsnest Pass. There is snow on the foothills, the river is mostly frozen and the spray from the partially frozen waterfall has left huge, fancifully shaped chunks of ice hanging on the side of it. Courtesy Jean McEwen Burns

A part of the Crowsnest Pass where the Crowsnest River, the highway, and the CPR go through a relatively narrow pass in the Rocky Mountains

The unpaved highway is in the near foreground; the river is beyond the highway. Where a river goes through a narrow break like this in the mountains the highway is built on one side of the river and the railway on the other side.

Here the railway winds along a narrow roadbed that runs along the bottom of the perpendicular rock face on the far side of the Crowsnest River. In such places the railway follows the contour of the riverbank and runs as close as possible to the river's edge.

Rock slides and avalanches are a constant danger to railways through the mountains. A rockslide shows in the centre middle background on the far side of the river. Nowadays, when a rockslide occurs warning signals are automatically turned on so that the train can stop in time thus avoiding a derailment. Washouts of stretches of railway track, caused by spring flooding in mountain rivers, made railway construction and maintenance difficult and dangerous in the early days of railroading in the mountains. Courtesy George and Shirley Tyson

Close examination of a Canadian Pacific Railway map over the Crowsnest Pass through the Rocky Mountains in southwest Alberta shows the twisting route of the CPR from Crowsnest on the Alberta border to Cranbrook, BC, which is about a 150-kilometre stretch.

For more than 12 months from spring 1897 to August 1898 the railway builders had to lay tracks along railbeds blasted out of mountainsides high above raging rivers. Throughout the winter, working largely with picks and shovels and horse and mule drawn equipment, the half-frozen workers clung to snowy, icy precipices along perpendicular mountainsides to complete yet another challenging task.

Turtle Mountain before the Slide.

Here is what Turtle Mountain in the Crowsnest Pass looked like before the Frank Slide came thundering down into the valley in 1903 obliterating the thriving mining town of Frank, AB.

My dad told me that when he came to Beaver Mines (in 1904) the year after the Frank Slide people resident in the area at the time told him that they heard the roar of the Frank Slide "forty miles out on the prairies."

In the foreground can be seen some of the houses and businesses that nestled at the very base of that sleeping giant. A full story of the Crowsnest Pass and of the Frank Slide can be found in a book about the history of the Crowsnest Pass by Vern Decoux, who was a district correspondent for the Lethbridge Herald *in the 1950s and 1960s.*

The slide, of course, also wiped out a section of CPR tracks that were laid by the Vroom brothers and their work crew friends only six years previously. There was no train service from Blairmore to Cranbrook until a trench was dug through the metres deep pile of rocks from the slide and the rail bed and tracks were rebuilt.

Nowadays a modern highway runs over the rubble from the slide, which extends more than one-half mile up the opposite side of the valley. A modern visitor centre located at the Frank Slide site shows photographs of the area and explanations of the geological phonemena that caused the disastrous slide. Courtesy Katherine Bruce

The train tracks make tortuous turns as they zigzag through the mountainous areas of southwestern Alberta and southeastern BC following twisting river valleys cut over the eons out of the granite rocks of the main range of the Canadian Rockies and several smaller ranges between the Continental Divide and Cranbrook, BC.

Little did the railway builders realize when they were laying the CPR tracks through the Crowsnest Pass in the winter of 1897-98 that in a few years, in 1903, a gigantic chunk of imposing Turtle Mountain would come crashing down into the valley below, wiping out the small mining town of Frank, AB, and killing all but one of the people who lived there.

A small child who habitually slept between her parents was found the next morning sitting atop a massive boulder a half mile up the east side of the valley. People who lived 40 miles out on the prairies heard the rumble when the thousands of tons of rock broke away from the east face of the mountain and slid into the valley below.

The Summit Hotel, located at the summit of the Crowsnest Pass was one of the earliest business establishments along the historic Crowsnest Pass route. The new Summit Hotel, shown here, was built in the 1920s after the first hotel burned down in 1920 or 1921. The Summit Hotel straddles the border between Alberta and British Columbia near the town of Coleman.

Members of the Summit Hotel staff came out on the second-storey balcony to pose for the photographer in this historic photo. Trophy heads of six whitetail deer, four Rocky Mountain sheep and one Rocky Mountain goat hang from the edge of the balcony.

"It's been suggested that Andy Good was a camp follower on the CNL and that he may have run a cook house for those who felt they deserved a break from Company cuisine. (Mr. Good) got this far in 1898 and went no further. Charmed by the beauty and significance of the locale, he and his wife, Kate, built their Summit Hotel between the twin outlets of Island Creek.

"One outlet flowed into Summit Lake in the Pacific watershed; the other outlet flowed into Island Lake in the Hudson Bay watershed. The couple liked to mention that rain falling on their roof ended up in two oceans.

When not seeing to the comfort of their guests or sorting mail in the post office, Andy and Kate wandered through their surroundings, hunting and exploring. The original hotel burned to the ground in 1921 or 1922, and much of the current structure looks to date from the subsequent rebuilding."

This information is from: http://www.crowsnest-highway.ca/cgi-bin/citypage.pl?city=SPARWOOD. The Old Summit Hotel and the New Summit Hotel may be seen on this website. Courtesy Katherine Bruce

Upon reaching Cranbrook, BC, already a thriving community in the East Kootenays in August 1898, the Vroom brothers stayed in the area. They took time to engage in some well-earned relaxation by socializing happily with the early residents of that area. The CPR tracks were laid as far as Kootenay Landing on the east side of Kootenay Lake in the fall of 1900.

In 1900, having left the CPR track laying crew, Claude and Ralph Voorhees Vroom, both of whom were carpenters, were engaged in the building boom of the time. Archie set up a blacksmith shop in Cranbrook. According to an advertisement in the *Cranbrook Herald* of February 7, 1901, by that time Archie was doing general blacksmithing and repairs, horseshoeing, wagon making and painting.

Years later, as reported in the *Cranbrook Courier* of July 26, 1946, when Archie visited friends in Cranbrook, the following items appeared in the *Cranbrook Courier.*

"Mr. and Mrs. Archie Vroom of Vancouver were overnight visitors in Cranbrook last week en route to Calgary. Mr. Vroom resided in Cranbrook many years ago and will be remembered by old time time friends. Mrs. Geldhart, also an old time resident of the city, who lives in Calgary, accompanied them.

"Archie Vroom, one of the early day blacksmiths of Cranbrook, was a visitor in the city this week, renewing old acquaintances. Archie was a partner in the smithing business with Jack Dezall in 1905, when he sold out and moved to other parts. He is now making his home in Vancouver. He admits the ranks of the old timers of his day are pretty well thinned out."

Married.

At the Methodist parsonage, February 2nd, by Rev. J. W. Bowering, B. A., Mr. Ralph Vroom, of Cranbrook, to Mrs. Marie M. Blanchard, of Boston, Mass.

Mr. and Mrs. Vroom will live in the new house just completed by Mr. Matheson, on Garden street. The Herald extends congratulations and wishes the happy couple prosperity and contentment.

This notice in the Cranbrook Herald, February 7, 1901, marked the marriage of Ralph Voorhees Vroom to Mrs. Marie M. Lacross Blanchard, of Boston, Mass., noting also that the young couple planned to live in a newly completed house on Garden St. and that Mr. Matheson was the builder. Ralph's sister Amanda "Minnie" married Dr. Clark Gould of Boston, Massachusetts. Ralph probably met and courted Marie Blanchard while visiting his sister. Marie was Ralph's first wife. We don't know where or why she died. There is a mysterious "Mrs Vroom" (no other name given) buried in the Pincher Creek cemetery. Courtesy George and Shirley Tyson

On October 18, 1911, Ralph Voorhees Vroom married his second wife, Elizabeth "Bessie" Angelina Newcombe in Vancouver, BC.

My great-aunt Bessie, seen here with my great-uncle Ralph Voorhees Vroom about the time of their marriage in 1911, was a dear, loving soul. She was my favourite great-aunt. I got to know her one time that she was visiting my aunt Marion Cyr. It just happened that I visited Aunt Marion Cyr as a young child while Aunt Bessie was there visiting. We took an immediate liking to each other.

Aunt Bessie was an expert knitter and while I was at Aunt Marion's that time she knitted a new red hat for me. I loved that hat and wore it constantly until it was practically in shreds. Author's collection

The Cranbrook Courier *Jubilee Edition on September 1, 1955, featured this group.   The newspaper identifies the people as: "A merry group of visitors at the Banks & Thompson shaft at Perry Creek." Photographed in 1902 by Prest, Cranbrook, Fort Steele, Moyie City, BC.*

A group of young people who were working in the Cranbrook area at that time had gathered at a favourite picnic spot for a few hours of fun and relaxation before returning to their respective jobs next morning. Perry Creek runs through a beautiful, forested valley about eight miles northwest of Cranbrook in the Purcell Mountains.

Archie Vroom, wearing a bowler hat, sits in centre above between two ladies. Note: Enlargement of photo shows Archie Vroom pulling cord attached to camera shutter release, presumably so photographer, Prest, could be in the photo.

The following ID of people is from the above-noted Cranbrook Courier:

On roof from left: (?); Thompson; Wes Ferris

Next row: Ernie Ryckman; (?); J. Dezall; (?); Gougeon (Mrs. Dezall); Post; C. Prest (photographer); H.A. McKowan; Delmar; Baker; Mustard.

Lower row: Ethel Ryckman (Mrs. D. Burton); Olive Ryckman (Mrs. Burge); Ethel Baker (Mrs. Johnson); Enid Cartwright (Mrs. Peck); Archie Vroom; Mabel Baker; Gail Thompson; B. Boyter (Mrs. Lee); Ella Johnson (Mrs. McKay) and leaning on her, Evah Cartwright (Mrs. H.A. McKowan); Hattie Patmore (Mrs. Harris); Rev. Thompson to the right of Mrs. McKowan; then Slater boy and Mrs. F. Slater.

In front: F. Slater's boy and two Thompson boys.

The newpapers in Cranbrook kept close tabs on Archie, reporting on his every move. The Cranbrook Courier telling in 1905 Archie Vroom, who was a partner in the smithing business with Jack Dezall, sold out and "moved to other parts". The Prospector of February 24, 1906, reported that Archie was visiting in Cranbrook and the Cranbrook Courier reported that in September 1906 (Archie) was "returning to Archie's ranch near Pincher."
Courtesy Peter Vroom

This group of men, women and children, dressed in their Sunday best, was taken on June 26, 1902, at a young peoples' picnic Perry Creek, BC, beside what looks like a good-sized barn built of large square-cut logs chinked with concrete.

Archie Vroom, with bowler hat tipped forward, is standing, centre, back row. Ralph Voorhees Vroom (hatless) is kneeling, centre, middle row, with his hands resting on the head of Claude Vroom, who is seated. Oscar Vroom, wearing a hat, is standing, far right, in the back row.

Oscar and Claude, en route from Clementsport, Nova Scotia, to Beaver Mines, NWT, visited their brothers in Cranbrook for a while before going to Alberta to take up homesteads. Courtesy Peter Vroom

In February 1901 Archie Vroom still owned his blacksmith shop in Cranbrook. Service offered to his clients, as shown in this ad in the Cranbrook Herald of February 7, 1901, included blacksmithing, horseshoeing, repairing, wagon making and painting.

Archie, a blacksmith before he left Nova Scotia in 1897, honed his skills further while working on the track laying crew building the CPR from MacLeod, AB, through the Crowsnest Pass to Cranbrook, BC, during 1897-1898. At that time, most breakdowns in equipment could be mended on site with Archie and Oscar combining their blacksmithing skills to get the job done.

Archie's blacksmithing business flourished so briskly that he had to take on a partner. In the Cranbrook Herald, March 20, 1902, the ad for Archie's business read: "VROOM & DEZALL Blacksmithing, Horseshoeing, Carriage Repair and General Jobbing". Courtesy of George and Shirley Tyson

On July 1, 1902, the Vroom brothers are with a group of friends on an outing at Pattons Lake, BC, which is two miles north of Cranbrook. Kneeling in the back row are Claude Vroom, far left, and Archie Vroom, second from right. Oscar Vroom, wearing a cap and having a dark mustache, sits second from the left in the front row. Courtesy Peter Vroom

With his blacksmithing business well established, Archie Vroom had time on weekends to enjoy the company of other young people of Cranbrook and their families. This is a fishing expedition on Lamb Creek, August 12, 1902. Lamb Creek is approximately 10 miles south of Cranbrook. Archie Vroom, in bowler hat, seated in the back row, far left, joins some young families. Courtesy Peter Vroom

This picture shows Archie Vroom, second from left, and Ralph Voorhees Vroom, second from right, entertaining guests at their bachelors' pad in Cranbrook on Christmas Day, 1902.

Oscar and Claude had gone to the Beaver Mines district in the summer or fall of 1902 to apply for homestead quarters. We do not know where Ralph's wife, Marie, whom he married in 1901, was at this time.

The cabin is sparsely equipped, but comfortable for the times. Dishes and cooking utensils sit neatly on open shelves along the wall and a banner cheerfully proclaiming "Our Happy Home" hangs across the back wall. The small cabin is heated with a wood heater with the chimney running straight up through the roof. Courtesy Peter Vroom

In 1902 Oscar and Claude went back to Pincher Creek and thence to Beaver Mines Creek Valley. Claude chose his homestead quarter in the same township as his brother, but east of Oscar's land over a range of foothills. Oscar and Claude settled on their land and did the work needed to qualify as homesteaders.

Archie and Ralph Voorhees Vroom stayed in Cranbrook until 1903. Ralph, who never did anything "cowboy-like," went from Cranbrook to Vancouver. There he initially met his second wife, Elizabeth "Bessie" Angelina Newcombe. Ralph went to Seattle later in 1903 where he continued working as a carpenter. In 1903 Archie joined Oscar and Claude at Beaver Mines, but he did not "prove up" a homestead.

Archie lived on the NW ¼ -35-5-2-W of the 5th, the quarter where I lived as a child, long enough that it became known as "Archie (Vroom)'s ranch," as noted in the *Cranbook Courier*, Thursday, September 13, 1906. Claude homesteaded the quarter directly west of Archie.

Archie, a carpenter as well as a blacksmith, and his brothers Oscar and Claude, also built a two-storey, four-bedroom log house on Oscar's homestead in Beaver Mines Creek Valley. It was the first two-storey log house in the district.

When the Vroom brothers finished building Oscar's two-storey log cabin, they turned their attention to getting Claude settled on and proved up on his homestead. Together Archie and Claude, and maybe Oscar, built a small log cabin for Claude. That little cabin, on our west quarter, was still standing when we lived on the ranch at Beaver Mines. It stood at least until the middle of the WWII years.

This is my grandfather Oscar Vroom on his Sunny Vale Ranche at Beaver Mines. Table Mountain, which is not shown in this picture, formed a perfect backdrop for Oscar's preferred way of life.

By the time of the 1901 Census of Canada, Oscar had moved back to Clementsport from Cranbrook and was living with Alena and four children. Oscar had just spent two years travelling to Mexico to visit his brother Herbert on his ranch.

His brother Claude, now of Cranbrook, accompanied Oscar back to Clementsport, NS, for a period of time, living with his parents, William and Sara, and his niece Jennie Louise Vroom.

*By 1902 the lure of the west took hold of Oscar again and he left Nova Scotia once more to head for the West, this time accompanied by his brother Claude. Claude also homesteaded southeast of Beaver Mines on NE ¼ -34-5-2-W5th, 26*Courtesy Adeline Cyr Robbins

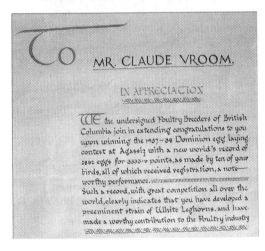

After proving up on his quarter, Claude sold his homestead to Charles "Charlie" Mitchell. Claude worked on the CPR mail train on the run from Medicine Hat through the Crowsnest Pass for a few years. In 1917, Claude moved to Surrey, BC, where he became a prize-winning egg/chicken farmer.

This manuscript certificate of appreciation was presented to Claude Vroom for winning the 1937-38 Dominion Egg-Laying contest at Agassiz, BC. Claude Vroom's obituary states: "He won especial fame for raising the pen of White Leghorn pullets which set a new world's record for egg production in the 1937-38 egg laying contest."
Courtesy City of Surrey Archives

This banner publicized the most desirable quality of chickens produced on the Vroom Farm at Surrey, BC. Claude Vroom's prize-winning chickens were "milk fed." Courtesy City of Surrey Museum.

Once they got Claude's cabin built, Archie put into operation his plan to get Oscar's family re-united. Archie knew that Alena, who was a schoolteacher before she married Oscar, would never move to a place where there was no school for her children.

To meet Alena's conditions for moving west, Archie executed his plan. In the absence of a regular school in Gladstone Valley, Archie set about building a schoolhouse. Assisted by his brother Claude, Archie built a schoolhouse on NW ¼ 35-5-2-W of the 5th, which we called the "east quarter" when I was a child. This assured that Alena would not have the excuse of "no school for the children" as a reason for not coming west.

The east quarter was in the Gladstone Valley School district. The children of the earliest settlers in Gladstone Valley, the John Truitt and the William Barclay families, for instance, attended the Archie Vroom School for several years until Gladstone Valley School opened in 1912-13 (*Unfolding the Pages*, 1992). This information was also stated in various conversations with oldtimers, such as with Adam "Dutch" and Hazel Truitt and my dad's recollections.

One sure sign that the house I lived in when I was a child had been a schoolhouse at one time was the fact that there was a two-sided toilet--one side for "Girls" and one side for "Boys"--in the house yard. Moreover, the two sides of the toilet building had various sized holes so as to accommodate children ranging in age from six years to at least 14 years of age.

When our house was used as the Archie Vroom School the classroom was likely an L-shaped room that included what was our dining room living room areas. Adam Truit brought to my attention the fact that the classroom was crowded as there were several children of William and Jane Barclay, John and Cinnie Truitt, and Harry and Bessie Truitt, out of families with as many as nine children each, who were of school age during that period.

There were also the school-age children of other families living in Gladstone Valley at that time. These could have been the older children of the Nash, Cesar, Elliott, Fred Strauss, and other early homesteader families in Gladstone Valley.

The schoolteacher boarded with people who lived on the Kubzsa place about one mile north of the Archie Vroom School and walked over the hills to get to school, according to Adam

Truitt in 2005. There was no school in the Beaver Mines Creek Valley either, so for a few months when my grandparents first moved west and until he turned 14 my dad also attended the Archie Vroom School.

Charlie Mitchell "proved up" his homestead on the Archie Vroom schoolhouse quarter, NW ¼ -35-5-2-W of the 5th. At the time, Charlie was still a bachelor so he lived with his parents less than a mile away on the Richardson place.

Charlie married Mary Ellen "Sis" Buchanan in 1914. Born in Glasgow, Scotland, "Sis" immigrated to Canada in 1910 and settled in Pincher Creek. She took a position as postmistress, working there until she married.

Like all women who immigrated to Canada in the early 1900s, "Sis" was strong and hardy. In addition, she possessed a robust Scottish sense of humour that never left her and enthusiastically embraced the idea of becoming a westerner. Charlie and "Sis" built a second storey onto the Archie Vroom School and lived there from 1914 to 1926.

In 1926 my grandmother Vroom helped my dad and mother to purchase the Mitchell land and the two-storey house became the home of the Ralph and Molly Tyson Vroom family.

MAP 2 Quarter Section Homesteads in Beaver (Mines) Creek Valley and Gladstone Valley, circa 1910

Oscar developed his homestead as a working ranch. When Oscar grew old and could no longer do the heavy ranch work, he turned his homestead over to his oldest son, Harold, whose own homestead abutted his father's land.

Oscar's second son, Ralph, chose the SW ¼ -28-5-2-W5th, the northeast corner of which just touched the southeast corner of Oscar's homestead. Unlike, Harold and Oscar's quarters, Ralph's quarter had very little flat arable land. What it did have and which Oscar prized was a thick stand of tall, straight trees of varying diameters, which blanketed the low foothills that covered most of Ralph's quarter section. Oscar, who was somewhat of a visionary, foresaw constructing ranch buildings and corrals using these logs. He lost no time in beginning the task.

This map shows the quarter sections located in Township 5 on which settlers had filed for homestead rights about 1910. There were a number of quarter sections northwest and southwest of Oscar's homestead that had not been filed on where a large herd of horses could be grazed at very little cost.

By 1904 settlers had homesteaded on most of the good land in the bottom of the Gladstone and Beaver Mines Creek Valleys. However, there were still a number of unoccupied quarter sections available as rangeland. These quarter sections were often on hilly land where the snow would melt off in the early spring providing a longer grazing period.

Some of these quarters could have been lived on, but not homesteaded yet, by single men, men with families, or men like Oscar Vroom who had a family in Nova Scotia and did not actually homestead his land until after his family came west in 1904. In fact, in the 1930s there was a group of unoccupied buildings still standing on a quarter section of land, the NE ¼ -33-5-2-W5th, about one mile due west of my childhood home. My dad talked about the Prentices when I was a child, but I never knew that family. Based on information from the National Archives of Canada, Western Canada Land Grants Website. Illustration by Edi-May Smithies, Cartography by Shelley McConnell

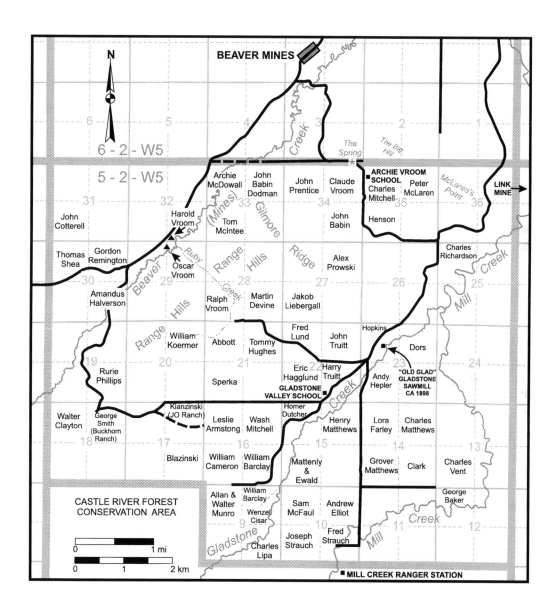

MAP 2 QUARTER SECTION HOMESTEADS IN BEAVER (MINES) CREEK VALLEY
AND GLADSTONE VALLEY, circa 1910

Archie Vroom's homestead cabin and barn circa 1911 on NW 1/4-35-5-2-W5th became part of the ranch buildings where I grew up (our east quarter). Archie probably built the homestead house and barn so he could live there while building the "Archie Vroom School."

However, Charlie Mitchell, not Archie Vroom, "proved up" the homestead on this quarter. Charlie undoubtedly paid Archie something for the buildings he had erected. That would give Archie enough cash to start his store in Watson, SK. Claude Vroom may have shared the barn with Archie at first, and then shared it with Charlie when Archie moved to Saskatchewan.

This cabin was moved a short distance south and a bit north and became Dad's carpenter shop. Archie's barn stayed where it was and became our goat house. Courtesy Ruby Jaggernath

Claude Vroom homestead cabin circa 1911 on NE 1/4 -34-5-2-W5th This *became known as Ralph & Mollie Vroom's "west" quarter. The cabin was still standing when I was a child.* Courtesy Ruby Jaggernath

RALPH VROOM: "I WANT TO BE A COWBOY"

While his younger brothers, Claude and Ralph, took work in the Cranbrook area and enjoyed the social life, Oscar could talk of nothing but the beautiful countryside southwest of Pincher Creek. Oscar told everyone he had resolved to return there and take up a homestead.

This is the village of Clementsport, NS, in the Annapolis Valley on the Bay of Fundy. Oscar and Alena Vroom and their family lived here until they came west to live in the Beaver Mines Creek Valley in 1904, one year before Alberta became a province. The Vroom family home is second from right.

For the first 10 years of their married life, Oscar lived a relatively settled life. He and Alena and their four children lived contentedly in the village. "We used to dig for clams," Dad told my siblings and me when we were young. "You could tell where there was a clam just beneath the surface, but as soon as it felt you starting to dig for it, the clam would burrow deeper into the sand. You had to dig real fast or the clam would get away on you," Dad assured us. Courtesy Sheila Wheelock

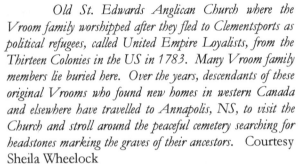

Old St. Edwards Anglican Church where the Vroom family worshipped after they fled to Clementsports as political refugees, called United Empire Loyalists, from the Thirteen Colonies in the US in 1783. Many Vroom family members lie buried here. Over the years, descendants of these original Vrooms who found new homes in western Canada and elsewhere have travelled to Annapolis, NS, to visit the Church and stroll around the peaceful cemetery searching for headstones marking the graves of their ancestors. Courtesy Sheila Wheelock

(On the left) *This is my great-grandmother Sara Ann Woodman Vroom, taken in Annapolis, NS. Marion Vroom Cyr recalled visiting with her grandmother, who was very kind and jolly, was never out of sorts, and was adored by all of her grandchildren.*

My aunt Marion said that her grandma Vroom preserved fruit from their garden and baked goodies that the children enjoyed eating. My dad, too, remembered his grandmother as being jolly and kind. Sara was very lonely for the children when they moved west. Before Alena and her family came to the West to live in a log cabin, albeit a two-storey log cabin, she lived very comfortably in the peaceful village of Clementsport located on the Bay of Fundy in Nova Scotia. Her father-in-law and mother-in-law lived nearby and took a great interest in the children and visited them often. Author's collection

(On the right) *William Voorhees Vroom stands in front of Oscar and Alena's fine home in Clementsport, NS. William, who attended church regularly, is dressed and ready to go to Sunday service.* Courtesy Peter Vroom

This is one of the chairs from the original set of six plus a love seat that was part of the furniture owned by my grandmother Alena Vroom and with which she furnished her lovely home in Clementsport, NS, and her four-bedroom log cabin on Oscar's and her Sunny Vale Ranche in Beaver Mines Creek Valley, AB.

Oscar and Alena's house in Clementsport had four bedrooms and was furnished with complete bedroom suites, which Alena's family had brought from Ireland. We had most of this furniture in our house on the ranch at Beaver Mines when I was a child. The chair frames were made of mahogany decorated with intricately carved designs. Author's collection

Here my great-grandfather William Voorhees Vroom stands in the midst of his cherished well-kept apple orchard. The carefully nurtured trees are laden with fruit. A field of wild flowers, seen in the foreground, bordered the orchard. Great-grandfather Vroom is dressed in his working clothes--a peaked cap, comfortable baggy trousers, a long-sleeved shirt and a vest with watch pocket so he will know when to go to the house for lunch.

My dad remembered how he did not like to help his grandfather pick the apples when the family lived close to their grandparents. However, he did love to eat the delicious apple pies, which his grandmother baked frequently. Whenever my dad visited his grandmother, Sara Woodman Vroom, or when he had picked a big basket of apples for his grandfather, his grandmother Vroom invited him in for a piece of fresh apple pie and a cool glass of milk.

However, after the family moved to the West my dad's appreciation for his grandfather Vroom increased immeasurably. Every fall his grandfather Vroom picked the apples alone, or with the help of neighbours, and shipped barrels full of apples to Alena and Oscar and their children in Alberta. Then Alena made pies for the family, and Ralph remembered with delight the mouth-watering smells from his grandmother's cozy kitchen. Courtesy Peter Vroom

In Cranbrook, Oscar made a new friend, William Barclay. William, his wife Jane and family had just moved from Cowley, AB. Oscar's enthusiasm for the Pincher Creek area was so convincing that the Barclays decided to pull up stakes again and take a homestead in Alberta.

In 1905, when William and Jane moved to their homestead, they were the third family to move to Gladstone Valley. Their homestead was about six miles south of where I lived as a child and only a few miles east of Oscar's homestead. The Barclays became close friends of the Vroom family and remained so over their lifetime. William Barclay was a pallbearer at Oscar's funeral.

In 1946 William and Jane Barclay celebrated their 50th wedding anniversary. Here they are flanked by seven of their adult children who were able to be with them on this memorable day.

As identified by Sonia Chiesa, shown here are: Standing (left to right) Lillian "Lil" Barclay who married Mr. Robbins and also married a second time; James "Charlie" who married Sonia Chiesa; Note: Charlie's name on his birth certificate was "James"; there is no mention of Charles on the certificate. Sonia doesn't know how he got the nickname "Charlie"; Elizabeth "Liz" who married Bill Bird; Helen "Nellie," who married Wallace Adam; Alexander "Alex (pronounced 'Alec'), who married Margaret Martin; Ann who married Mr. Kemp first and, secondly a Mr. Cameron. Mr. Cameron owned a gas station on Main St, Pincher Creek. William, Jr. "Bill" Barclay stands on the right. Missing Agnes Barclay (deceased).

To differentiate between father and son, William Barclay, Sr. was always called "William," while his son William was known as "Bill". Courtesy Dorothy Archibald

On February 2, 1901, Ralph Voorhees Vroom married his first wife, Mrs. Marie M. Lacross Blanchard of Boston, Massachusetts. They lived in a new house on Garden Street, which was just completed by a Mr. Matheson, as reported in the *Cranbrook Herald*, February 7, 1901. Claude and his brother Ralph Voorhees had steady work in construction in Cranbrook, according to the reminiscences of Archbishop M.C. O'Neill.

About the same time, the Vroom brothers' sister Amanda "Minnie" married Dr. Clark Gould of Boston, Mass.

Oscar spent about two years before 1901 visiting with his brother Herbert at his ranch in Mexico. The Census of Canada records that by 1901 Oscar had moved from Cranbrook back to Clementsport and was living with Alena and the children. Claude, who went back to Nova Scotia with Oscar, was living with his parents and his niece Jennie Louise Vroom in Clementsport.

Archie lived away from Cranbrook for a period of time in 1901, but the ads for his blacksmith shop continued to run in the *Cranbrook Herald* until at least November 1901. There are family photographs showing Archie in Cranbrook in 1902. And, in the *Cranbrook Herald* of July 31, 1902, Archie's ad still read: "*VROOM & DEZALL Blacksmithing, Horseshoeing, Carriage Repairing and General Jobbing, Outside Orders Promptly Attended To.*"

Impromptu sports days, and the inevitable contests that these entailed, were held at some of the big ranches around Pincher Creek. Here two democrat outfits, each pulled by one team of fast horses, vie for first spot in a democrat race at the fairgrounds in Pincher Creek in the summer or 1928. Here one driver is taking the outside of the racetrack on a straight stretch by pulling past two outfits that are in front of him.

Driving in a democrat could be dangerous. A number of people were injured when thrown out of a careening democrat pulled by a frightened team that bolted and ran away. The driver, unable to stop the runaway team, held on as best he or she could, but often passengers were thrown out. Mrs. Nellie Gladstone Riviere died from injuries received when she was thrown from a buggy in about 1940.

David Ballantyne father of homesteader and long-time Beaver Mines postmaster George Ballantyne, died after "his driving horse bolted and he was thrown and dragged." (Friesen 1974) Courtesy Katherine Bruce

"Oscar came west from Nova Scotia in 1902. He located on Crown Land 18 miles west of Pincher, where he looked after Crown Brand horses." (Friesen, 1974) This is an understatement of Oscar's involvement with the West. We now know that Oscar travelled in the West as early as 1886.

When Oscar returned to the West in 1902, he brought his brother Claude with him. They first went to Cranbrook to visit Archie and Ralph. Then, in the summer or fall of 1902, Archie and Ralph Voorhees remained in Cranbrook, while Oscar and Claude went on to Pincher Creek.

Robert "Bob" Lang's homestead was about half way between Pincher Creek and Beaver Mines. Bob recalled (Lang, Ellis, 1961 interview) that in 1903 he had a four-day visit from Oscar and Archie Vroom. The two brothers had attended the First of July Sports Day in Pincher Creek and were heading back to their homesteads when they got caught in a torrential downpour. "We used to call them 'cloud bursts'," Bob said.

Being close to Bob's homestead Oscar and Claude pulled in there to visit for what they thought would be only a couple of hours. Other ranchers passing by also called in at Bob's place. The whole crowd of them was at Bob's place for four days, stranded there until the rain ceased.

During their four-day stay, Mr. Lang said, he also told Archie and Oscar Vroom that in 1901 he "put up 55 tons of hay where Judge McLaughlin lives at present (in 1961) west of Beaver Mines [on the Harold Vroom homestead] at $3.50 a ton." Harold Vroom sold the land to Judge McLaughlin. Judge's widow, Rosalie Biron McLaughlan, was living on that quarter as late as 2005 when I called on her during a visit in the area to renew old acquaintances.

Mr. Lang, like other bachelors in southwestern Alberta, enjoyed a lively social life. He attended parties at Beaver Mines and played euchre with the Catholic priest who held services there. George Ballantyne and W. J. A. "Wash" Mitchell played against Bob and the priest. When Bob and the priest won, the priest would say, "It's hard to beat a Catholic priest and a good Orangeman."

In the fall of 1904, Mr. Lang remembered that the Indians from Brocket went past his homestead on their way up Mill Creek to shoot deer to get meat for winter. Upon their return, Mr. Lang bought a whole side of venison for $1.25. "It was nice deer meat," he assured me. Bob also told of Indians from the Peigan Reserve at Brocket passing his homestead every summer to go up Mill Creek fishing.

In 1903, Archie Vroom left Cranbrook to take up a homestead. Archie built at least three buildings on the "east quarter" (NW ¼ -35-5-2-W of the 5th). These buildings included a homestead cabin, a barn and the Archie Vroom School, the first school in the district. Homestreaders' children from Gladstone Valley and Beaver Mines Creek Valley attended the Archie Vroom School from about 1904 until Gladstone Valley School opened (Truitt, Ellis, 2004 interview).

RALPH VROOM: "I WANT TO BE A COWBOY"

My dad, too, often told me that the Archie Vroom School was the only school that he attended in the West. He rode about five miles from his parents' homestead to the school that his Uncle Archie built only a couple of years before my grandmother Alena Vroom brought her family west in 1904. Archie sold these buildings to Charlie Mitchell when Charlie homesteaded NW ¼ -35-5-2-W of the 5th. Charlie added another storey to the Archie Vroom School. Charlie and Sis Mitchell and their son, Jack, (in this 1924 photo with Wash Mitchell on right) lived in the resulting "big box type house," decribed as such by Jack Mitchell (2000). In the 1930s my dad used Archie's barn as a goat house and his homesteader cabin as a carpenter shop. Courtesy Ruby Jaggernath

(Above left) *Archie Vroom went through the motions of becoming a homesteader Archie's horse brand was* capital 'NS' *(for Nova Scotia) on the left flank.*

(Above right) *Archie Vroom's cattle brand, 'Anchor A', was capital 'A' with an arrow down and a bar over. The 'A' was for Archibald; the down arrow reminded Archie of an anchor—he never forgot the sea. Archie's cattle brand was reminiscent of his childhood spent beside the Bay of Fundy in Nova Scotia.* Illustrations by Edi-May Smithies, based on 1907 Alberta Brand Book

Archie's main aim in building the Archie Vroom School was to get Alena and the children to come to the West from Clementsport. All the time he was working in the West, Archie kept in touch with Alena. He knew that she would never move to anywhere that there was not a place for her children to go to school.

Oscar was quite happy with the situation as it was, but his brother Archie had strong feelings on the subject. When Archie had done everything he could think of to get his brother's family reunited in the West he went to Clementsport himself, determined to escort Alena and her four children to the West. Once there, he convinced his sister-in-law Alena that she should move her children to the West to join their father as soon as possible.

Alena soon realized that it would be better if she and her fast-growing family came west to join Oscar on his homestead. Then one day Ralph, who was by then a rambunctious pre-teenager, declared to his mother, "I want to be a cowboy!" That did it. Alena made up her mind to join her husband in the West.

Alena wound up her Nova Scotia business affairs, selling as many items as she could to raise money for her new home. She shipped her cherished Irish mahogany living room suite, maple dining room suite, and four complete bedroom suites by freight to Cowley, NWT, the nearest railway station to Beaver Mines.

To the spectators at a Castle River Stampede in the 1930s the chuck wagon race looked like a dangerous activity. Pulled by a vigorous four-horse team the light wagons used in this race slewed to one side when rounding the racetrack corners while the driver and his partner hung on for dear life and the crowd cheered wildly for a favourite driver.

Here four chuck wagon outfits are trotting up to the starting line on the stampede race track in front of the judges' stand. The two close-up outfits are in clear view, but the two back outfits are almost obscured by the dust kicked up by the first two teams.

The steep white cliffs on the west side of the Castle River where it flows north past the stampede grounds show beyond the trees on the east side of the river. Courtesy Katherine Bruce

Alena, like thousands of other women with families travelling on the train to join husbands in the West, had to bring enough food to feed herself and her children for the five-day journey. The family rode in a colonists' day coach sitting on uncomfortable hard wooden benches as the train puffed and steamed across the vast expanse of Canada.

The children loved the excitement and made up lively games to entertain themselves. At night the family slept on bunks at the end of the car using bedding that they brought with them from Nova Scotia. Marion Vroom Cyr remembered they "got off the train at Cowley in July and went straight to the farm at Beaver" travelling by democrat and team.

When the Alena and her four children arrived in the west, Harold was nearly 16 years of age, so he was old enough to work away from home. At first, various ranchers who were already established in southwestern Alberta hired Harold to help with the ranch work.

As soon as the family had moved into their log cabin on Beaver Creek, the three younger children had to start school. The nearest school, the Archie Vroom School, was five miles away.

Alena decided that Marion and Alfred were too young to ride so far, but since she and Oscar could not afford to send Marion and Alfred to school in Pincher Creek, Alena taught them both at home for nearly three years--from 1904 until the spring of 1907.

Upon the death of her mother, on November 2, 1906, Alena inherited a considerable amount of money from Elizabeth's estate, enabling Marion and Alfred to school in Pincher Creek.

The first time Alena visited Pincher Creek after arriving in the West in the spring of 1904 she was aghast at the size of the settlement. It consisted of less than 100 houses and a few businesses on either side of the Main Street. She wondered how they would ever survive. Alena, however, had a good spirit. She soon adapted to life in the West, and saw to it that her children fitted in, too.

Taken "looking west" in 1908 and showing the main street of Pincher Creek four years after Alena and her children arrived in the west. By this time there was a telephone system, operated by Alberta Government Telephones, in place in Pincher Creek. (Cashman, 1972)

Five telephone poles with at least eight wires strung on the crossbars march along the north side of Main Street showing that a number of people in Pincher Creek, and some people living in rural areas, had telephones.

The street looks muddy, indicating a recent heavy rainfall. There is a wooden sidewalk on the south side of the street, but none on the north side.

The building in the near right foreground is the livery stable, a well-used service in the early days of Pincher Creek. Settlers came to town by saddle horse or by team and democrat or team and wagon. Their horses had to be fed and watered before the return journey to the ranch. The livery stable provided this accommodation.

A team, still hitched to a democrat, is tied to a hitching rack just outside the livery stable. This is the type of conveyance that Oscar used when he met Alena and the children when they arrived at the train station in Cowley, AB, in the spring of 1904. Courtesy Bill Link

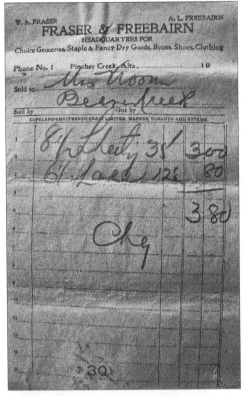

Making their homestead houses into homes necessitated the women of the day becoming very good seamstresses. Alena used what household effects she brought with her to furnish her new home in Beaver Mines Creek Valley, but in a couple years she sewed more sheets and pillowcases for her four-bedroom log house.

This circa 1906-1908 receipt from Fraser & Freebairn of Pincher Creek for the purchase by "Mrs. Vroom of Beaver Creek" of 8 ½ lengths of sheeting at $0.35 per length, rounded off to $3.00, and 6 ½ lengths of lace at $0.12 per length, rounded off to $0.80 for a total of $3.80. This purchase indicates that Alena intended to make new sheets to furnish the four bedrooms in their two-storey log house on Oscar's homestead on Beaver Creek.

The receipt can be dated 1906-1908 because Beaver Mines did not appear as a name until Census of Canada 1909. Fraser & Freebairn's phone was No. 1 meaning that these partners had the first telephone ever installed in Pincher Creek.

For years, when I was child, we had some of Alena's homemade, lace-trimmed pillowcases. We did not use them everyday, but saved them to use when we had overnight company. Author's collection

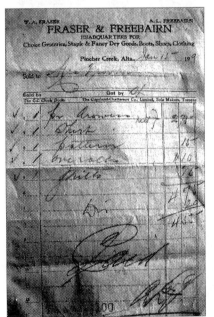

This receipt from Fraser and Freebairn notes that on January 15, 1909, Alena purchased:

1 pr. drawers (long underwear)	....	2.75
1 shirt pattern	....	0.15
1 pr. overalls	....	1.10
1 pr. mitts	....	0.75
	Total	4.75
		0.20
		4.55

The receipt advertises that Fraser and Freebairn sell "Groceries, Staples & Fancy Dry Goods, Boots, Shoes, Clothing." Eventually the Fraser & Freebairn business split up. Mr. Fraser went into business with Mr. McRoberts and started a department store across the street from Freebairn's ladies' ready-to-wear shop. Both these stores operated until about the 1960s. Courtesy Margaret Coulter Vroom and Bob & Isabel Vroom

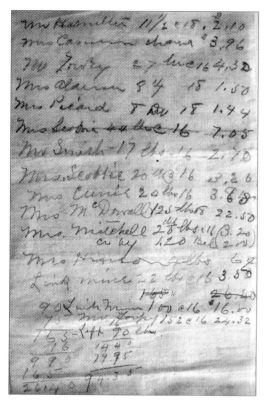

Cash was hard to come by in homesteader days. The wives of homesteaders were ingenious at "stretching a dollar."

Alena hit upon the idea of canvassing her neighbors to see if they would like to buy fresh cuts of prime beef from her. Finding that she had a ready market Alena had Ralph butcher a steer. From notes that Alena made on the above list it appears that she delivered the meat herself. This would mean driving by democrat to her various customers.

Some of these people, the Link Mine for instance, were nearly 10 miles away. Not everyone was able to pay for the meat when it was delivered, which would mean a return trip at some time, so this endeavor required a considerable amount of time. Courtesy Margaret Coulter Vroom and Bob & Isabel Vroom

The receipt above gives the names of people to whom Alena sold various amounts of different cuts of meat. Alena's customers on this list are:

Mrs. Hamilton	....	11 ½ lb. @ .18	....	2.10
Mr. Cameron	....	charged	....	3.96
Mr. Lowry	....	27lb @ .16	....	4.30
Mrs. Alainson	....	8 ¼ lb @ .18	....	1.50
Mrs. Picard	....	8 lb @ .18	....	1.44
Mrs. Scobie	....	44 lb @ .16	....	7.05
Mr. Smith	....	17 lb @ .16	....	2.70
Mrs. Scobie	....	20 lb @ .16	....	3.20
Mrs. Currie	....	20 lb @ .16	....	3.60
Mrs. McDowall	....	125 lb @ .18	....	22.50
Mrs. Mitchell	....	20 lb @ .16	....	3.20}
			Cr 1.20 Bal	2.00}

The total of this list was over $50.00, which alot of cash in those days.

The blast of a steam whistle has a timbre like no other. The regular sounding of steam train whistles on the CPR line west of MacLeod could be heard for several miles on cold, crisp winter days.

The almost mournful wailing of the CPR steam engines making their long climb to the summit of the Crowsnest Past became as familiar as an old friend's voice. The whistle's moan lessened the feeling of isolation and loneliness experienced by early settlers in the West.

The periodic shattering of the vast prairie silence was also a signal of hope for settlers living on isolated homesteads in western Canada--perhaps on that train there was a long-expected letter from a loved one in a distant land bringing news of family members left behind. Courtesy Jean McEwen Burns

J. M. J.

Our Lady of St. Michael of Kermaria Convent
PINCHER CREEK, ALTA.

Sep. 1907

MONTHLY REPORT.

Miss *Marion Vroom*

CONDUCT *Excellent*		DRAWING *Fairly Good*	
RELIGIOUS INSTRUCTION "		MUSIC *Satisfactory*	
ENGLISH *Satisfactory*		FRENCH *Very Satisfactory*	
ARITHMETIC *Fairly Good*		PAINTING *Satisfactory*	
HISTORY *Fairly Good*		SINGING	
GEOGRAPHY *Satisfactory*		DOMESTIC ECONOMY *Satisfactory*	
HYGIENE *Good*		BOOK-KEEPING	
NEEDLEWORK *Very Good*		APPLICATION *Satisfactory*	
GRAMMAR *Very Fair*		HEALTH *Very Good*	

Mother St. Bridget   *Mks 5 21/1000*

Marion Vroom's September 1907 report card indicates that Alena felt it was very important for her daughter to have a well-rounded education. She and Oscar strove very hard to see that Alena's wishes were met. They invested a considerable amount of money in Marion's room and board and art and music lessons.

Marion entered Kermaria Convent in Pincher Creek in the spring of 1907 at the age of 14 years, while Alfred entered in January 1908 at the age of 13 years. They attended St. Michael's School.

Marion's September 1907 report card, issued by Our Lady of St. Michael Kermaria Convent for, reflects Marion Vroom's aptitude for a foreign language, in this case French, and in artistic endeavours. Marion received a mark of "Very good" for needlework, French, painting and singing. Her marks in more prosaic subjects received, in general, a "satisfactory" or "good" mark.

Marion's granddaughters, Edna, Doris, and Anita, children of Gerald and Adeline Cyr Robbins inherited their grandmother's talent, with Edna and Anita presently playing all the liturgical music for St. Michael's Roman Catholic Church in Pincher Creek. Courtesy Margaret Coulter Vroom and Bob & Isabel Vroom

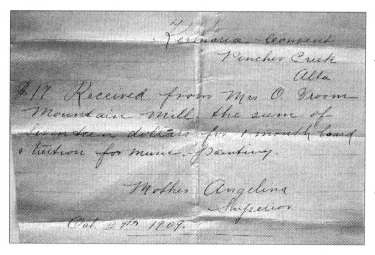

This receipt of January 15, 1908 for one month's board, signed by Mother Angelina, Convent Superior, was for the first month that Alfred Vroom boarded at Kermaria Convent in Pincher Creek and went to St. Michael's School. Courtesy Margaret Coulter Vroom and Bob & Isabel Vroom

Alena wanted to ensure that Marion came out to be a well-rounded young lady. Alena paid for art and music lessons for Marion while she boarded at Kermaria Convent and attended St. Michael's School.

In addition to tuition for art and music lessons this money paid for the cost of painting, art and needlework supplies, such as drawing paper, a palette, canvas, use of books, use of ink blotting paper, and other incidental supplies. Courtesy M. Coulter Vroom and Bob & Isabel Vroom

Oscar needed help with the ranch work. Of the four children of Oscar and Alena, Ralph was the only one who was really interested in becoming a cowboy, so he willingly took over the role of looking after Oscar's livestock—mostly cattle for the first few years they were in the West.

The legal age for children leaving school was 14 years of age at that time, so Ralph had to go to school even though he had to ride five miles on a trail through the hills that followed a section line. In the winter time there would be three or four feet of snow. During spring run-off Beaver Mines Creek was full to the brim and often flooded large areas. In 1904, on the day he turned 14 years old, Ralph quit school, rather dramatically, and adopted the life of a cowboy.

This 1935 scene illustrates some of the difficulties that Ralph faced, when 14 years old, in riding to the Archie Vroom School. Here swollen Beaver Mines Creek overflows its banks during spring run-off and floods a large part of Harold Vroom's land, which was adjacent to Oscar's homestead.

In general, Beaver Mines Creek Valley has a gentle slope to it. All along the creek when I was a child there were thick stands of willows. Often these willows were standing in two or three feet of water. What we kids called the "short cut" was the route my dad took when he rode the five miles to the Archie Vroom School.

That route eventually became impassable for our ponies. Beaver dams in the slow flowing creek made the creek overflow its banks. The soil became soaked with water and turned into slimy mire. Our ponies had to struggle to keep from slipping and falling into the muck. Sometimes they lunged along.

By 1935 Uncle Harold had cleared the willows from along the creek banks and had turned the land into a productive hay field that yielded many tons of high quality feed each year. A few tall trees that had survived the yearly flooding were left standing to help prevent erosion of the creek banks. Courtesy Ruby Jaggernath

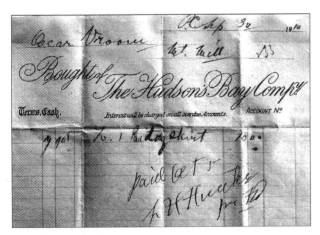

While Alena was concerned with Marion's education in the arts, Oscar was more concerned that she learn to ride horseback well and that she should be stylishly attired when doing so. L. H. Hunter, a clerk at the Hudson's Bay Company store in Pincher Creek issued this receipt when Oscar bought a riding skirt for Marion on April 30, 1910.

Both Marion and Alena learned to ride sidesaddle. Elva Ballantyne McClelland recalled that "they were a pretty sight" when they rode together to visit friends or to attend various social functions. I remember as a child we had two sidesaddles that Alena and Marion had ridden 15 to 20 years previously. Courtesy M. Coulter Vroom and Bob & Isobel Vroom

While in BC and Alberta, Archie led a full life. He participated in the social life of a lively group of young people in the Cranbrook, BC, area for a few years; helped his brothers Oscar and Claude to build houses on their homesteads; built a temporary schoolhouse for Oscar and Alena's children to attend when Alena moved west; and went back to Nova Scotia himself to escort Alena and her four rambunctious children on their train trip to the West.

Archie loved people and was a skilled tradesman in carriage-building and finishing carpentry. He worked joyously along with his brothers Claude and Oscar helping to build the Mountain Mill Church, which celebrated its 100th anniversary in June 1906.

On June 11, 2006, members of the Ralph and Mollie Tyson Vroom family, descendants of Oscar and Alena Munro Vroom, attended the 100th anniversary celebrations of Mountain Mill Church.

(Left to right) Donald Vroom, Edith Annand Smithies, Rodney Vroom, Bessie Vroom Annand Ellis, Jim Annand, Evelyn Annand Lailey.

The 100th anniversary commemoration activities and ceremonies were organized by a committee of descendants of the original members of the Mountain Mill Church. Over the past century each new generation of descendants of the founders of the church have lovingly cared for this jewel in the valley, keeping it clean and in good repair. Their work bees finished, the congregation often puts on potluck suppers at the church. Services are held at the Mountain Mill Church on a regular basis and are attended by almost every one in the community.

The first minister to serve Mountain Mill Church was Rev. Gavin Hamilton. "On June 7, 1906, the church was dedicated to the work of God by Rev. Gavin Hamilton who was their minister until 1910. Rev. Hamilton was somewhat of an eccentric but he and his wife were the moral backbone of the Community. On dedication day the church was debt free. The first Board of Managers were J.J. Skene, W.R. Lees, J.S. Ledingham, and R. (Robert) Lang." (George, 1996)

Mrs. Hamilton played the organ, which was purchased through fund-raising efforts of the Ladies Aid. This original organ accompanied hymn singing at the 100th anniversary celebrations of Mountain Mill Church in June 2006. Mrs. Hamilton was my teacher in grades three and four at Gladstone Valley School. There was a pump organ in the classroom. Every morning we children gathered around Mrs. Hamilton while she played the organ to accompany our singing of several hymns before starting our lessons for the day. Courtesy Lee and Doug McClelland

A number of great-grandchildren of the community-minded pioneers who built the Mountain Mill church attended the 100th anniversary of the church in June 2006.

Billy Gladstone, William IV, son of Leonard and Anna de Geest Gladstone of Pincher Creek, spoke on behalf of the Gladstone family. Billy's great-great-grandfather was William Shanks "Old Glad" Gladstone (William I). Old Glad was a generous man. He "donated 4.11 acres of land for the church (part of the N.W. ¼ of section 7, township 6, range 1, west of the 5th meridian" (George, 1996) who stated further, "The church was built on a timber foundation, the logs being hewed by hand with a broad axe wielded by the Gladstone boys. Teams and wagons were used to hall the doors and windows from Blairmore. Mr. George Ballantyne and Mr. William Gladstone were the building foremen... Albert Link was one of the carpenters, along with many other volunteers."

The land donated by Wm. Shanks "Old Glad" Gladstone was a part of his homestead quarter that was cut off by Mill Creek from the bulk of the quarter.

In the photo on the opposite page, behind the watering cans, in front of Mr. and Mrs. Burton is a treadle sewing machine. It looks like a Singer sewing machine, a very desirable brand for Prairie homemakers.

My grandmother Elizabeth Mary Tyson owned a Singer sewing machine when I was a child. During World War I ladies of the Fishburn district met regularly at the largest home in the district. There they packed various knitted items and other comforts to send to Canadian soldiers serving in the Canadian Army Overseas. For each meeting Grandpa Tyson loaded Granny's sewing machine into the back of the democrat and drove Granny to the meeting where she sewed patchwark quilt squares together so the busy homemakers could do the quilting as a group.

When not in use the Singer sewing machine folded neatly into the top of the stand, which then looked like a low table. The stand was generally covered with a crocheted or embroidered cloth to keep off the ever-present prairie dust. The machine rested on a metal stand with the treadle near the floor in the middle. There were two drawers placed handily on either side of the machine in which were kept various colours of thread, scissors, and other sewing accessories.

To use the machine Granny lifted the lid on the top and laid back on the left-hand side, forming a small flat surface on which to lay the material she was sewing. After the lid was folded back to the left Granny lifted the machine up out of the well where it was stored and secured it in place. She put the belt around the flywheel on the right-hand side and the machine was ready to operate. Granny then seated herself at her sewing machine and started sewing. When she had the item she was working on that day positioned underneath the sewing machine needle, Granny pressed up and down with her feet on the treadle which activated the belt which made the flywheel turn which made the sewing machine operate. As if by magic, to my young eyes, pieces of garments, or other items, were neatly stitched together.

Eventually various makes of sewing machines became available to western Canadian homemakers. Miraculously, and unlike today, the needles seemed to fit whatever make of sewing machine a homemaker owned. This saved a great deal of frustration and maybe anger, or even despair. Many homemakers lived three hours or more by team and wagon or by saddle horse away from a general store where sewing machine needles were available.

Even though he had a horse brand and a cattle brand in Alberta, Archie was not committed totally to being a homesteader/rancher at Beaver Mines. Or perhaps he thought his intended bride would not be inclined to be a rancher's wife. In any case, satisfied that Oscar's family was safely settled and well established in the West, Archie felt free to pursue his own dreams.

By 1908 he had bought a partnership in a Vroom and Burton General Store in Watson, SK. Archie's partner was a Mr. Burton. Watson, SK, was a thriving town on the railway line that ran straight north from the Union Railway at Culbertson, Montana, USA, to Watson and Wolleston Lake, SK (Bramley Books. 1989). After getting himself set up in business in Watson, SK, Archie's next move was to return to Nova Scotia to marry his longtime sweetheart, who had waited patiently for this day. On December 31, 1908, Archie married Alberta Annetta Butler in Weymouth, NS. Archie brought Alberta back as a bride to Watson.

This 1908 picture shows the interior of the Vroom and Burton General Store in Watson, SK, a small town located on a railway line which connected northern Saskatchewan with the Great Northern Railway at Culbertson, Montana, and thence with the very extensive USA railway system which led to Chicago and other big centres in the eastern USA and Canada, as well as with USA cities in the south and west of the country.

On the right hand side of the store are glass showcases displaying silverware and other small items. Various items, including what look like pieces of yard goods, hang from the ceiling. The two people standing behind the sewing machine are likely Mr. and Mrs. Burton. Archie Vroom, still wearing his trademark bowler hat, stands behind the huge cash register on the right. There are several other people in the store, too, including a male clerk standing behind the glass showcase and a woman in a stylish puff sleeve blouse and dark skirt leaning against the counter near the back of the store. Another man is standing behind that woman.

Two more men, obviously customers and wearing a Stetson hats, are perusing the items offered for sale. Details of the merchandise on the left-hand side of the store are also shown. On a slightly raised platform, center front, various sizes and styles of handheld watering cans are featured. These cans enabled gardeners to spray precious water on only the plants that they wished to thrive. No water was wasted spraying pieces of garden soil where no edible plants were growing. Courtesy Peter Vroom

However, life in Watson, SK, did not suit Archie and Alberta. In 1911 they moved from Watson to Vancouver, BC (Kerrisdale area). Archie had apprenticed as a carriage builder in Nova Scotia and wanted to try his hand as a contractor and build houses.

Ron and Nat Vroom, Archie and Alberta's two children are sitting on a fur rug watching the cameraman with absorbed interest in this charming photograph taken while on a 1914 visit to Weymouth, NS from their Vancouver home. Courtesy Peter Vroom

(L to r) Alberta (Mrs. Archie) Vroom and her children, two bonnie wee lads, Nat and Ron, sitting in a four wheeled, one-horse carriage when the family lived in Clayton, BC, in 1915.

In 1922, Archie and his family moved back to Vancouver. Archie was a contractor who built modest family homes living in each home until he sold it and then moving on to build another. Courtesy Peter Vroom

In 1911, Mary McLaren (Mrs. Claude) Vroom and her sister Miss McLaren of Boston stand beside a small shed on Archie's ranch at Beaver Mines.

After Claude and Mary married (before 1911) and settled on their homestead across the road from Archie, Mary's sister came west for a visit. Courtesy Ruby Jaggernath

HOMESTEADS BECOME HOMES

Intrigued by Oscar's vivid descriptions of his "Sunny Vale Ranche" in southwestern Alberta his mother, Sara Ann Woodman Vroom, decided to make a pilgrimage from Nova Scotia to Beaver Mines.

Oscar chose his homestead with an eye to the wonderful natural beauty of Beaver Mines Creek Valley as well as to the practicality of the location. Massive Table Mountain dominates the valley and is visible from many points in the valley. In a 1908 letter to her daughter Maude, Oscar's mother Sara, wrote that Oscar had named his homestead quarter "Sunny Vale Ranche." This reflected how optimistic Oscar felt about his new home and how he loved the long sunny days of southwestern Alberta. Sara Ann travelled west by train in 1907 and found the west as thrilling as she expected.

Oscar's quarter was situated in the relatively flat bottom of Beaver Mines Creek Valley; his land straddled Beaver Creek, which provided ample water for animals and for domestic use. He built his house on the east side of Beaver Mines Creek and north of Ruby Creek, which runs from the east and joins Beaver Mines Creek where Oscar built his log house.

This photo is taken from his son, Harold's, quarter section looking towards Oscar's homestead. Harold and Ruby Vroom's ranch house was to the left, in the creek bottom. Courtesy Edi-May Smithies

In the early 1900s, scattered throughout the hills where four Vrooms, Oscar and his brother Claude and sons Harold and Ralph, filed on homesteads in the Beaver Mines Creek Valley there were some 20 quarter sections which either abutted the Vrooms' homestead quarters or touched the next one on the corner. Many of these quarters were available as pasture for Oscar and Alena's herd of horses, which Ralph looked after. (See Map 2, Volume 2, *Quarter Section Homesteads in Beaver (Mines) Creek Valley and Gladstone Valley, circa 1910.*)

The first homestead of Oscar's eldest son Harold on SE ¼-32-5-2-W5th was immediately north of Oscar's homestead in flat bottom of Beaver Mines Creek Valley. Both Oscar and Harold's homesteads were located in the rich, hay-producing bottom land of Beaver Mines Creek Valley, making them suitable for raising feed for livestock.

Mae Vroom Peters in California, 1937 Mae was the only child of Harold and Ruby Mitchell Vroom

My cousins Adeline Cyr (Robbins) and Mae, when they were in their early teens, often walked over to look at Oscar and Alena's old house, which was about one-quarter mile from Harold and Ruby's house. Oscar and Alena's log house was located at the confluence of Beaver Mines Creek and a little creek called "Ruby Creek" that was named after Ruby (Mrs. Harold) Vroom. Ruby made herself a beautiful, private, peaceful sanctuary among the willows there. Sometimes the girls sat in Ruby's sanctuary talking quietly.

Years later Adeline returned to the site. The house was falling down, but inside she found Mae's old sewing kit. Still later, my brother Bill visited the site of Oscar and Alena's homestead house. He said that by then all that was left of their two-storey house was "a pile of logs."

In 1937 Mae Vroom left Beaver Mines and Pincher Creek. She moved to California with her uncle and aunt, Dave and Glenn Mitchell. Mae married Miles Peters. Their granddaughter, Ruby Jaggernath, graciously supplied many of the pictures used in this book. Courtesy Ruby Jaggernath

My dad's homestead, on the other hand, was located on the east side of Beaver Mines Creek Valley. It abutted the west side of Martin Devine's homestead. The northwest corner of Ralph's homestead quarter just touched the southeast corner of Oscar's land, so the three quarters were close together. Ralph's homestead, located on the dry, rocky hills on the east side of the valley, provided tall, straight logs to build Harold's homestead cabin, a two-storey log house on Oscar's homestead and two large hay barns, one on each of Harold's two homestead quarters.

During winters when sleighing was good some of the logs from Ralph's homestead were hauled to the ranch where I lived as a child. There they were used to build a cabin for my great-uncle Claude Vroom on his homestead, in about 1902.

Claude sold his homestead quarter to W. J. A. "Wash" Mitchell, who later sold to my dad. My great-uncle Claude's homestead cabin, still containing some of his bachelor's housekeeping equipment, was standing on his homestead quarter when I was a child. Sometimes we played in it.

Family friendships forged in the homestead years lasted a lifetime. This 1917 photo shows Adam "Dutch" Truitt and "The Hagglund clan," as Linnea Hagglund Goble (Mrs. Frank) described them many years later. The child on the lower right may be Hilding Hagglund, who was born 1914. The picture was taken in front Eric and Olga Gavelin Hagglund's home in Bellevue, AB. After homesteading in Pleasant Valley Eric Hagglund worked in the mine in Bellevue until he was injured. The Hagglunds then moved to Waterton Lakes National Park where they lived most of the rest of their lives. Courtesy Adam and Hazel Anderson Truitt

(Left to right) circa 1922/1923, John and Melcina Truitt in front of the Truitt home on their farm in Pleasant Valley, AB. The living room windows faced east toward Gladstone Valley. They presented a stunning view across Gladstone Valley toward Victoria Peak in the Rocky Mountains, which ran southwest at that point.

John and Melcina Truitt, parents of Adam "Dutch" Truitt, raised their family in this log house, which was built by John in 1912.

Lawrence Truitt, who suffered from rheumatoid arthritis, spent much of his time in the 1930s gazing out from these true picture windows and enjoying his magnificent view of the surrounding landscape.

It was while sitting looking out this window that Lawrence taught my brother Bill some language that my mother considered very unacceptable (Ellis, 2006 and 2003). Courtesy Adam and Hazel Anderson Truitt

Homemade music was a very important part of many homes during the homestead era. The Truitt family was truly blessed in that all of their sons played the violin beautifully. Some of the Truitt boys played more than one instrument. Here in this circa 1922/1923 family picture are (l to r) Dewey Truit (playing guitar) and Lawrence Truitt (playing violin). The picture was taken in front of their home on the farm in Pleasant Valley, which looked east across Gladstone Valley. Courtesy Adam and Hazel Anderson Truitt

The Bruces' farm, when they lived immediately southwest of Beaver Mines at the northwest end of Beaver Mines Creek Valley, produced an abundant hay crop. Here Ronald Bruce, standing on top of the load and Gordon Hamilton pitching the hay onto the hayrack, gather in the 1927 hay crop. This was the kind of land, where the natural grass grew "belly deep on a horse," that attracted Oscar Vroom to the Beaver Mines Creek Valley when he first saw this country in 1886.

In this hay-gathering operation the loose hay is piled on the hayrack in a special way so that the part of the load that is above the sides of the hayrack does not slide off while the load is being taken to the barn or to a stack, to be stored for the winter.

Looking directly east here, the hill in the background is the hill that I called "the big hill" when I was a child. The hill in the background in this picture is straight north of my parents' ranch two and one-half miles southeast of Beaver Mines.

Here ranchers can raise the large crops of hay necessary to feed livestock over the winter months. Oscar was wise to choose land in Beaver Mines Creek Valley so that he could grow hay to feed the big herd of horses he intended to purchase when Alena and the children came west. Oscar, Harold and Ralph Vroom's homesteads were about five miles south of here. Courtesy Katherine Bruce

Having his homestead abutting Harold's homestead, and having Ralph who wanted to be a cowboy to look after his livestock, was an ideal situation for Oscar who wanted to raise horses for sale. Along with his brothers, Claude and Archie, who were skilled in woodworking and house building, Oscar, a blacksmith by trade, first cut enough logs to construct a four-bedroom, two-storey log house for himself and his family.

He expected Alena to come west with their four children as soon as the house was ready. Oscar wanted their house to be large enough to accommodate the family and the fine furniture that Alena wanted to move west when she came.

By 1904 the house was almost ready for Oscar's family to move in. Oscar just wanted to put a few more finishing touches on the house and to start building the corrals which he knew they would need right away. In the spring of 1904 Archie volunteered to travel east and help Alena get packed and finish up the family's affairs in Clementsport.

As soon as the family arrived in the west, Harold, who was 16 years old by then, went out to work for various ranchers in the district. Alena taught Alfred and Marion at home until they went to Kermaria Convent.

Ralph had to ride five miles to take grade five at the Archie Vroom School located on the NW ¼ -35-5-2-W5. However, he did not like school. He tried to get himself kicked out, but the teacher had unending patience. Finally, after several unhappy months at school and on the day that he turned 14, the legal age for leaving school, young Ralph executed a plan he had hatched over the winter.

Ralph had trained his saddle horse to kick viciously when he goosed her in the ribs. On the morning of his 14th birthday, after another run-in with the teacher, he jumped on his saddle horse and backed it up to the door on the south side of the school.

Ralph dug his heels into the horse's ribs, making her give a powerful kick. The horse's hind hooves hit the schoolhouse door with full force, splintering the door into small pieces. Ralph made a hurried departure. He rode off for home confident that his mother would not send him back to school.

From that day onward Ralph worked like a man. He helped his dad with the ranch work, which included cutting and stacking hay on the rich bottomland where Oscar's homestead was located. He assisted Oscar in looking after all the livestock that they owned at that time. The 1906 census showed that Oscar had 25 horses, 50 cattle, and 5 hogs.

Ralph enjoyed working outdoors, as opposed to sitting in an enclosed classroom, but he was still not doing what he really wanted to do. When Ralph exuberantly declared, "I want to be a cowboy!" he had envisioned himself flying over the foothills on a fleet-footed saddle horse chasing a herd of other fleet-footed horses at breakneck speed. He had not thought of himself as milking cows, cleaning cow manure out of the barn, hauling feed to hungry livestock on a cold winter's day, branding kicking, struggling horses and cattle on a scorching-hot summer's day, nor any of the other back-breaking, as well as mundane, tasks that are a large part of being a cowboy. But he did not complain.

Even though Ralph and Harold were working hard as ranch hands, they still had time for youthful hijinks. Two of their more spectacular adventures occurred in 1909, when a shot from a revolver wonded Harold's left hand; and in 1911, when Ralph rode a borrowed saddle horse across the long, high, half-finished wooden railway trestle across Mill Creek at Mountain Mill.

Vroom, Mitchell, Tyson and Annand family brands (see illustrations pages 71, 86 and 134)

Alena made considerable sacrifices and worked very hard so that Alfred and Marion could get a good education. When the Vrooms came west in 1904, Alena was not in a financial position to buy the large herd of horses that she knew Ralph longed to have. Like many women of that era, she worked long, hard hours.

To help make ends meet, she had Oscar butcher a fat steer on a regular basis. Alena canvassed the neighbours to see what cut and the quantity of beef they wanted to buy. She delivered the meat by driving from neighbour to neighbour by horse and buggy, or by team and sleigh, weather and roads permitting.

In pioneer days, as on ranches today, women often owned livestock brands. In the absence of a large bank account, owning livestock gave a woman a measure of economic security. Each brand was registered with the provincial department of agriculture providing proof of ownership. Whenever livestock was bought or sold or moved to a different location a provincial brand inspector checked the brand of each animal to ensure that the person selling or moving the animals was indeed the owner.

In order to carry on her beef sales business Alena had a cattle brand to prove that she actually owned the cattle that she was butchering. Since Oscar was raising horses, he, too, needed a brand. Oscar acquired his 'Crown on left shoulder' brand when he purchased a herd of some 300 head of Crown brand horses being sold off when the owner lost interest in raising horses; Oscar subsequently had the brand transferred to his name.

Oscar purchased the Crown brand horses in the fall of 1906 on the strength of the fact that Alena inherited quite a bit of money when her mother, Elizabeth Munro Dodge, died November 2, 1906. It took several months for Alena to settle Elizabeth's estate and Oscar had to have a bank loan to pay for the horses, which Ralph then looked after. Oscar had some difficulty repaying the loan, but eventually paid it back.

It was also the custom for parents to give their children a few head of livestock as starter herds. The four children of Oscar and Alena, Harold, Ralph E, Marion and Alfred all owned brands. Harold's wife, Ruby Mitchell Vroom, registered both a horse brand and a cattle brand soon after she and Harold were married in 1910.

From 1914 to 1918, Ruby Mitchell Vroom had a cattle brand for which on December 31, 1918, she received a letter of registration. This renewal means her brand was originally issued at least four years prior in 1914. She renewed her cattle brand for the last time December 31, 1951, having owned it for over 40 years.

Oscar Vroom's brothers, Archie and Claude, also owned cattle and horse brands, as did Claude's wife, Mary Malain Vroom.

Alena did not renew her horse brand, described as Bar XV on the right thigh (stifle), when it came due December 31, 1925, so the brand was suspended and finally cancelled in 1929.

In an October 18, 1928, letter to the Inspector (Recorder) of Brands Mollie (Mrs. Ralph) Vroom advised the inspector that "on her (Alena's) death last December (1927)" Alena Vroom had bequeathed a number of horses with the Bar XV brand to her son Ralph, Mollie's husband. Mollie asked the Recorder of Brands to please transfer the brand to Ralph or to her. An October 28, 1928, letter from the Recorder of Brands, Edmonton, to Mrs. Ralph E. Vroom advised her that the brand was unavailable at the time but that a similar brand, XV bar on the right thigh (stifle), was available right away. Mollie settled for the XV bar brand and filled in the application forms for the new brand, receiving it in due course, and that is why Dad's horse brand when I was a child was XV bar on the right stifle and not bar XV.

Mollie applied for and received the cattle brand half diamond heart on the left rib in 1928. I kept the 'XV bar' brand paid up for a number of years, eventually purchasing the Ralph Vroom brand when the Alberta department of agriculture retired that brand for historical purposes. Illustrations by Edi-May Smithies, based on Alberta Brand Books

1906 Alena Vroom

1928 Mollie Vroom

1906 Oscar Vroom *"Crown"* brand

1906 Alena Vroom

1906 Ralph Vroom

1937 Ralph Vroom

My great-grandmother Elizabeth Dodge lived on her own for seven years after the death of her second husband, "Grandpa" C. C. Dodge, in 1899. When Grandmother Dodge became ill she had to be cared for by her family.

In 1905 Elizabeth's son-in-law, Oscar, travelled back to Nova Scotia to bring Elizabeth to live with him and Alena on Oscar's homestead, Sunny Vale Ranche, in Beaver Mines Creek Valley. Oscar built two rooms onto their two-storey log house as accommodation for Elizabeth, who lived with Oscar and Alena from the spring of 1906 until November 2, 1906, when she took ill and died at Sunny Vale Ranche. Oscar and Alena accompanied her body by train back to Annapolis, Nova Scotia, for burial in the family plot in the cemetery there.

The 1906 Census of Canada also showed that there were eight people living in the Vroom home. These people were: Oscar, Alena, Harold P., Ralph E., Marion M. and Alfred S. Vroom, as well as Elizabeth Dodge, who was Oscar's mother-in-law and Alena's mother, and H. I. White, a prospector from Pincher Creek with one horse.

The census showed Elizabeth Dodge's post office address as Mountain Mill, as was the Vrooms', so she must have considered she lived there. "Mountain Mill" was the address of all the homesteaders in Beaver Mines Creek Valley and in Gladstone Valley until Beaver Mines Post Office opened.

Two lifelong friends, Marion Vroom (Mrs. Dominic Cyr), left, and Elsie Belle Crosbie (Mrs. Edward Joyce), right, in 1909

This view looks east across the Beaver Mines Creek Valley. In 1903, at the age of 10 years, Elsie came to Beaver Mines from Butte, Montana, with her parents, brothers George and Charles, and sister Mildred. My grandfather Oscar Vroom was already living in Beaver Mines Creek Valley and made friends with the Crosbies right away. My dad often talked with great affection about the Crosbie family.

Elsie married Edward Joyce and had one son, Jack. Mrs. Joyce was active in the Beaver Mines Women's Institute and became friends with my mother then. They both attended meetings regularly.

When I was a child Joyces lived just behind Mr. and Mrs. Frank Holmes. Mrs. Joyce was always kind and friendly towards me; I didn't know that she had been a friend of the Vrooms since 1904. In the 1930s, Jack Joyce, and his family also lived at Beaver Mines. Courtesy Adeline Cyr Robbins

Alena, who worked very hard as a rancher's wife with a growing family, was very sad when her mother died so suddenly. During the previous year, they had been able to spend very little time visiting and enjoying each other's company.

Settling her mother's estate required several months of letter writing back and forth with lawyers in Nova Scotia. Eventually, however, things began to move along. Alena had to deal with a number of legal documents before she finally received her inheritance some time in 1907.

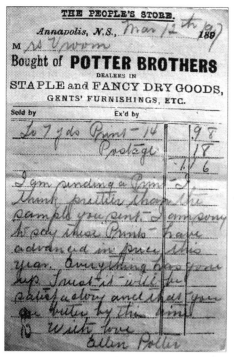

Alena kept busy using her considerable dressmaking skills to make dresses for her daughter, Marion, and herself.

At one time, as shown by this sales slip, Mrs. (Alena) Vroom ordered seven yards of print material from Potter Brothers, Dealers in Staple and Fancy Dry Goods, Gents' Furnishings, Etc., Annapolis, NS. In those days the price of dressmaking print was only 14 cents per yard. Postage of eighteen cents was charged to mail the print to Alena. The print material referred to in this receipt was probably used for a summer dress for Marion.

Mr. Potter also wrote a note on the bottom of the bill, saying: "I am sending a Print—I think prettier than the sample you sent—I am sorry to say these Prints have advanced in price this year. Everything has gone up. Trust it will be satisfactory and that you are better by this time. With love, Allen"

Alena lived about 15 miles (3 hours by team and democrat) from Pincher Creek, so did not get into town very often. As well, there may not have been a wide selection of materials for women's summer dresses at the few dry goods stores that were operating in Pincher Creek at that time.

Looking ahead to that situation, Alena must have brought samples of material for dressmaking with her when she moved from Annapolis, NS, to Sunny Vale Ranche in 1904; or she could have mailed a sample of material that was available at Fraser and Freebairn's Dry Goods Store, thinking that she could get a better price on it from Potter Brothers in Annapolis, NS. Mr. Potter obviously thought his dress print material was prettier than what was available to Alena in Pincher Creek and sent what he had. Courtesy Margaret Coulter Vroom and Bob & Isabel Vroom

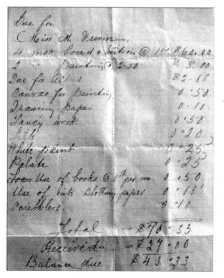

This is an invoice for board, tuition, art lessons, "fancy work" material for embroidery, art supplies such as "canvas for painting", "drawing supplies" and a palette, scribblers and book rentals. These were for Miss Marion and Alfred Vroom at Kermaria Convent. The invoise was sent to Alena Vroom in about the spring of 1908.

Marion entered Kermaria in spring 1907 and received a report card in September 1907. Alfred entered Jan 7, 1908. Adeline Robbins said that at one time she had five oils on canvas paintings done by her mother, Marion, as a student at Kermaria.

Another one of Adeline's daughters also has a pillow embroidered by Marion at Kermaria, but we have no photo of it. Courtesy Margaret Coulter Vroom and Bob & Isabel Vroom

Alena used her resources to provide a better life for her children. Dividends from the Valley Telephone Co., Ltd. comprised one source of Alena's income. Alena received quite a bit of money from her mother's estate. She invested it in making a better life for her three younger children.

Besides being able to buy a large herd of horses for Ralph to look after, the money inherited from her mother enabled Alena to send her two youngest children to school in Pincher Creek.

Almost immediately upon receiving her February 1908 dividend payment, Alena paid Kermaria Convent the sum of forty-two dollars for two month's board; the receipt was signed by Sr. Angelina, Superior.

Oscar and Alena wanted their daughter to become a well-rounded young lady, so arranged for Marion to have art and music lessons.

Marion Vroom (Cyr) painted this oil on canvas painting in about 1907-08 while she was a student at Kermaria Convent. This oil painting now hangs in the home of its proud owners, Marion's granddaughter and her husband, Doris and Larry Bruder, who are collectors of paintings. Adeline said, "Marion also took piano lessons and did beautiful embroidery." Courtesy Adeline Cyr Robbins

The number of homesteaders and settlers increased yearly. Finally it was decided that the community needed a Protestant church. So the concerned families of the district got together to make plans for their church. The men would do the building construction. The women sewed, crocheted and embroidered fine linens for the altar. The Vroom brothers, Oscar, Archie and Claude, skilled in various trades, along with all other available men took to the task with gusto. In three months the church building was completed and the official opening service was held.

My grandmother and grandfather Vroom and their children, my dad and his three siblings, excitedly mounted saddle horses and the family democrat and travelled the six miles from Sunny Vale Ranche to the Mountain Mill Church for the joyous service. A community picnic following the service completed the day.

In 1906 the entire Vroom family, as well as every other family and many bachelors in the community, attended the opening of Mountain Mill Church.

This is a view of the steep wall on the west side of Mill Creek Canyon a short distance upstream from Mountain Mill, and almost directly west of the Mountain Mill Church, where a huge wooden railway trestle spanned Mill Creek 1909 to 1920. The canyon wall is now covered with a thick growth of evergreen trees. The scene is dramatically framed by one of the arched windows of the Mountain Mill Church. "The trestle was there in 1919-20, when I attended the Mountain Mill Church," stated Marguerite Link Bennett (2004). "I started school in 1920 at Coalfields School. Shortly thereafter they started taking the trestle down."

In June 2006, three of my four children and I and my brother Donald and his wife Doreen and nearly 150 descendants of homesteaders with whom my dad's parents were friends attended celebrations commemorating the 100th Anniversary of the Mountain Mill Church. The church, which was constructed with the volunteer labour of people of the community, has served the Beaver Mines-Gladstone Valley community continuously for the past 100 years. The Mountain Mill Church has become affectionately known as the "Church in the Valley." (George, 1996) Courtesy Edi-May Smithies

Sgt. Harold P. Vroom (left, standing with another soldier somewhere in France during WWI.

Harold's handwriting on the back of the picture states: "I don't know if you will recognize me here. Sam Bijaird (illegible handwriting) and I had this taken in what was left of a little town next day after the Armistice was signed."

Although my uncle Harold did not seem to be a quarrelsome type, nor a person who would get himself into a scrape in Pincher Creek on a Saturday night, he did, indeed, get involved in a fracas one time.

WWI army records show that when Harold enlisted in 1917 he told the recruiting officer that the scar on the palm of his left hand was the result of the 1909 revolver shot in Pincher Creek, AB. As far as I can remember the incident was never talked about when I was a child. Courtesy Ruby Jaggernath

Mr. and Mrs. Oscar Vroom

Request the pleasure of your company at an

At Home

On Friday evening, July 22nd, 1910.

Mr. and Mrs. Harold Vroom will receive

from Eight to Ten

at their residence.

Dancing.

In 1910 Alena turned her mind to happier thoughts--her oldest son, Harold, became engaged to marry Ruby Mitchell. Alena set about making plans for a big party celebrating Harold and Ruby's engagement. She ordered 24 invitations and 100 invitations from the Pincher Creek Echo to Harold and Ruby's wedding and sent invitations to all of their neighbours and friends to come to an "at Home" party at their Beaver Mines Creek Valley home July 22, 1910.

The "at Home" at their home in Beaver Mines Creek Valley celebrated the July 5, 1910, marriage of their son, Harold, to Miss Ruby Mitchell, daughter of Wash and Belle Mitchell, who homesteaded in Gladstone Valley, just a couple of miles over the hills from the homesteads of Oscar, Harold and Ralph Vroom. Courtesy Ruby Jaggernath

The Pincher Creek Echo published an article detailing Harold and Ruby's wedding that read: "Monday, July 4, (sic) 1910. **VROOM-MITCHELL.** At Mountain Meadow on Monday, July 4 (sic), Reverend J. F. Hunter officiating, Harold Vroom to Ruby Mitchell, both of Mountain Mill."

The earlier error regarding the date of Harold and Ruby's wedding was corrected in a second article in the July 21, 1910 Pincher Creek Echo, that elaborated on the news item relating that the young couple "departed for a tour of western cities including Seattle and Vancouver, (and will) be at home to their friends after July 20th in a neat little cottage near Mountain Mill, erected by the groom."

Over the years other members of Harold's family used his "neat little cottage" as well. In 1979, Margaret Coulter remembered that "during WWI" Oscar and Alena lived at Mountain Mill, not in Oscar's homestead log house on Beaver Creek. They found Oscar's homestead in Beaver Mines Creek Valley to be too isolated to live on while Harold, their closest neighbour, was Overseas in the Canadian Army.

From the *Pincher Creek Echo*, July 7, 1910:

:

"Vrooms (sic) *- Mitchell*

"The hovering of Cupid around the house of Mr. and Mrs. W. Mitchell resulted in the (consummation) of a happy marriage on Tuesday, July 5th. The contracting parties were their daughter Miss Ruby Irene Mitchell and Harold Vrooms (sic), son of Mr. and Mrs. Oscar Vrooms (sic).

The bride, who is noted for her sweet personality, has a host of friends in this vicinity. The groom is well and favorably known by his acquaintances. Rev. Hunter, of Blairmore, performed the beautiful and innovative marriage ceremony. The bride was tastefully attired in white silk; the groom in conventional black.

About fifty guests partook of a sumptuous feast prepared by relatives and the mother of the bride.

Mr. and Mrs. Vroom departed amid showers of rice for a short tour of the western cities, including Seattle, Vancouver and other points of interest. They will be "at home" to their friends after July 20th, in a neat little cottage near Mountain Mill, erected by the groom.

The article ended with a few lines of poetry by the writer, probably W. D. McDowall, the Beaver Mines-Mountain Mill correspondent for the Pincher Creek Echo for many years, who wrote: *"O'er roses may their footsteps move/ Their smiles be smiles of love/ Their tears be tears of joy/ Is the wish of their many friends.'"*

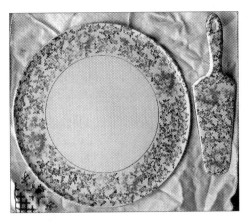

This two-piece set of beautiful antique china, a cake plate and a cake server, was given as a wedding gift to Harold and Ruby Mitchell Vroom by Harold's parents Oscar and Alena. It is still in the possession of Ruby and Harold's great-granddaughter and Oscar and Alena's great-great-granddaughter, Ruby Jaggernath.

An intricate pattern made up of various shapes representing leaping sheep, unicorns and other fanciful creatures forms the wide outside border of the plate, while the whole of the server is decorated with the same pattern. Interspersed amongst these shapes are delicately coloured white and pink roses.
Courtesy Ruby Jaggernath

Ruby Mitchell was a tall, handsome woman taking after her dad, W. J. A. "Wash" Mitchell, in height and temperament. Here in 1910 Ruby is wearing a high-collared white blouse. Her moderately short dark hair, which may have been naturally curly, frames her oval face. Ruby's only jewellery is a simple brooch at the neck of her blouse.

As I recall, Aunt Ruby had a sharp sense of humor, not always appreciated by my dad, who was her brother-in-law. Here Ruby gazes steadfastly out of dark eyes, her sense humor showing on her face.

Mr. and Mrs. W. D. McDowall and members of their family would most certainly have been invited to Harold and Ruby's wedding. Oscar met Mr. McDowall when he was returning from Nova Scotia in 1906 after the funeral of Alena's mother. At that time Mr. McDowall was travelling alone, intending to set up a dry goods business in Winnipeg. Oscar persuaded him to take a homestead in the Beaver Mines area. Mr. McDowall did that and the family has owned the homestead property ever since. The Vrooms and McDowalls were lifelong friends. Courtesy Ruby Jaggernath

Taken circa 1906, (left to right) Emma Mary Price McDowall (Mrs. W. D.) with Marjorie and Elsie McDowall in London, England

In April 1907, Emma left London to travel to Beaver Mines with eight children—Douglas, Archie, Leslie, Roy, Hector, Malcolm, Marjorie and Elsie. There the family joined, W. D. McDowall, head of the family, who had gone ahead a year before. Two more sons, Kenneth and Neil, were born in Canada.

The McDowall family was the heart and soul of the Beaver Mines district. Emma McDowall was an accomplished pianist. She played for dances at the Beaver Mines Women's Institute Hall along with two other local musicians--Michael Bruce, who played banjo, and John Babin, who played the violin.

In addition, Mrs. McDowall played the organ at Mountain Mill Church and accompanied the singing of Coalfields School children for elaborate Christmas concerts staged by the local teachers.

I remember the whole class of 40 children walking or riding horseback on very windy days to rehearse with the piano at Mrs. McDowall's home. There was no piano in the school. Courtesy Ina Kokkila McDowall (Mrs. Ken) and Mary Lou McDowall

(Above left) *Archie McDowall, second son of W. D. and Emma Price McDowall, circa 1923, at about 30 years of age. During his youth my dad spent a lot of time with the McDowells from 1910 onward. Ken McDowell's older brothers, Douglas and Archie, became Ralph's very good friends.* Courtesy Ina Kokkila McDowall and Mary Lou McDowall

(Above right) *W. D. McDowall, born circa 1865, looks about 70 years old here. This is the image I have of Mr. McDowall from my childhood. Mr. McDowall conceived the idea of the Castle River Stampede and served on the stampede committee for many years. He wrote a weekly column for the Pincher Creek Echo for some 60 years.* Courtesy Ina Kokkila McDowall (Mrs. Ken) and Mary Lou McDowall

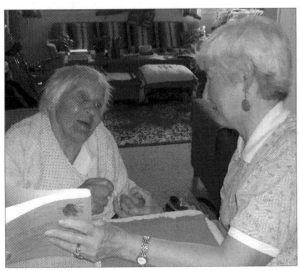

(Left) Ina Kokkila McDowall (Mrs. Ken) (Right) Bessie Vroom Ellis in August 2003. Ina was still living at the McDowall family home, "Windymere" ranch, northeast of Beaver Mines.

Bessie is showing Ina the story she wrote about Ina and her husband, Ken, in her book Volume 1, The Vrooms of the Foothills: Adventures of My Childhood.

The friendship of the Vrooms and McDowalls continues to succeeding generations. Mary Lou McDowall, youngest child of Ken and Ina expressed how fond she and her siblings were of my dad and how much they anticipated his next visit when she stated, ""We knew when he was coming into the ranch yard because we could hear him whistling long before he came down the lane (riding on horseback). We all joyfully ran out to greet him."
Courtesy Edi-May Smithies

Taken at the homestead of Dominic and Marion Vroom Cyr east of Fish Lake and south of Pincher Creek in 1918, the above photo shows (l to r) Adeline Cyr, Marion Vroom Cyr, Eugene Cyr (baby) and Marie Alberta Cyr. Marie Alberta was five years old, Adeline three years old and Eugene, one year old.

In the background may be seen: Marion and Dominic's log cabin; their log barn with a shed built on the side of it along with a high pole corral to use when handling livestock. The homestead is still in the Cyr family. A good part of the land is covered with scrub brush, having open meadows where livestock can graze. A small stream runs through it.

When coal was discovered at Beaver Mines southwest of Pincher Creek, Dominic Cyr was one of the enterprising young men of the district. In 1910 Dominic, along his brother Theodule, established a livery stable business in the thriving, new town of Beaver Mines. Dominic's dealings with the Vrooms began when he purchased hay from Alena to feed horses that were stabled with him. A few years later Dominic became very involved with the Vroom family when he and Marion, only daughter of Oscar and Alena Vroom, fell in love, courted and married on June 25, 1913, making Marion the second of Oscar and Alena's children to leave home.

After a few years of living at Beaver Mines Dominic applied for a homestead northwest of Twin Butte, the young couple moving there in 1915. They lived in a log cabin on the homestead for six years then moved elsewhere for a few years. In the meantime, Dominic proved up on his homestead and the young couple had six children, Alberta, Adeline, Eugene, Esther, Vera and Rita. They bought a farm one and one-half miles southeast of Pincher Creek, retiring to live in Pincher Creek in 1946.

Dominic and Marion were very kind to Alena, building a room onto their house so that she could live with them for a few years before she died.

The financial picture of other homesteaders in southwestern Alberta was similar to that of the Vrooms. Their fortunes ebbed and flowed, but with each gain they added to the comfort of their homes and added to the well being of their families.

Over the years the Cyr family gathered at Dominic's homestead to hold family picnics and reunions. I once attended such a family gathering in about 1943 during WWII. Courtesy Adeline Cyr Robbins

(Above left) *Dominic Joseph and Marion Vroom Cyr on their 40th wedding anniversary. They were married June 25, 1913, St. Michael's Church, Pincher Creek, AB. Courtesy Adeline Cyr Robbins*

(Above right) *To ensure that their families felt at ease in a fine dining situation, women regularly brought out their finest china, silverware and table linens and laid them out in a formal fashion, as shown above. Courtesy Jean McEwan Burns*

Here Wm. Shanks "Old Glad" Gladstone (William I)) holds his fourth child, Nellie "Babe" Riviere. The baby is dressed in what looks like a christening gown. Mr. Gladstone wears a suit and a white shirt for the occasion.

The location of the picture is unknown. However, the room is finely furnished with floor-length drapes, a varnished wooden chair, and a small table covered with a fancy cloth upon which is sitting a vase of flowers. Courtesy Lorraine Riviere Pommier

Homesteaders' families and early settlers engaged in many activities to bring liveliness and gaiety into their lives and lives of other members of the community. Here Mabel Bruce is dressed in a clown costume while her eldest son, Ronald, is dressed as a Scotsman. Mabel, is demonstrating how high she can kick while standing on one leg

Ronald, her oldest son, is pretending to be her ballet partner. This picture may have been taken shortly after a masquerade ball at the Beaver Mines Women's Institute Hall, which shows in the distant background. The remains of an early fall snowstorm still lie on the ground, characteristic of southwestern Alberta during the fall and winter. Courtesy Katherine Bruce

As well as bringing their treasured home furnishings from their family homes, the wives of homesteaders bought their deep sense of the importance of maintaining family ties and forging new friendships in their adopted land.

The above 1916 photo, titled "A Sunday Gathering" by Linnea Hagglund Goble (Mrs. Frank), shows just such an occasion. Shown here, (Back row left to right): Gunnar Lund, Washington Mitchell, Erik Hagglund, Fred Gavalin, Lawrence Truitt, Dewey Truitt, Swan Hagglund, "Doc" Truitt, Fred Lund, Alex Barclay;

(Front row left to right) Iona Truitt, Olga Hagglund, Hilding Hagglund, Aggie Barclay, Bessie Truitt, Minnie Barclay, Nellie Barclay, Anna Lund, Indgred Lund, Melcina (Mrs. John) Truitt, Adam "Dutch" Truitt. Courtesy Frank and Linnea Hagglund Goble

Marietta "Etta" Irwin McRae holds Kay, while young son Ken stands beside her. Taken on the McRae homestead in 1913, this shows the broad sweep of the prairie stretching eastward from the Rocky Mountains in southwestern Alberta. Mrs. McRae focused her photographer's eye on the beauty of this vast land and took many pictures, which are still treasured by her descendants. Mrs. McRae, like many other homesteaders' wives, kept her children dressed in immaculate white clothing, including a hat for shade from the sun, in the summer time.
Courtesy Kay McRae Leigh

MAP 3 Village of Beaver Mines, circa 1910 to 1950

Shown are: 1 Jack Morden residence; 2 Colin Currie residence; 3 Andrew Scobie residence; 4 Picard & Gamache Blacksmith Shop; 5 Beaver Mines Hotel; 6 Bill Bremner Store; 7 Elsie Joyce and Jack Joyce, son, residence; 8 Mine building or butcher shop, Hern Liddell Store; Frank & Mrs. Holmes residence; Ken & Ina McDowall Grocery Store; 9 St. Anthony's Roman Catholic Church; 10 Empty lot; 11 Bran shed; 12 One-truck garage, 1920s; 13 Dominic Cyr livery barn; 14 Ballantyne's Store and post office, 1920s; Keeping's Store; 15 Blacksmith shop (owner unknown); 16 Church (Unknown denomination); Women's Institute Hall, 1920's; Stella's Restaurant, 2004; 17 Dominic Cyr & Theodule Cyr Butcher Shop; 18 Theatre & dance hall; 19 Kootenay & Alberta (K & A) Railway water tower; 20 Beaver Mines Tennis Club; 21 Bakery; 22 Western Coal & Coke (miners' houses); 23 Edward "Ted" & Mabel Bruce residence, 1930s; Leskosky residence; 24 K & A Railway equipment storage and maintenance sheds when railway was in operation to Beaver Mines; barn and hay storage when Bruces lived there in 1930s. 25 Mike Prozak's residence, 1930s; Jack Noble's residence, 1950s; 26 K & A Roundhouse; Jenks' residence, 1930s; 27 Andy Wojtula residence, 1930s.

Also shown on this map are: Road to: 1) "Chicken Coop" School, 1938 – 1942; and 2) "Old" Beaver Mines School, 1942 – 1955; and 3) Castle River Forest Reserve; Beaver Mines Creek; the swimming hole where my brother and I swam; the deep beaver dam in which we swam our horses in the 1930s; "Old" road and rebuilt road to Ralph and Mollie Vroom's ranch and Gladstone Valley; the Frank Holmes coal mine, which the Vrooms called the "#1 mine."

When my brother Don and I were about 8 and 6 years old, we used to "draw" a map similar to this in the snow in front of our kitchen window so that our mother could look out the window and see our efforts. Don, the map creator, would make a track representing the road to Beaver Mines by taking tiny steps forward. I tramped it down by inching sideways along Don's tracks.

When Don and I went to Coalfields School we took a shortcut past the Andrew Scobie residence and past the Colin Currie residence. The flat piece of ground in that area was often a sheet of glare ice in the springtime. Beaver Creek overflowed because of the beaver dams and the water froze overnight. It was nearly impassable on horseback unless one's horse was sharp shod. On the way home from Coalfields School, which was more than five miles from our home, Don and I frequently stopped at Mrs. Holmes's home. She always gave us a cup of hot chocolate and cookies before starting us on our way home again. On mail days we picked up the mail at the Beaver Mines post office as we went by. Illustration by Edi-May Smithies, Cartography by Shelley McConnell

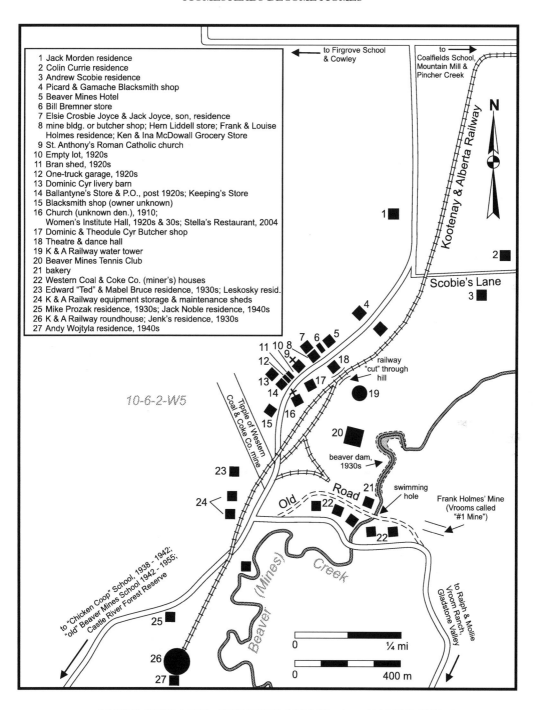

1 Jack Morden residence
2 Colin Currie residence
3 Andrew Scobie residence
4 Picard & Gamache Blacksmith shop
5 Beaver Mines Hotel
6 Bill Bremner store
7 Elsie Crosbie Joyce & Jack Joyce, son, residence
8 mine bldg. or butcher shop; Hern Liddell store; Frank & Louise
   Holmes residence; Ken & Ina McDowall Grocery Store
9 St. Anthony's Roman Catholic church
10 Empty lot, 1920s
11 Bran shed, 1920s
12 One-truck garage, 1920s
13 Dominic Cyr livery barn
14 Ballantyne's Store & P.O., post 1920s; Keeping's Store
15 Blacksmith shop (owner unknown)
16 Church (unknown den.), 1910;
   Women's Institute Hall, 1920s & 30s; Stella's Restaurant, 2004
17 Dominic & Theodule Cyr Butcher shop
18 Theatre & dance hall
19 K & A Railway water tower
20 Beaver Mines Tennis Club
21 bakery
22 Western Coal & Coke Co. (miner's) houses
23 Edward "Ted" & Mabel Bruce residence, 1930s; Leskosky resid.
24 K & A Railway equipment storage & maintenance sheds
25 Mike Prozak residence, 1930s; Jack Noble residence, 1940s
26 K & A Railway roundhouse; Jenk's residence, 1930s
27 Andy Wojtyla residence, 1940s

to Firgrove School
& Cowley

to
Coalfields School,
Mountain Mill &
Pincher Creek

Kootenay & Alberta Railway

N

Scobie's Lane

10-6-2-W5

Tipple of Western
Coal & Coke Co. mine

railway
"cut"
through
hill

beaver dam,
1930s

swimming
hole

Frank Holmes' Mine
(Vrooms called
"#1 Mine")

Old   Road

to "Chicken Coop" School, 1938 - 1942;
"old" Beaver Mines School 1942 - 1955;
Castle River Forest Reserve

to Ralph & Mollie
Vroom Ranch,
Gladstone Valley

Beaver   (Mines)   Creek

0   ¼ mi

0   400 m

MAP 3 VILLAGE of BEAVER MINES, circa 1910 TO 1950

Then, as now, some women used their artistic skills to enhance the lives of their families and neighbours. Artistic women of note in the area southwest of Pincher Creek included: Marietta "Etta" Irwin McRae, a photographer, and Lorenda Russell (Mrs. Harold Russell and Andy's mother), an artist, who painted daffodils on the living room walls of her log house. Kay Leigh, remembering that Lorenda was "a great talker," recalled how much Lorenda enjoyed visiting with neighbours. This photo was taken and developed by Marietta "Etta" Irwin McRae in the summer of 1913. Malcolm McRae in buckboard; Mrs. Harper standing on porch; Etta Irwin McRae and daughter, Kathleen, standing at garden gate. Courtesy Kathleen "Kay" McRae Leigh

Constance "Connie" Warburton Holroyd, right, stands with her husband, J.C. " Bo" Holroyd, on a rocky promontory overlooking Pass Creek Valley Waterton Lakes National Park. Bo was the chief warden in Waterton for a number of years. Mount Blakiston, a nine-mile-long monolith, fills the background of the picture. In this summertime picture Connie is riding an English saddle. Her saddle horse is sleek and shiny, evidence of the good care that it receives at Connie's hands. Courtesy Jack Holroyd

Constance "Connie" Warburton (Mrs. Bo) Holroyd, mother of Arthur, Dorothy, Jack, Nora and Alice, was another artistically accomplished woman who lived in the area south of Pincher Creek. One time Constance drew a mountain goat using charcoals on a lean-to at the warden's cabin at Red Rock Canyon when "Bo" was a warden there. Constance was also a photographer, developing her own photos. Constance described her developing process to Jack who used the process himself and described it thusly: "As for the picture developing, I only made prints from negatives although it was possible to process film at home with some very simple equipment. My mother had a bit of a kit with chemicals to mix up fixer and developer. Also she had sensitized (light sensitive) paper as well. You could buy the paper in some drug stores I think.

"In any event, you mixed up fixer in one pan and developer in another and a third pan held water for washing prints. A piece of light sensitive paper was fixed in a sort of frame, much like a picture frame, against glass. The negatives were put in first - then the paper. You put in a back, which sandwiched the negatives and paper in place. This all had to be done in the dark so as not to expose the sensitive paper before you were ready.

"When ready you simply exposed the glass side of the frame with negatives and paper to a light for a few seconds. Then back in the dark to take the frame apart and place the paper in the pan with the developer fluid, after which you rinsed it in water then into the fixer solution. This was sort of a slow, tedious process. Timing was everything with the exposure. You gradually learned by looking at the density of the negatives beforehand, about how much exposure they would need. I used to mess around and make a few prints that way."

Jack described how he tried to emulate his mother's printmaking, "Many years later I did set up a proper darkroom complete with enlarger and developing tanks for film rolls, where I carried the black and white processing a bit further, but of course by that time we had electricity which was much easier to work with than the old kerosene lamps we used originally. Actually black and white is a fun medium to work with because there are so many tricks to learn to enhance the quality of one's photos. I am sure the printmaking I did in the 30s and early 40s was pretty much the same process that others used then and earlier. I can remember the photo paper came in thick, black lined envelopes, which you never opened in the light, or you would expose, and so ruin, the paper."

This curio, which was prominently displayed in Mrs. Bruce's home at Beaver Mines when I was a child, is still in the Bruce family.

Made of unknown material the curio features two huge bull elk standing at the bottom of an elaborate structure representing a tree of some kind.

One elk is bugling to announce his presence to other male elk in the area, while the other bull grazes on the grass of the knoll where the elk are depicted as standing.
Courtesy Katherine Bruce

1906 Miss Marion Vroom

1906 Alfred Vroom

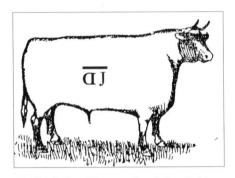

1915 Marion Vroom Cyr (Mrs. D.J.)

1906 Claude Vroom

1906 Mary Vroom (Mrs. Claude)

1906 John George "Kootenai" Brown

RALPH BECOMES A COWBOY

In his book *THE CANADIAN COWBOY* (Russell, 1993), Andy wrote about my dad:

> *"I met and worked with a lot of cowboys over the years. Some of them stand out very distinctly from the rest and one of these was Ralph Vroom. Ralph could be as wild as they got... He would give a friend his shirt if that friend needed it but, given reason, he could be an implacable, dangerous enemy. He wasn't very big as men go but he was tough, colourful, and a showy rider without being a show-off, though he loved to entertain people. He could get on and off a horse like a flash, never seeming to touch a stirrup....*
>
> *"He had a good-looking palomino stud that he rode on special occasions and I remember him coming into Pincher Creek one time riding this horse that he had trained to buck. He was wearing a pair of white woolly batwing chaps ... (and) made quite a picture as he rode the prancing horse down Main Street. All of a sudden the horse blew up and Ralph went over his head to come down on all fours in front of his horse making great buck jumps with the horse trailing and bucking behind him. Then like magic Ralph was back in the saddle, the horse never missing a step as it pranced on down the street heading for the livery barn....*
>
> *"I had seen and heard enough of Ralph and horses to believe just about anything. When he was courting Molly (sic, Mollie), his wife, and she agreed to marry him, he bought a fancy buggy and driving harness and then looked over his horses to pick a suitable team...a matched pair of five-year-old chestnut mares that had silver manes and tails...they weren't even broke and the wedding was only two days away...by evening he had them answering the rein after a fashion....*
>
> *"Next day (he headed) for Molly's home to pick her up and then take her to the parson who was due to perform the ceremony...made another circle, this time stopping the horses for moment to give him time to reach down and pick her up to set her on the seat beside him."*

Dad could transfer his knowledge of living in meagre circumstances to any situation in any part of the world. Looking at a picture of my dad, shown on the next page, at his wild horse camp in British Columbia when he was a young man, perhaps in his early twenties, reminded me of the campsite that Dad set up near the Canadian Army base in southern England while serving Overseas in WWII. Dad used a thickly wooded vale near his Army camp to hide well-bred horses not used as workhorses, which otherwise would have been slaughtered. By then, Dad was a 45-year-old man. He loved horses, and stayed young at heart all of his life.

Ralph Vroom at his campsite in the East Kootenays in British Columbia, where he was chasing and catching wild horses. He is standing beside two wild horses that he caught and tamed. Two of the saddlehorses that Ralph used to chase and catch wild horses are standing beside the tent in the middle right background. The set-up of Ralph's camp indicates that he intended to be there for a considerable time. The smoking chimney leads from a stove of some kind that is in the tent. Ralph would use the stove both for cooking and for heat on chilly autumn nights.

The inscription on the reverse of this picture promises Mollie a saddlehorse, as Ralph writes: "Our camp on Dutch Creek and Ralph holding three wild horses, Cake Walk, Stranger and Clutche, also Fish and Rick (saddlehorses)...the dogs are Peter and Jocke, the collie pups that I was going to send to ... I did not mention anything about your saddlehorse. She is four in the spring and she will make you a nice one. Please show these to old Bill H. (Billy Huddlestun) and the rest." Signed "R". Author's collection

Ralph Vroom, 1922, is holding a 2-year-old colt at Mountain Mill where he and Mollie lived when they were first married. Cowboys had to look after all the livestock on their ranches whether it was winter or summer. Dad generally never rode a young horse that he was breaking until it was three years old. Although he could ride the roughest bronco, Ralph preferred that a horse he was breaking never buck with him. Instead, he liked to work with a horse from the time it was a young colt, halter breaking it and getting it accustomed to different situations. Here, Ralph is trying to teach a puppy to ride on the back of a colt, while at the same time teaching the colt to stand still until the puppy gets balanced on its back.

Generally, when my dad finally mounted an unbroken horse the horse did not buck with him. It might stand there quivering nervously, but Dad's quiet voice and calm assurances made the horse settle down and finally start off down the road without ever bucking. Courtesy Marion Vroom Grechman

Ideal conditions do not always exist when one is camping out in the mountains. The weather can change overnight. Taken in October 1927 taken after a fall snowstorm in the foothills, this shows the wet snow clinging to the delicate branches of deciduous trees. It shows the fairyland created by such a snowstorm. But it does not show the wet wood or camping equipment that would add some discomfort to the experience. Courtesy Katherine Bruce

Being a mountain guide entails dealing with adverse weather conditions and keeping up the spirits of guests who are on such an outing. A wet snowfall often occurs in the foothills and mountains of southwestern Alberta during hunting season in the fall. While an early snowfall means colder weather, it also enables a hunter to track animals and improves the chances of having a successful hunt. My dad was an excellent tracker. He was able to tell how many animals were in a herd and when the animals were on a certain trail by looking at their tracks.

Trees and shrubs covered with a heavy snowfall of soft, fluffy snow look like big piles of absorbent cotton. If a rider or a person on foot even touched such branches the snow would dump on top of the person. Then the person was wet for the rest of the day if not adequately protected by wearing a water repellent jacket.

Looking southwest from the Beauvais Lake district, one sees the area of the Christie Ridge where the Christie coal mine, the Good coal mine and other coalmines were located. Castle Mountain, located south of the Ralph Vroom ranch, is visible in the background. Courtesy Alvina Bond Clavel

Ralph came upon this magnificent view looking south from Hector Cote's ranch southwest of Pincher Creek toward a section of the Rocky Mountains while riding south of what became the Hector Cote ranch. At this location Pincher Creek flows north of the west (right) side of the rocky outcrop. The creek then turns and flows eastward. Alvina and Wilbrod Clavel's house (not visible in this photo) was nearby, just beyond the Cote buildings, in the trees halfway to the rocky outcrop.

Looking from left to right one sees the Cote ranch buildings on the west side of Pincher Creek, then Pincher Creek, which has low bushes along its banks to help prevent erosion of the banks. Beyond the creek ones sees the road running south from Pincher Creek to the Alberta Ranch buildings. Beyond the road, hidden in a clump of trees is the Clavel ranch house.

The high, dome-shaped mountain in the distance is Drywood Mountain. To the right (west) of it is Pincher Ridge. Still further west is Comer Mountain, now called Prairie Bluff. Victoria Peak is behind Prairire Bluff.
Courtesy Hector Cote

Alena, like most ranch wives of the time, was very busy. Home schooling Marion and Alfred, as well as keeping a watchful eye on them, was very stressful. In addition, having her mother staying with her, and then having her become ill, put a lot more work on Alena's shoulders.

So when Ralph quit school, Alena would often prevail upon him to look after Alfred and Marion for a few hours in an afternoon. Tiring very quickly of that task, Ralph figured out what he thought was the perfect solution to his problem. He would take Alfred and Marion with him on his forays through the hills, but how to do it was the question.

Ralph hit upon the idea of carrying Alfred and Marion in panniers fastened on either side of a packhorse. The idea worked fine the first few rides. Marion and Alfred, who stood peeking over the sides of the panniers, enjoyed their peaceful rides through the hills.

But one day Ralph loaded them into panniers on either side of a bronc he was breaking. Something startled the half-wild horse. It ducked its head and started to buck.

Marion bounced out on the first jump, but Alfred - "John Chinaman," as Ralph had nicknamed him - slid further down into the pannier and wedged tightly in the bottom of the wooden box. The bronc, tired of bucking but still in a mood to escape, yanked its halter shank out of Ralph's hand and took off kicking and running into the hills.

Ralph thought the packhorse would go home by itself after a while. He picked up Marion, who had landed unharmed in the bushes beside the trail, seated her behind his saddle and together they rode off for home.

"Where's Alfred?" demanded Ralph's mother when the Ralph went into the house.

"Oh, John'll be OK," Ralph replied jauntlly. "He just went for a little ride with my packhorse."

Alena was angry with Ralph for his behaviour and worried about Alfred lest something happen to him. When it came dark and the packhorse had still not returned to the home ranch, Alena told Ralph sternly, "Go and look for Alfred, and don't come back until you find him."

Ralph searched until late evening, looking for the horse at the most likely water holes first, finally finding the packhorse standing quietly in a grove of trees. Alfred had cried himself into an exhausted sleep. Ralph, thankful that his younger brother was safe, pulled Alfred out of the pannier carefully and carried him home doubledeck on his saddle horse.

Alfred was so traumatized by the incident that he would not go riding with Ralph again and never did take to the idea of being a cowboy.

This 1997 panoroma of Beaver Mines Creek Valley shows the foothills country west-northwest of Oscar and Alena's homestead. The picture was taken from the east side of Beaver Creek, from about the location of Oscar's two-storey homestead house on the north side of Ruby Creek.

One can see why Oscar named his ranch "Sunny Vale Ranche". Looking towards Beaver Mines this shows the general area where Alena's large herd of horses ranged and where Alfred, scrunched down in the bottom of a pannier on a runaway packhorse, was lost for several hours.

By the 1930s Harold had purchased this land from the original homesteader and had built a large chicken coop there. To raise cash for everyday living expenses Harold and Ruby pedalled eggs and butchered chickens to people living in Crowsnest Pass towns some 15 to 20 miles north of here.

The McLaughlin family now owns this property. Their ranch buildings are hidden behind the trees.
Courtesy Edi-May Smithies

Work crews, using teams of horses for hauling the heavy loads, built the right of way for the Kootenay & Alberta Railway in February 1911. As construction on the trestle proceeded, lore surrounding it grew. The trestle was the longest wooden railway trestle for its height in Canada at the time. It was located just north of the Mountain Mill Church and was built about five years after the church was opened.

To take this 1914 photo Mabel Bruce stood on the side of the hill on the east side of Mill Creek and faced upstream.

Young Ralph, fascinated by the wooden trestle from the day the construction began, vowed to ride a saddle horse across the top of it. In the late spring of 1911, on a bet with another local man, Ralph carried out his vow and rode the bronc he was breaking at the time across the Kootenay & Alberta Railway trestle that spanned Mill Creek Valley at Mountain Mill. The horse had to place its hooves carefully on the railway ties to avoid falling through between the ties. Adam "Dutch" Truitt confirmed that the iron rails for the railway track had not been laid on the trestle when Ralph rode the bronc across it.

As he rode across that massive structure my dad no doubt looked down on the sturdy little church nearly 1000 feet below and thought of the occasion when he and his parents attended the opening of the church regarded with such love and pride by the entire community. Perhaps Ralph said a prayer for his own safety as he took his precarious ride across the towering railway trestle on that day. Fortunately, Dad made it safely across and this story became part of the lore of that part of Alberta.

By June 25, 1912, the railway tracks were laid into Beaver Mines. However, the huge coalmine development expected at Beaver Mines never occurred. By 1915 the coal had gone "soft" so mining at Beaver Mines ceased. The mines closed and trains stopped running to Beaver Mines. The trestle fell into disrepair and, according to Bill Link, was dismantled in 1923, with the timbers being hauled to Pincher Creek and sawed into lumber.

When I was a child in the 1930s the approaches to the trestle were still very prominent. Even in 2008 the eastern approach can still be seen. Both the east and west approaches to the railway trestle are now overgrown with trees and brush. Courtesy Katherine Bruce

In about 1921 Ralph sits astride one of his favourite saddle horses beside the cottage at Mountain Mill where he and my mother lived when they were first married. Dad is wearing his prized white woolly chaps and his trademark 10-gallon Stetson hat, a tanned elkskin jacket, embroidered with colourful designs, and a pair of beaded elkskin gauntlet gloves.

"My mother, Nellie (Mrs. Henry Riviere) may have made the jacket and gloves for Ralph", said Frances Riviere McWhirter (2003). Or, he may have gotten it by trading with the Indians who frequently travelled through that area on hunting trips into the foothills.

To complete his cowboy regalia, Ralph has a coiled lariat tied just below the pommel. The saddle is equipped with saddle pockets.

The stirrups feature leather tapaderos. These keep the rider's foot from slipping through the stirrup, preventing the rider from being hung up in the stirrup should he ever be thrown. Author's collection

Members of the Vroom family and their descendants remained active in the affairs of the community. In this letter dated June 11, 1956, my mother, Mollie Tyson Vroom, writes to her cousin Ruth Tyson Brandes:

"We got the car license on June 2, and the road is good just now. We were out yesterday to a 50th anniversary service at the Mt. Mill church. Ralph was at the first service in it. About 75 people were there, possibly half of them old timers. The ladies served a bounteous potluck supper in the church following the service.

"On Sat. we went to the Horse Show, which was quite good."

One of the main organizers of the 100th anniversary celebration of the Mountain Mill Church was Lee Gingras McClelland (Mrs. Douglas McClelland), daughter of my cousin Vera Cyr Gingras (Mrs. Homer Gingras), daughter of Marion Vroom Cyr (Mrs. Dominic Cyr), daughter of Oscar Vroom. Author's collection

The young people of the Beaver Mines district had a lively social life. Tennis was a famourite sport amongst homesteaders. This is the Beaver Mines Tennis Club circa 1909. Back from left, Frank Holmes, Mr. Moodie, Mr. Morrison (holding racket, student minister, Mountain Mill Church); Samuel McVivar, Mgr., Beaver Mines coal mines, is second from right.

Front row, second from left is Louise Riley Holmes (Mrs. Frank) in a white dress; next is Mrs Moodie wearing a hat, with unknown small girl; Elsie Belle Crosbie (Mrs. Edward Joyce) and Mrs. Morrison, each in a white dress and helding a racquet. Edna McDonald (Mrs. Malcolm "Mickey") is fifth woman from right (hat and tennis racquet); Mrs. Gertrude McVicar is the third woman from the right (no hat); and the two women on the extreme right, are my aunt, Marion Vroom (Mrs. Dominic Cyr) in a white hat, and her mother, Alena Munro (Mrs. Oscar) Vroom, who is on the end of the row wearing a dark hat. Courtesy Adeline Cyr Robbins

MAP 4 Village of Mountain Mill, circa 1870 to 1976

Shown on the map: Dave and Marjorie Clemens Link residence, ca 1934; McLaren ranch barn/original location of Fred Link ranch; stone grist (flour) mill, 1883; McLaren saw mill; boom diverting water to water wheel; new location of Link ranch barn (moved and reoriented by Bill Link in the 1950s); McLaren bunk house; McLaren ranch house; mill office; post office; Fred Link ranch house; worker/lumberjack log house; R. & M. Vroom house, 1921); worker/lumberjack frame houses; Mountain Mill church, est. 1906; Wm. Shanks "Old Glad" Gladstone's homestead and root house; Edward and Elizabeth Pope Gamache first cabin; Alex White's homestead cabin; Ed and Mary Gamache Buchanan residence; Tommy Hughes residence; Ken & Jessie Gamache residence, 1954-1970.

Also shown are the "old" road to the Roodee Ranch and Pincher Creek; the "new" road to the Roodee Ranch and Pincher Creek; the road that was the main road from Beaver Mines and Coalfields School to Pincher Creek when I was a child; the Mountain Mill Trestle of the Kootenay & Alberta Railway; and two quarters owned by Peter McLaren.

The map shows where Old Glad and his family lived after he donated his land in the bottom of the Mill Creek Valley for the location of the Mountain Mill Church.

Dave and Marjorie Clemens Link's house shown in this map was where Don and I rode to visit them one sunny, chilly March day in 1935. I dearly loved "Miss Clemens" when she was my grade one teacher at Coalfields School, and pestered Don until he finally rode the eight miles to Mountain Mill with me to visit her.

Alex White's homestead quarter was NE-12-6-2-W5th. Peter McLaren's quarters were SE-13-6-2-W5 and SW-18-6-1-W5. Wm. Shanks "Old Glad" Gladstone's homestead cabin was on the northwest corner of NW 7-6-1-W5. Illustration by Edi-May Smithies, Cartography by Shelley McConnell

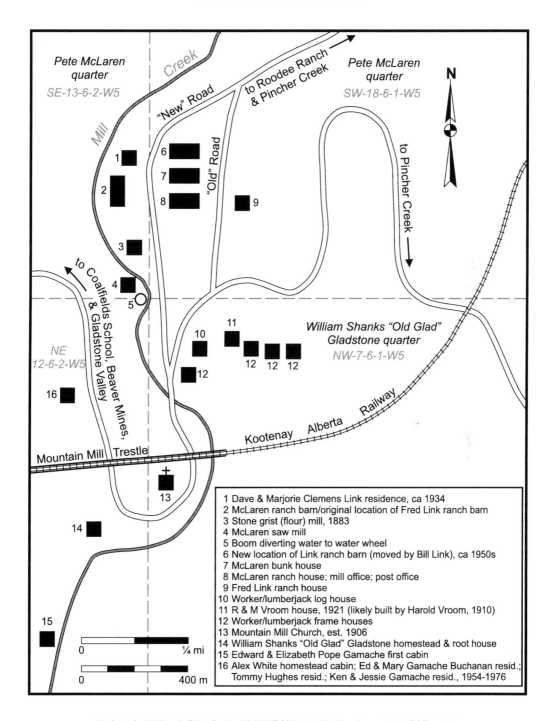

MAP 4 VILLAGE OF MOUNTAIN MILL, circa 1880 TO 1976

This modern post card of Chateau de l'Epinay, PLESSE (Loire-ATL.), France shows where Henri Arnous Riviere was born January 13, 1867. Henri Arnous "Frenchy" Riviere was the patriarch of the Riviere family who lived southwest of Twin Butte, AB, in the 1930s and 40s. Some descendants of Henri and Nellie Gladstone Riviere still ranch in that area, said his daughter Frances Riviere.

Henri Arnous "Frenchy" Riviere, named after his father, Henry-Guillaume Arnous [Arnoss] Riviere and a descendant of the French aristocracy. Frenchy's job at a Montana ranch took him into southern Alberta and as far north as Edmonton. Frenchy fell in love with the rolling Alberta foothills. Courtesy Lorraine Riviere Pommier

My dad met the Rivieres when he first came to the West and was just learning to be a cowboy. By then, Henri Arnous "Frenchy" Riviere, who was descended from an aristocratic French family, was already an old timer in the Pincher Creek area, having arrived there in the late 1800s after working his way from his parents' home in Mobile, Alabama, to a ranch near Deer Lodge, Montana. En route Frenchy learned to be a skilled horseman, an all-round cowboy and an accomplished marksman.

A letter to the editor by Frenchy Riviere in the March 25, 1954, *Pincher Creek Echo*, explained how Frenchy came to the Pincher Creek area in 1886 acting as packer and manager for Colonel Marshall, a British army officer, who had come from England to join Lionel Brooke on a game and salmon hunting trip in the Columbia country.

A. Primeau in her book *Frenchy Riviere* said that Frenchy came to Pincher Creek in 1888 "night herding bulls for I. G. Baker …hauling hay from Halifax bottom, east of Pincher Creek, to Lethbridge."

Frenchy next got a job working for Donald Bell, co-owner of the Alberta Ranch with his brother Lachlan. His horsemanship skills immediately became evident and Frenchy was given the job of breaking horses on the Donald Bell ranch near Beauvais Lake southwest of Pincher Creek. . Don Brestler in his *Shell Waterton News* said that by 1894 Frenchy was breaking horses for the Bell Ranch.

Frenchy soon realized that he would be a lot better off with a wife. Moreover, he knew that in order for his family to survive the harsh frontier life he would need a wife with special survivor skills, a wife who could bear many children and knew how to survive in a remote area with few or no amenities. As good fortune would have it he met just such a young woman. She was Nellie Gladstone, a beautiful Metis girl.

Nellie was like a princess in a long line of European royalty, only her lineage was based on the plains of North America and was a mélange made up mainly of French and Cree Indian blood mixed in various amounts in various generations.

Nellie Gladstone Riviere, at age 18 soon after she married Henri "Frenchy" Riviere, a frontiersman, in Fort Edmonton, AB. Over the years Nellie and Frenchy had eleven children, one of whom, Emilie, died of spinal meningitis at the age of three years. At the time, Henri and Nellie were taking goldrushers, their equipment and supplies to the Yukon. There was no doctor and most of the children in the village died, recalled Lorraine Pommier.

Nellie Gladstone was born March 17, 1876, in Bow River, NWT, later called Macleod and now known as Fort Macleod, AB. However, there is some disagreement about Nellie's birthplace. Henri Riviere's death certificate of 1938 and the Kootenay Region Metis Association Pedigree Chart both state Nellie's birthplace as Calgary. But, Nellie's obituary in the Pincher Creek Echo of August 22, 1940, states that Nellie "died at 64 yrs; born in Macleod". **C**ourtesy Lorraine Riviere Pommier

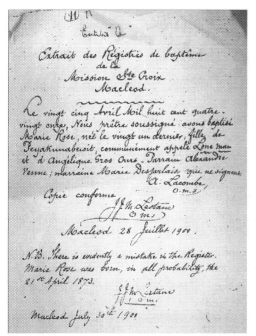

The baptismal certifcate of baby "M. Rose," daughter of Lone Man, a Cree Indian, and Angelique Big Bear,, daughter of Cree Chief Big Bear. "M. Rose" became "Marion" Johnson when her father, Lone Man, got tired of the Indians and moved to the Crowsnest Pass where he took the name "Sam Johnson." Marion "Johnson" married George "Bull" Gladstone. George was Nellie Gladstone Riviere's cousin. Lone Man was the brother of Nellie's mother, Mary Samat Vandal "Johnson."

The English translation states: "Extract of Baptismal certificate 25 April 1891 of M. Rose born 21 March 1891, girl of Peyaronabewit, aka Lone Man, and Angelique Big Bear; Baptism performed at Mission St Crois, Macleod--Godfather: Alexandre Verne, godmother: Marie Desjarlais; Baptism performed and original certificate signed by A. Lacombe, O.M.I. (Father Lacombe)"

Noted on the original extract: "Marie Rose was born, in all probability, the 21 April 1873" Courtesy Lorraine Rivierre Pommier

At the end of his time as an Indian, Lone Man visited Nellie Riviere at their Victoria Peak ranch. He was wearing a feather in his hair and riding his pinto pony, remembers Frances Riviere McWhirter. Frances was a small child when Lone Man visited Nellie, but still shudders at the memory, saying, "I was scared to death of him… I hid under a bed the whole time he was there."

Here circa 1905 are: Seated: Madeleine Gladstone, Nellie's sister. (Back row, left to right) Henri Riviere, b. 1899, six years old; Nellie Gladstone Riviere, b. 1879; George Riviere, b. 1902; about 3 years old being held by his grandmother Mary "Marie" Samat Vandal Johnson Gladstone (Nellie's mother) who is also holding baby Mary "Girlie," b. 1904; about one year old. Jessey Nellie "Babe" who was 7 months old in the 1906 census was not born yet.

 Nellie's mother, Mary Samat Vandal Johnson Gladstone, a very handsome Cree Indian woman, was from North Battleford, near Fort Pitt, SK, on the banks of the North Saskatchewan River. Mary was the wife of Wm. Gladstone II, who was an interpreter for the North West Mounted Police (RNWMP). Mary was also the sister of Lone Man, the Indian who when he was an old man visited his niece Nellie Gladstone Riviere. Frances Riviere McWhirter, Lone Man's grandniece, was a child at the time. She was " nearly scared to death" of her uncle.

 This is an excellent photo of Mary (Marie) Samat Vandal Gladstone, Nellie's mother, widow of William Gladstone II who died in 1891. William Gladstone III was born in Macleod, NWT, in 1891. Frances Riviere McWhirter said that Nellie always sat around the kitchen table and talked about life with her children. Frances tried to do the same with her children. My dad as a young man knew and was fond of Nellie Gladstone Riviere and Mary Samat Vandal Gladstone, who died when she lived with her daughter and son-in-law Dave and Madeline Carpenter. The Carpenters tried to rush Nellie to hospital in Pincher Creek in wintertime. Both of these kind, generous ladies treated my dad like a son, and he loved them as a son loves his mother.

 Mary Samat Vandal also took the surname "Johnson," and so became Mary Samat Vandal Johnson. However, she used the name 'Mary Gladstone' when she took out her homestead north of Drywood Creek on SW ¼ -18-4-29-Wth4. This was located two quarter sections directly east of George Gladstone and three quarter sections directly east of George Annand, spanning Drywood Creek on the north and south side. Her children were Nellie; William III, born 1891 in Macleod, NWT; James, born March 1893, Macleod, NWT; George, born February 1885, Calgary, AB; Alexander, born 1888 (Willow Tree Website). Courtesy Frances Riviere McWhirter

In his book, *The Gentle Persuader: A Biography of James Gladstone, Indian Senator*, (Dempsey, 1986), Dempsey implies that as a token of their affection for William Gladstone II the people of Calgary gave Marie a tent to live in and a place to put it—likely for the winter as well as for summertime. The land that Marie was given may have been her homestead quarter, although at first Marie was given a place to live for only only year. After that she was expected to work outside her home to support her children.

Frances Riviere McWhirter also told Edi-May Smithies that Mary Samat Vandal Johnson Gladstone and her children, roamed in a wagon living on handouts from friends and relatives for a period of time. Nellie, who was their oldest child, was forced to quit school to travel with her mother and siblings. When she was 18 years old, Nellie met and married Henri "Frenchy" Riviere, escaping a life of poverty as a female Metis teenager who had no way to support herself.

My dad also knew Louise Spence Gladstone, wife of William Gladstone III and mother of Leonard Gladstone.

Frances McWhirter said Mary "Marie" Gladstone (Nellie's mother) and Louise Spence were from North Battleford, SK, which was near Fort Pitt, SK, on the banks of the North Saskatchewan River.

Here, in this circa 1915 photo, "Kookem" (Grandmother) Margarette Louise Spence holds Tommy, born circa 1914, and about one year old in this picture taken at the Spence homestead on the north side of Yarrow Creek. The Spences' homestead was adjacent to that of William Gladstone III and his wife, Louise Spence Gladstone. The children, standing left to right, are four-year-old Jerry Spence, born circa 1911, and six-year-old Joe Spence, born 1909.

Jerry Spence was a cousin of Frances Riviere McWhirter, related to her by marriage only. Jerry's mother died when he was young, so kindly "Kookem" Spence raised him. Jerry Spence was the grandson of "Kookem" Spence, and the son of a half-sister of Louise Spence Gladstone, who was Leonard's mother. Nellie Gladstone Riviere also looked after the children of Louise's half- sister when they were young, even though they were not related by blood to Nellie.

Frances looked at this picture and said: "This is the mother of my Aunt Louise Spence Gladstone." Frances' Aunt Louise was the wife of William III and mother of Leonard Gladstone. Frances said that Louise Spence was a Cree from North Battleford, SK, and that she died prior to about 1936, when Jerry rode with James and Frances at Red Rock Canyon because "Kookem" Spence had died.

Huddlestun (circa 1969), also attesting to "Kookem" Spence's kindness and generosity, stated, "West of Billy's (Billy Huddlestun) was Mrs. Spence. Living with Mrs Spence was John Lawrence, known as "Bone," and his family. His children were Jerry, Joe, Tommy and Mary. After Mrs. Spence's death, the Lawrence family moved to the Mountain Mill district." Courtesy Frances Riviere McWhirter

Like many early families in southwestern Alberta, the Gladstones and their relatives homesteaded on quarter sections that were close to one another, often in the same section of land. This provided companionship and extra help for family members in times of need.

Margarette Spence homesteaded NW ¼ - 1- 4-30-W4. Steve Gladstone homesteaded the SE ¼-1-4-30-W4th, adjacent to William Gladstone III on the south side of Yarrow Creek. Steve was the son of Harriet Gladstone, sister of Nellie. The 1901 Census shows Steve at 15 years of age living in Standoff, AB, as a "lodger" with his brother and sister, James and Lucy.

"Old Glad" worked for the Hudson's Bay Company for several years and then was self-employed as a carpenter in several locations and as boat builder in Fort Edmonton. "On May 6th, 1855, Old Glad married a native girl, Harriet Leblanc at Fort Edmonton." (Friesen, 1974) They had seven children, William II, Harriet, Mary, Sarah, Robert, Jack, and Harry.

Old Glad continued as a carpenter, working at one time working time near the gold mines at Fort Benton, Montana. Upon returning to Canada Old Glad built a sturdy trading post west of Lethbridge to replace one that had burned down. The new trading post eventually became known "Fort Whoop-Up." When the Royal Canadian Northwest Mounted Police (RNWMP) came west, Old Glad moved to Macleod and set up his carpenter shop there. When that community became too large for his liking Old Glad moved his family to Mountain Mill, AB, in about 1880, where he continued working as a carpenter and living there for the rest of his life. "Old Glad died at Mountain Mill on April 8th, 1911. Mount Gladstone and Gladstone Creek are named after him." (Friesen, 1974)

William Shanks Gladstone (William I) was born December 29, 1832, in Montreal, PQ. He married Harriet Leblanc May 6, 1855, in Fort Edmonton, said Lorraine Pommier. Harriet died before 1901 (she was not on the 1901 census) and was buried at (unknown at this time).

The 1906 Census of Canada noted William S. Gladstone as living in Mountain Mill P.O. district and "Babe" as being on a ranch in Pincher Creek P.O. district.

1910 photograph of the first five children of Henri "Frenchy" and Nellie Gladstone Riviere. Left to right, back row, standing: Henry born 1899, George born 1902 and Jessey Nellie "Babe born 1906. Front row seated: Robert "Bob" born 1907 and Mary "Girlie" born ca 1904.

In subsequent years Henri and Nellie had five more children about 2 1/2 years apart. Emilie (Mimi) born circa 1897, died circa 1900; Nellie's first-born child; "...died in the north at the age of 3 years." (Friesen, 1974) Courtesy Lorraine Riviere Pommier

When my dad, Ralph, met the Henri Riviere family he took an immediate liking to Nellie Gladstone Riviere. Their friendship ended in 1940 when Nellie died as the result of injuries received in a tragic accident. Nellie's democrat team ran away with her while going down a steep hill south of Pincher Creek. Nellie died from injuries sustained when she was thrown from the vehicle. My dad was grief-stricken.

Nellie and Frenchy Riviere were generous, friendly and helpful. Nellie was especially kind to children. By 1912 when my dad visited Nellie Riviere he found that she had six children of her own, as well as three other children from the area whose own parents were not able to care for them.

This photo was taken in the summer of 1912. Left to right are Charile; Nellie Gladstone Riviere, holding James; George, in a big hat; Nellie "Babe"; Mary "Girlie"; and an unknown girl. They are on the Whipple Ranch, which is the land Frenchy bought from the government before he homesteaded on his Victoria Peak ranch. The land in this photo was sold to a man named "Whipple" and was subsequently referred to by the Riviere's as the "Whipple Ranch". Courtesy Frances Riviere McWhirter

When my dad first met Nellie and Frenchy, perhaps as early as 1904, they were living on the Lauchie Bell ranch where Frenchy was breaking horses for the ranch. They had three young children--baby Mary, George, and Henry--so Nellie was not able to travel around the countryside very much. Nellie and Ralph would sit and "talk for hours," said Frances Riviere McWhirter. Nellie appreciated my dad's visits, which helped to combat the loneliness of pioneer times, and my dad was totally enthralled by Nellie's accounts of her experiences while living on the western plains of Canada in the time of her ancestors.

In those years, when Frenchy was often away for weeks at a time, Nellie valued my dad's visits even more. According to Nellie's daughter Frances, "Can I give you a hand, Nellie?" were always the first words out of Ralph's mouth after initial greetings were over whenever he came to visit the Rivieres. "Then he would hustle around and help Mother get dinner ready," Frances continued. "He'd wash pots and pans as they went along and after dinner he'd wash up all the dishes in short order."

"When the family was fed, the dishes washed and all the children were settled down your dad would talk with my mother for hours," Frances continued enthusiastically. "Your dad loved to hear the old, old stories of when Mother was young" and lived with her parents. Nellie was related to the Cree Indians of Saskatchewan through her mother, Mary "Marie" Samat Vandal Johnson Gladstone, wife of Wm. Gladstone II, an interpreter for the Northwest Mounted Police (RNWMP).

My dad watched with interest as the children of Henri and Nellie Riviere grew older, all of them learning to ride at a young age. The Riviere boys became expert horsemen.

To break horses to be reliable saddle horses Frances used the technique developed by her dad during his many years working with horses. My dad as a teenager watched Frenchy breaking horses when he visited the Rivieres.

Dad was a fast learner and soon had the method down pat. When breaking a wild young horse Dad talked in a soft, patient tone of voice and worked the nervous animal over quietly with a blanket before ever riding them, something like the main character in the movie The Horse Whisperer.

Dad taught us children to break horses in this soft-spoken way. The aim, though it did not always work that way, was to break a horse without it ever bucking with you.

Seen here in 1912, George Riviere, 10 years old at the time, stands in the ranch corral gently holding an appaloosa colt, distinguished by the patch of white hair on its rump. Hand written information on the reverse of this picture states: "George born 14 Feb 1902; died 29 Dec 1995." Courtesy Lorraine Riviere Pommier

Although George's obituary says he was born **in** Twin Butte on February 26, 1902, he was likely born on what became the Whipple ranch west of Twin Butte, where Rivieres were living in 1902. Frances Riviere McWhirter said, "Nellie's mother, Mary Johnson, acted as midwife and for most of George's life, Mary Johnson and her daughter Madeleine raised him" (although Madeleine died not many years later).

When George Riviere was born his grandfather, "Old Glad", was living in Macleod and was growing tobacco--the plants had "great big, green leaves," as related by Frances McWhirter, who was told this by her mother, Nellie. In 1902 "Old Glad" had George baptized in the Church of England in Macleod. In 1901 Mary Samat Vandal Johnson, Nellie's mother, was living in Macleod. That may have been why George was baptized there in 1902, Frances continued. George's birth certificate showed the same information when he applied for Old Age Security.

Shown here is Robert "Bob" Riviere at about 18 years of age. Bob is dressed in his best cowboy regalia, complete with a wide-brimmed Stetson, a colourful neckerchief, a beaded buckskin vest that was made by his mother, Nellie Gladstone Riviere,.

Leather gloves, his prized white woolly chaps, and with a holster, complete with pistol, at his waist.

The pommel of his bronco-busting saddle just shows above his horse's withers. Nellie made a beaded vest for each of her sons. Robert married Mary Burns. Their children were Frances, Rose, Bobby, Lois, Zilda and Wanda. Courtesy Lorraine Riviere Pommier

Frances was the only one of the Riviere girls who became an expert horsewoman. For several years after she left home Frances made her living breaking broncs for other ranchers as far away as Claresholm. For another few years she helped her brother James take pack trips out into the mountains west of their home.

Here, in 1937, are (left to right) Frances Riviere (18 years old) and her brother James Riviere. They had just arrived home from a pack trip in the mountains and were dirty and sweaty, but someone wanted a photo of them, Frances said. The photo is taken on the south side of Drywood Creek in the homestead houseyard of Nellie Riviere's brother George Gladstone. At the right of the photo is the hitching rail used to tie up saddle horses.

In the background is the road coming down the hill to the house where, in 1939, Nellie and Maggie Clark (Mrs. George) Riviere had a serious buggy accident with "Dolly," a runaway horse. Nellie was thrown from the buggy and, in 1940, died from the injuries she sustained. Frances grieved for her mother for many years thereafter. Courtesy Frances Riviere McWhirter

(Above left) *Even the best cowboys and cowgirls get old, but they never lose their sense of pride in their achievements as young people in the prime of life. Here at her home in Kimberley in August 2003, Frances Riviere McWhirter holds the bridle and spurs that she used as a teenager and young adult. Frances Riviere was as good a rider as any of her brothers, breaking her own horses from a young age and earning money by breaking horses for other people. These mementos are some of Frances's most treasured possessions reminding her of an adventurous youth.* Courtesy Edi-May Annand Smithies

(Above right) *George, second oldest Riviere boy, nears the end of his life. George spent most of his life ranching near Wasa, BC. One time George came down from Barkerville, BC, where he was working and stopped to visit Frances Rivieer Mcwhirter, his youngest sister. George fell in love with the country around Kimberley. He bought a ranch north of Kimberley at Wolf Creek, near Wasa, BC and ranched there for many years. As a teen, Ralph Tyson of Kimberley visited George on this ranch.* Courtesy Frances Riviere McWhirter

KLONDIKERS

I n his memoirs Anthony Bruce said, "Dad's father was one Alan Cameron Bruce-Pryce (the Pryce was later dropped), a well-known and highly respected barrister in Cheltenham (England), who married one Louisa Slade. They had six children, Dad being the second (child, and a twin with Alan Cameron) and a brother of one Charles (of him, more later). Dad was born on September 29, 1874, and later, for a while, was a lieutenant in the 2nd Inniskillen Dragoons, which he later left. His full name was "Edward Maunsell Bruce".

Edward Bruce in Yukon garb--a thigh-length, fringed buckskin jacket with handsewn bead designs on the sleeves and yoke and a pair of fur mittens in the Klondike circa 1898.

Edward is wearing his glasses, which he wore full time when I knew him, and is smoking a very handsome straight-stem pipe. He holds his rifle, safely sheathed in its leather scabbard, in the crook of his right arm. The well-worn scabbard, fastened with leather thongs, is also decorated with handsewn bead designs.

Edward likely purchased this jacket from a Yukon Indian during his sojourn there. He brightens up his jacket with a colourful sash around his neck. Two leather straps criss-cross his chest. One strap likely holds his field glasses, while the other is for carrying small items and light rations.

Edward also has a leather belt around his waist from which hang two muskrat pelts, evidence of his prowess as a trapper.

With his neatly trimmed, waxed and twirled mustache and his beautiful, straight-stem pipe clenched between his teeth Edward looks every bit the English gemtleman transplanted into the wilds of North America. In the lower right-hand corner of the picture are the handwritten words "Kla-horoya! Taricuhu." (There is an upside-down 'v' above the 'c'.) Courtesy Katherine Bruce

Like Edward Bruce, Mabel Noyes Bruce had a very interesting and adventurous life before she moved to Beaver Mines where I knew the family in the 1930s.

In an unpublished paper "For Nigel & Carolyn" Anthony Bruce, youngest son of Edward "Ted" and Mabel Bruce wrote: "Mother was born (I believe) in England, on October 28th, 1876, her maiden name being Mabel Katherine Elliott Noyes. The family was transferred to Malta, where her father (Col. Noyes) was in charge of the British garrison there. It was there that (Mabel) learned to swim," stated Anthony. "She was an excellent swimmer."

In his memoirs Anthony continued, "When Mother was about 10 or 12 years of age, they were again transferred, this time to Halifax, Nova Scotia, for her father to take charge of the Garrison there, for 5 years. From there, he retired from the army, and the family returned to England, taking up residence in a place called "Parkfield Lawn" in Cheltenham, where Mother completed her education."

This 1892 photo, taken in Halifax, NS, shows Mabel Katherine Elliott Noyes (Bruce) as a teenager. Here Mabel is dressed in a fancy gown, perhaps in readiness for a special occasion. As a very attractive, lively young woman Mabel would have enjoyed the attention of the young army officers in her father's command, but she did not choose one of them as her lifelong mate. Photo taken by: Gauvin & Gentzel, Artists, Halifax, NS. Courtesy Kevin and Heather Bruce Grace

When I was a child I had no idea of the thrilling, even dangerous, adventures of our neighbours Edward and Mabel Bruce when they were young.

Edward Bruce, a mining engineer, spent 10 years in the Klondike from 1894 to 1904 during which time he owned a riverboat and transported thousands of gold rushers and their equipment and supplies from St. Michael's, Alaska, to Dawson City, Yukon, using the mighty Yukon River as a highway. When he left the Yukon, Edward walked out over the trail from Dawson City, to Dyea, Alaska.

My great-uncle Herbert Vroom took a different route. He drove a herd of some 300 cattle from Ashcroft in the Cariboo-Chilcotin area of British Columbia, to Telegraph Creek and on to Dawson City, Yukon. This was an alternate route that was followed by hundreds of people heading to the Yukon in the hopes of finding a rich lode of gold and becoming wealthy.

Edward Bruce was in the Klondike for ten years. During that time he wrote detailed letters to his father, Alan Cameron Bruce-Pryce of Chelthenham, England, telling of the hardships that he and fellow Yukon trekkers endured. Most of the trekkers were men, though there were some women. Edward's father typed out Edward's letters and sent them to the *Cheltenham Examiner*. The letters were printed in the *Cheltenham Examiner* on November 23rd, 1898, and in December 1898.

KLONDIKERS

We have no actual map showing the route taken by Edward Bruce up the Yukon River from St Michael's, Alaska,, to Dawson City, YT, and back out to Dyea, Alaska, and by Herbert Vroom from Ashcroft, BC, to Dawson City. However, the reader is referred to the book, *Klondike: The Last Great Gold Rush, 1896-1899*, 1972, by the eminent Canadian writer, Pierre Berton, for several excellent maps of routes to the Klondike.

In his memoirs Anthony continued, "Dad was educated in Cheltenham, and took a further course in mining at a university in (I think) Frankfurt, Germany. He was a born linguist, and could speak, read and write English, French, and German, and could get by in Italian and Spanish, and learned two or three Indian languages and Eskimo, whilst in the Yukon, where he went as a mining engineer from 1894 to 1904. He was there right through the 'Gold Rush.'"

The Bruce family's story in Canada started about 1911 when they moved to a farm southeast of Calgary, AB, at a place called Cluny, which is near Gleichen.

The land at Cluny was flat and barren, but Mabel found activities of interest to herself and of historical significance to the rest of us.

Anthony stated in his memoirs: "Going still further back, I remember Mother telling me that when they first went to Cluny, the country was so unsettled that one could have ridden in three directions from the farm, for 150 miles and not meet a fence. Directly across from the farmhouse (that is, across the road allowance) was the Blackfoot Indian Reserve, with the Indians still living in teepees."

Women of the Plains Indian tribes, who were responsible for setting up the teepees when a group of people moved to a fresh campsite, became very skilled at the task. In this scene of sports day activities, women of the Blackfoot tribe at Gleichen, AB, are having a contest to see who can erect a teepee the fastest. In the background an audience of bystanders cheers on the contestants. Courtesy Kevin and Heather Bruce Grace

The teepees of ordinary Blackfoot Indians were very plain.
Courtesy Kevin and Heather Bruce Grace

Blackfoot Indians on the Siksika Reservation near Cluny and Gleichen, AB, performing the Sun Dance in their annual Sun Dance celebrations. Cluny, AB, is a few miles East Southeast of Calgary, on the North bank of the Bow River.

The Siksika (Blackfoot) Reservation is immediately across the Bow River from Cluny (and near Gleichen). A Siksika medicine man, dressed in full costume, is performing a sacred dance at the sun dance ceremonies of the Siksika Indians near Gleichen, AB.

At the annual Sun dance ceremonies held by the Plains Indians the Medicine Man's teepees were set up in a prominent location. Courtesy Katherine Bruce

The Blackfoot Indians of the Siksika Reservation near Cluny and Gleichen, AB, gathered for their annual Sun Dance celebrations circa 1910.

Blackfoot Indian Chief, Chief Big Snake, from the Siksika reserve wears his full chief's costume.

As well as wearing an eagle-feather headdress, the chief hung a string of eagle feathers from his horse's bridle. The horse is also decked out in other special regalia for the occasion. Courtesy Katherine Bruce

The Bruces lived right across the road from the Siksika Reservation, which is near Cluny and Gleichen, AB. Mrs. Bruce took a keen interest in the life and customs of the Plains Indians. Always a fine rider, she bought herself a saddle horse and visited the Blackfoot Indians who lived near Cluny, AB, when the family lived on a farm there when first coming to Canada in 1911. Mabel soon gained the Indians' respect and confidence. Before long she was invited to observe some of their most sacred rites and rituals. She photographed many of them.

The Plains Indians used various herbs in treating illness. The "Medicine Man" in each tribe usually had this knowledge. The Medicine Man, as photographed above, was a highly esteemed member of the tribe. To help maintain his prestigious position, the Medicine Man did not share with the regular members of the tribe, but let them believe that he alone had magic powers over didease and sickness.

To further convince fellow tribesmen of his magical powers the Medicine Man wore a special costume and performed special dances when curing a sick person. Courtesy Kevin and Heather Bruce Grace

Exterior of the two teepees of the "Medicine Man" at the Sun Dance on the Blackfoot Reserve, near Cluny, AB, in the 1920s. The teepees are painted in bright, solid colours. Simple designs, perhaps depicting the number of sick persons successfully treated by the Medicine Man, decorate the bottoms of the near teepee.

Another custom of the Plains Indians was that when a member of their tribe died other tribe members erected a death teepee (see image following) in his or her honour. Cooking utenslis, a hand-decorated case for carrying small items, a bundle of clothing, and other items that the deceased would need in "The Happy Hunting Grounds" are piled around the coffin.

Cluny, AB, is a few miles East Southeast of Calgary, AB, on the north bank of the Bow River. The (Blackfoot) Reservation is immediately across the Bow River from Cluny (and near Gleichen). Courtesy Katherine Bruce

Blackfoot Indian death teepee that has a coffin and all the equipment for the deceased in "The Happy Hunting Grounds", Siksika Reservation near Cluny and Gleichen, AB, 1911. Death teepees always have no skin covering on them. The deceased person's belongings and coffin, open to the skies, are inside the circle of teepee poles that would support the covering of a regular teepee.

Bob Lang told me (Lang, Ellis, 1961 interview) the Blackfeet Indians believed they should bury their dead on home soil. Once, in 1904, Mr. Lang related, an old man took sick.

His companions turned around to take their sick friend back to Brocket, but he died about one mile down the road at Mr. Sparks' home near Mountain Mill.

The Indians rolled the dead man up in a blanket, tied each end of the blanket to their saddle horns and took him to the top of a nearby hill. There they slung their friend's body between two trees. The Indians came back the next day, tied each end of the blanket to one of their saddle horns, and took their friend's remains away with them. Courtesy Katherine Bruce

This circa 1910 postcard shows a small group of Siksika Indians, a man and two women, standing watching ongoing events with great interest. The people are dressed in a mixture of traditional clothing and Europan clothing showing the influence of Indians' dealings with early furtraders, for example, plaid blankets.

One of the women has a papoose tucked inside her blanket.

The picture looks as if it were taken at a fairground or in a small town, perhaps at Cluny or Gleichen or at Brocket in southwestern Alberta. Printing on the reverse side of the postcard states simply: "POST CARD."

A banner in the background reads: "B. T. Beatty"

The medicine man, not seen here, is getting ready to perform a secred dance at the sundance ceremonies. Courtesy KatherineBruce

Mrs. Bruce was always particular about the way her horses were groomed and about the quality of riding tack that she used on her regular outings by saddle horse.

The Siksika Indians are very skilled at leather and beadwork. Shown here are two finely crafted bridles (with bits & reins), two sets of spurs with rowels, and a riding crop.

These items, possibly a gift from the Siksika to Mabel Bruce, are draped artistically on a background of fabric that is hanging on a wooden chair back. Courtesy Kevin and Heather Bruce Grace

In his unpublished short essay, "For Nigel and Carolyn," Anthony Bruce wrote: "When Uncle Michael was born, the Chief of the Indians (Chief Big Snake) was so thrilled at there being a white "papoose" (baby) there that he had his two squaws make Uncle Michael a tiny pair of moccasins—but they were beaded on the soles, which was his way of saying that he hoped that Uncle Michael would never have to walk anywhere— he would always have a horse to ride." (Anthony Bruce, circa 1994) Courtesy Katherine Bruce

(Above left) In the early 1900s it was the custom for a christening ceremony to have the baby, whether a boy or a girl, dressed in a long, white christening gown. Here in 1911 Mabel Bruce, seated on a wooden chair, holds baby Michael who is wearing a long, white christening gown. Michael is lying on a large, fur throw on Mabel's lap. The chief of the Sikska was very pleased to have a new white "papoose" living so close to the reservation. He gave this fur throw to Mabel.   Courtesy Kevin and Heather Grace Bruce

(Above right) This oil painting was done by Mabel Bruce while the Bruce family lived at Cluny. It shows two huge Buffalo bulls, behemoths of the plains, engaging in a battle for supremacy. When the struggle ends, one buffalo bull will take over as leader of the herd; the other will be vanquished. As well as being interested in the people of western Canada, Mabel Bruce, a talented artist as well as a photographer, was keenly interested in the wildwilfe that inhabited these untamed lands. Courtesy Katherine Bruce

The three Bruce children, Ronald, Michael and Anthony, sitting on their travelling conveyances beside their house on the Roodee Ranch, 1915

In this photo, taken while the Bruces lived on the Roodee Ranch, Ronald and Michael proudly display their riding expertise on their new tricycles, while Michael sits happily in his stroller. The picture was taken in April or May when cool spring breezes necessitate the wearing of warm coats. The older children children are clothed in neat coats and Michael is covered with a white, furry blanket. Courtesy Kevin and Heather Bruce Grace

Mabel Bruce, 1917, feeding a handful of grain to "Pedro," with four white socks and a white blaze on his nose. The Bruces' little white dog "Nellie" sits near Mabel. Courtesy Kevin and Heather Bruce Grace

"Battleaxe," one of Mabel Bruce's saddle horses, distinguished by his white left hind foot and a white blaze on his nose.

Here in about 1917 Mabel is showing off "Battleaxe," then about a two-year-old colt, by having him stand in his best horseshow stance. Courtesy Katherine Bruce

This is a mature "Battleaxe" standing near a grove of trees in the Bruces' pasture at Beaver Mines in the 1930s.

Mrs. Bruce, often accompanied by her son Michael, visited my mother frequently in the early to mid-1930s often riding her favourite saddle horse, Battleaxe, shown here in midsummer, his coat sleek and shiny from eating the nutritious foothills grass.

Mrs. Bruce always kept Battleaxe's tail, shaped straight across like a girl's bangs and long enough to reach below the horse's hocks so that he could switch the flies off when they settled on him in a sunny meadow such as this. The characteristic markings of Battleaxe: a narrow blaze starting beneath his forelock that widened to a broad, white splotch on his nose with a piece of it spreading into his right nostril, a white left hind foot and mane falling to the left. Courtesy Katherine Bruce

Mabel Bruce was a lovely rider and this is a beautiful picture of her. Here, wearing leather chaps and rowelled spurs, which you can see sticking out behind her boot in the right hand stirrup, Mabel is dressed for ranch work or for a trip to town to get some groceries. A note in Mabel Bruce's handwriting on the back of this picture states: "Self on Pat. Note the chapps (sic) and quirt." This picture was taken looking west or northwest from a few miles south of Cowley, AB, on the Roodee Ranch, which was located on the west side of the Castle River, a few miles northwest of Mountain Mill. The photographer braved a chilly west wind to take this early spring photo. There are still patches of snow lying around that were left by the most recent Chinook wind. Courtesy Katherine Bruce

Mabel Bruce painted this miniature painting of the Mountain Mill Church (opened June 1906) at Mountain Mill, AB, during the summer or fall of 1914 after she moved to the Roodee Ranch. Mabel gave this painting to her friend Sarah McJanet Ballantyne (Mrs. George) before Christmas 1914.

The Roodee Ranch was east of Mountain Mill, so the Bruces likely attended this "little white church in the valley". Edward left the Roodee Ranch to join the army in 1915. The Kootenay & Alberta Railway trestle, built just north of the church, was still in good condition when Mabel painted this close-up picture. She likely sat a short distance north-northwest of the church with her back against the lowest struts of the trestle where a grove of poplar trees and a fairly old house now stand. Courtesy Lee and Doug McClelland

Mabel Bruce was an accomplished artist, art instruction being an important part of her education. Mabel's specialty was miniature pictures using watercolour. Her special talent lay in realistic, and sometimes fanciful, paintings of various animals in action, especially animals often in various comical poses, though she also painted scenery and other subjects. Mabel made Christmas, and Easter and birthday cards, often featuring whimsical paintings, to present to her special friends. I still have some of the cards that Mabel gave to my mother in my collection. The card on the previous page with the painting of the Mountain Mill Church, which was an integral part of Ballantyne family life, is still treasured by Lee and Doug McClelland. Doug is a grandson of George and Sarah McJanet Ballantyne.

The Bruces left the Roodee Ranch early in 1921, moving across the (Castle) River to live with McDougalls for a few weeks and thence to "Chipman Creek". The Bruces moved several times before settling in Beaver Mines for about 10 years, as described by Anthony, ca 1994, below:

"Early in 1921 (I think that I was about March or April, but no later) Clarkson suddenly arrived and accused Dad of planning to leave without paying rent (it had always been paid on time) and gave him about 3 days to clear out. This we did, and moved across the river (Castle River, then known as the Old Man River) to live in the home of one McDougall. (It was said that it was lucky that Mr. and Mrs. McDougall had married, or otherwise they would have spoiled two homes, instead of only one.) "We were there for only a few weeks, and then moved to a place called "Chipman Creek," southeast of Pincher Creek, Anthony stated.

"Later, the same year, we moved to Mountain Mill, which is about three or four miles east of Beaver Mines. "Our fortunes were steadily going downhill, and after three years at Mountain Mill, we moved to a place called "Hugh's" (sic—Tommy Hughes), not very far away for one year, and then to a place owned by one "Brown," for one year, and then on to Beaver Mines.

Interestingly, at the same time as Edward Bruce was in the Klondike, my great-uncle Herbert Vroom (1865-1932), left Clementsport, NS, to seek adventure and fortune. Herbert avidly followed newspaper and word-of-mouth accounts of the vast quantities of gold in the Klondike and carefully studied the map of British Columbia and the Klondike. Knowing the gold rush trekkers needed food, when he heard the CPR had reached Cranbrook, Herbert bought a ticket to the end of steel. In Cranbrook in 1897 he bought enough cattle to make up a herd of some 300 head, hired some cowboys to help, and drove the cattle north to the Klondike. He followed the BC overland route into the Yukon, going from Ashcroft in the Cariboo-Chilcotin, BC, to Telegraph Creek and on to Dawson Creek.

Almost as fast as it had started, the Klondike gold rush ended. By 1898 it was pretty well over. Very few of the Yukon trekkers struck it rich in the gold fields. Many of them stayed in the Yukon and took up other businesses, but the vast majority left the Yukon never to return. Only a few hardy souls stayed on searching for gold (Berton, 1972).

Herbert Vroom was one of the people who went elsewhere. When the gold rush ended he sold his cattle and headed for Mexico where he bought a ranch. Returning to Clementsport, NS, for the final 20 years of his life Herbert conducted a successful business until the outbreak of WWI at which time he enlisted as a commissary serving until the end of the war. After WWI, Herbert worked in Clementsport as Collector of Customs and Stipendiary Magistrate.

W.J.A. "WASH" MITCHELL: OVERLAND BY COVERED WAGON

As the soon as the Yukon Gold Rush ended another gold rush of sorts, the settlement of the western prairies, started. The rush for quarter sections of free land in western Canada, called homesteads, started in earnest about 1900 when the trickle of settlers coming by horseback, mule train, covered wagons, and on foot turned to a flood of immigrants pouring to western Canada aboard Canadian Pacific Railway passenger trains. By 1914 tens of thousands of settlers had poured in and were living on their small, quarter section farms.

One quarter section was not large enough to make a decent living for a family, so as soon as the settlers had proved up on their original quarter sections many sold out to others who were more anxious to spend their lives as farmers or ranchers in western Canada.

Some of the homesteaders who sold out, like Mr. A. L. Freebairn, established businesses in Pincher Creek. Mr. Freebairn had a ladies ready-to-wear business until after World War II.

One of the earliest families to settle in Gladstone Valley was the family of W.J.A. "Wash" Mitchell, who had been an adventurer in his young years.

This inscription on the frontispiece piece of the family Bible of Timothy and Mary Ann Mitchell, parents of Washington Mitchell, reads:

Children of Timothy and Mary Ann Mitchell -

Washington John Abraham Mitchell was born at West Burlington, Otsego Co (New York) on the 3rd day of July about half past eight o'clock in the evening in the year of our Lord one thousand eight hundred and fifty-four. Dated: *Monday, July the 3, 1854* Courtesy Ruby Peters Jaggernath

The inscription on their family Bible is earliest record we have of the Washington John Abraham "Wash" Mitchell family. The inscription reads, "Children of Timothy…" but only Washington is listed. He inherited the family Bible, and was the only Mitchell of his generation to homestead in Gladstone Valley near my childhood home. Perhaps someone who reads this book will be able to answer this question. In November 2003 the Mitchell family Bible was in the possession of Ruby Peters Jaggernath, granddaughter of "Wash" and Aravella "Belle" Mitchell.

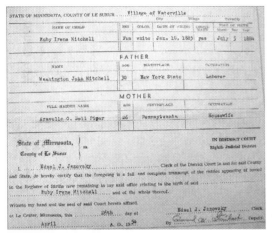

The transcript issued April 26, 1945 by the State of Minnesota records the Register of Birth for: Ruby Irene Mitchell. Born: July 5, 1884, Village of Waterville, County of Le Sueur, State of Minnesota. The baby's father is recorded as Washington John Mitchell, Age: 30 years, Born: New York State, Occupation: Laborer.

Her mother is recorded as Aravella C. Bell Piper, Age: 26 yrs, Born: Pennsylvania, Occupation: Housewife. As a small child Aravella was called "Belle" by her parents. The name was used by family and friends for the rest of her life. Courtesy Ruby Jaggernath

Before his marriage Wash Mitchell earned his living in various ways. Here, a solitary Wash Mitchell, circa 1877, herds a packtrain of mules through mountainous terrain somewhere in the Southwestern United States (possibly in Arizona).

Jack Mitchell (2000), grandson of Wash Mitchell, stated, "My granddad ran pack trains and wagons from California to Washington State." Photographer: Daniel A. Markey of Markey and Mytton, Fort Grant, AZ (photographers). Courtesy Ruby Jaggernath

The ranch buildings of Wash and Aravella "Belle" Mitchell in Meridian, Idaho, USA, about 1906, just before the family left by covered wagon for Mountain Mill, AB. An addition was built onto the original settler's cabin to accommodate their growing family and another building, seen in the right center of the picture, is under construction.

The whole family is ready to go, perhaps to a farewell get-together for the Mitchell family. The two women mounted on fine saddle horses are Ruby Mitchell and possibly her friend Edythe. The man is a neighbour. The two people in the fashionable democrat are likely Belle Mitchell and her younger son, Dave. The Mitchells' older son, Charlie, holds the reins of the spirited team to keep them still. Two other neighbours are driving a light wagon. Wash Mitchell holds his white prize stallion. In Gladstone Valley Wash became a noted horse breeder. Courtesy Ruby Jaggernath

Family birth, marriage and death records for the Mitchell children give the following information: Wash and Belle Mitchell's oldest child, Bessie, was born March 5, 1880, in Waterville, LaSueur, MN. Bessie married Harry Lemuel Truitt January 18, 1899, in Boise, ID. She died April 9, 1956, Moses Lake, Grant, WA. Wash and Belle's second oldest child, Ruby, was born on July 5, 1884, in the Village of Waterville, County of Le Sueur, State of Minnesota.

Ruby married Harold Vroom July 5, 1910 at Beaver Mines, Alberta. Ruby died November 11, 1968, in Coquitlam, BC. There are no details of the exact date and place of birth of Wash and Belle's third oldest child, Charles "Charlie," nor of the their youngest child, David "Dave."

However, family records show that Charlie was born in 1887 and Dave was born about 1890, more than 10 years before the family moved to Gladstone Valley.

An "In Memorium" card for the funeral of Belle Mitchell bears the inscription: "*In loving memory of Arvilla (sic) Calfernah Belle Mitchell Beloved wife of Washington J. A. Mitchell who died on Wednesday, June 11, 1919, at 10:20 a.m. at the age of 61 years*" (that is, born 1858).

Three men stand in front of a neatly organized tent set in a heavily forested, mountainous wilderness area. A third man, dressed in what may have been a Civil War uniform, stands to the left of the tent with one leg resting on what looks like a pile of gravel. Although this photograph is undated it appears to be of the same era as the previous photo showing "Wash" Mitchell herding a string of pack mules through the mountains.

The tent, obviously owned by the two unidentified men standing in front of it, is furnished with a table and chairs that might have been carried in from San Francisco These two men could be miners seeking a fortune in Arizona. The photographer apparently arrived at mealtime since the miners' table is set with factory-made dishes and look like they are being used for a meal at the time the picture was taken. For nighttime illumination a coal oil lamp hangs on the front tent pole.

The man wearing a uniform could be vintage Arizona photographer Charles O. Farciot. According to Jeremy Rowe, Farciot served in the United States Army and in the USNavy. After being discharged Faricot travelled to remote areas of Arizona where he "visited many of the mines and growing new settlements during their heyday and made striking photographs of the soldiers, settlers, and scouts that called Arizona home" and sometimes took self-portraits.

The full article for the above information is found in "FOLLOWING THE FRONTIER FROM ARIZONA TO ALASKA: The Photographs of Charles O. Fawcett" by Jeremy Rowe, 2002. The Internet. Search for "charles o farciot vintage photography". More information on Arizona Photographers 1850-1920 is found in www.vintagephoto.com, which mentions Daniel A. Markey, Bisbee, AZ and Ft. Apache, AZ. Courtesy Ruby Jaggernath

Harry Lemuel Truitt and 19-year-old Bessie Mitchell, on their wedding day in Boise, ID, January 18, 1899

Bessie's gown, likely of white satin and probably sewn at home by the bride and/or her mother, featured a high collar, a fitted bodice and long, fitted sleeves.

A close-up shot of detail of this photo shows that the shoulders have ribbons attached to resemble army officers' epulets, a style popular at the time.

A wide waistband and a floor-length A-line skirt complement Bessie's small waist. On her head Bessie wears a fitted lace cap with a short veil down the back.

Little did the young couple realize that in a few years they would immigrate to Canada and settle on a homestead in Gladstone Valley close to the Rocky Mountains in southwestern Alberta. Courtesy Ruby Jaggernath

Washington J. A. Mitchell stands with his three older children in Meridian, Idaho, about 1885, a number of years before the Mitchells immigrated to Canada in 1906.

The children, seated in a wheelbarrow, on the treeless land that was their Idaho home, are (left to right) Charles, born in 1887, Ruby, born in 1885, and Bessie, born in 1880. Wash and Belle Mitchell's fourth child, David "Dave", born about 1890 is not in this picture. All four of the children of Wash and Aravella "Belle" Mitchell were born when the family lived at Meridian, Idaho.

The children are wearing homemade clothes, hand sewn by their mother. Both girls are wearing dresses over thick stockings—for warmth as well as protection against scratches by bushes and bites by insects—and have stylish bows holding back their long, dark hair. Courtesy Ruby Jaggernath

A mustached, partly bald, middle-aged Washington John Abraham Mitchell, well groomed and wearing a stylish suit, about 1900. The Mitchells left for Mountain Mill in 1906. Photo by Rex Gallery of Boise, Idaho

"Wash" was born July 3, 1854, in West Burlington, Otsego County, NY. His parents were Timothy and Mary Ann Mitchell. Wash married Aravella Calfernah "Belle" Piper, who was born in Pennsylvania in 1858. The date and place of their marriage is unknown at this time. Aravella died June 11, 1919, in Pincher Creek (about the same year Jack Mitchell, grandson, was born); Wash died in 1943.

"Wash" Mitchell, as he was commonly known, was tall and wiry. He stood erect and rode tall in the saddle until the end of his long, adventurous life.

Jack Mitchell, Charlie and Sis Mitchell's son, in an interview by Ruby Jaggernath in 2000, said that his grandfather's name was Washington "Carver" ("W.C.") Mitchell. However, as recorded in his parents' family Bible, he was christened Washington John Abraham Mitchell. Courtesy Ruby Jaggernath

Before they left Meridian, Idaho, for their new home in Alberta the Mitchell children had photos taken with their best friends. From left to right above is a woman friend of the Mitchells, Charlie Mitchell, Ruby Mitchell and a man friend of the family. Unfortunately, the friends' names are unknown.

Taken in Boise, Idaho, about 1905, this obviously marks a special occasion. The two women have their luxurious long, dark hair specially coifed into a bouffant upsweep and wear crisp, white long-sleeved blouses, while the men wear three-piece suits with wide-collared white shirts fashionable at that time. Both men have their longish hair neatly parted and worn with loose waves around their faces. Charlie wears a bow tie, slightly askew, while his friend wears a four-in-hand. Courtesy Ruby Jaggernath

Mary Ellen "Sis" Buchanan Mitchell, in 1905, when she was about 15 years of age. Photographer: Hampton, 195 1/2 Argyle St., Glasgow, Scotland

Sis was likely born about 1890, emigrating from Glasgow, Scotland, to Pincher Creek in 1910, where she was postmistress until she married Charles Mitchell in 1914.

As I remember "Sis" she was a short, jolly lady, who retained her delightful Scottish accent and her sharp sense of humour to the end of her days. Charlie and "Sis" Buchanan Mitchell's only child, Jack, born in 1920, was a young teenager attending Coalfields School when I started there in 1934. Jack Mitchell in his Memoirs, September 2000 recalled: "I was six years old when we left (what was to become the Ralph and Molly Vroom ranch) in 1926."

For the pie-eating contest at local picnics Sis always made rhubarb pies, but with no sugar!

Photographer: Hampton 195 ½ Argyle St., Glasgow.
Courtesy Ruby Jaggernath

The Mitchell family stopped for lunch while making their trek by covered wagon from Meridian, nine miles from Boise, Idaho, USA, to Gladstone Valley, Alberta. For their midday repast the family chose a sunny, boulder-strewn gully that had scraggly evergreen trees clinging to its steep sides.

To protect themselves from the hot late-spring sun Belle, Ruby and Charlie wear hats. Charlie's is a broad-brimmed, dark-coloured hat, while Belle and Ruby wear bright cotton "poke bonnets" which were fashionable at that time, as well as being very practical. Belle and Ruby wear long, full-skirted dresses, while Charlie is dressed in sturdy pants.

Shown are Aravella "Belle" (Mrs. W. J. A. "Wash") Mitchell (center), son Charlie (left), and daughter Ruby (right), two of her four children.

Although Wash and Belle were in their 50s, they followed Harry Truitt, who married Bessie Mitchell in 1899, and George Smith both of whom had moved from Boise to Gladstone Valley in 1905. The Mitchells lived up Gladstone Valley, and had Mountain Mill post office for an address, before April 1907. See a postcard, inserted in text on following pages which was addressed to Miss Ruby Mitchell, Mountain Mill, AB, and which was postmarked April 29, 1907, Meridian, Idaho. Mitchells would have travelled by covered wagon the previous spring or summer, not in the winter (Friesen, 1974).
Courtesy Ruby Jaggernath

Aravella "Belle" Mitchell (center) and her two daughters, Bessie Mitchell (Mrs. Harry) Truitt (left) and Ruby Mitchell (right), in 1906. The Mitchells, accompanied by their married daughter Bessie Mitchell Truitt and her four oldest children Ruby, John, Sarah and Alice, travelled through the mountains of Montana, USA, en route from their old homes in Idaho to their new homes on homesteads in Gladstone Valley, Alberta.

Since there were no coolers, refrigerators nor iceboxes in 1906, the trekking family could not carry fresh meat with them. The task of shooting a bird or animal for daily meat fell to the person in the group who was the best shot with a rifle. In the case of the Mitchell-Truitt trekkers the unchallenged hunter was Charlie Mitchell.

There were also no inside toilets and no hot running water for showers. They did their daily ablutions in a small, shallow pan of icy water from a nearby mountain stream, much like we children were expected to do when on camping trips in the mountains with my dad many years later. Courtesy Ruby Jaggernath

MAP 5 1906, Mitchell Family - by covered wagon from Idaho to Gladstone Valley, Alberta

This shows the most probable overland route followed W. J. A. "Wash" Mitchell and his family when travelling overland by covered wagon from Boise, ID, to Gladstone Valley southwest of Pincher Creek, AB, in 1906, a journey of some 875 miles, or 1400 kilometres.

After equipping and supplying their covered wagon for the journey the family left Boise, ID, in the spring of 1906, first travelling east along the Snake River and then northeast to Idaho Falls and the Targhee Pass. From there they followed the Missouri River north to Helena, MT, then went northeast to Fort Benton, also on the Missouri River, to hook up with the Fort Benton-Whoop-Up Trail, first travelling a short distance northeast to the Marias River. After crossing the Marias River they followed it northwest to Shelby, MT, and north to the border crossing into Canada at Sweetgrass, MT, then on to Fort Whoop-Up, Canada.

The final leg of the Mitchells' overland journey by covered wagon was southwest to Pincher Creek, AB, and thence to Gladstone Valley, where "Wash" Mitchell and his son Charles took out homesteads. Wash's son-in-law Harry Truitt (married to Bessie Mitchell) homesteaded in Beaver Mines Creek Valley.

The homestead of John Truitt, brother of Harry, was in Pleasant Valley, an east-west valley that ran west off Gladstone Valley. "Wash" Mitchell and John and Harry Truitt families were amongst the earliest homesteaders in Gladstone Valley in southwestern Alberta. They were related to me through my aunt Ruby Mitchell (Mrs. Harold) Vroom.

The William Barclay family, who arrived in 1905, were the third homesteaders in Gladstone Valley. Adapted from 1983 Georgia Fooks map. Illustration by Edi-May Smithies, Cartography by Shelley McConnell

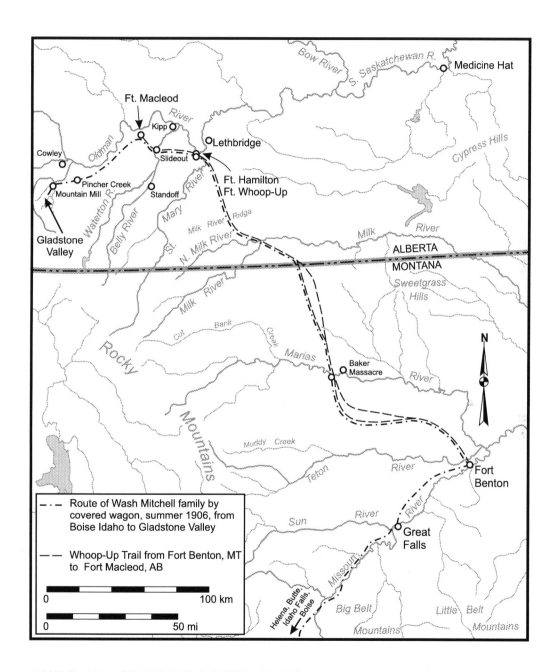

MAP 5 1906, OVERLAND ROUTE of MITCHELL FAMILY, IDAHO to ALBERTA

The Mitchells and Truitts were part of the thousands of immigrants and people from eastern Canada and other countries and who flooded into western Canada. They took advantage of the free land offered to settlers under the Dominion Lands Act of 1872, known as Canada's Homestead Act.

By 1905, Harry Truitt, along with George Smith, was in southern Alberta filing for homestead rights in southwestern Alberta. Harry homesteaded in Gladstone Valley, while George's homestead was just over the ridge to the west in Beaver Mines Creek Valley (Friesen, 1974).

In 1906 Wash Mitchell filed on a homestead, NE ¼ -16-5-2-W5th. This quarter was near the south end of Gladstone Valley close to the main range of the Rocky Mountains. It was a good five miles south of the Archie Vroom School. Their children Bessie, Ruby, Charlie and Dave Mitchell were older than school age so none of them ever went to the Archie Vroom School. Their daughter Bessie (Mrs. Harry) Truitt lived with her family on Harry's homestead. Dave, the youngest, sought work elsewhere.

In 1910 Wash and Aravella's daughter Ruby married Harold Vroom and left home. Wash and Aravella continued living on their homestead in Gladstone Valley, proving up on it in 1911. A National Archives of Canada, Dominion of Canada Homestead Grant dated February 20, 1914, shows that on February 19, 1914, Washington Mitchell received the patent for his homestead, NE ¼-16-5-2-W5th, Occupation: *Farmer.*

By 1911 Wash and Aravella found their homestead to be too remote. All their children were living lives of their own, except for Charlie who spent some time at home. So Wash and Aravella moved to the Richardson place. This was handy for Charlie since he buildings on the Richardson place were only about two miles from Charlie's homestead. In 1926 Charlie sold his homestead to my parents, Ralph and Mollie, and it became their home quarter.

Wash Mitchell knew that Charlie would inevitably leave home to start his own family. So in 1912 Wash bought the Shurts quarter (NW ¼-12-6-2-W5th). The Shurts homestead quarter was located east of Beaver Creek and west of Mountain Mill and was in the same section as Fred Doubt's homestead. "In 1909 the Kootenay & Alberta Railway line was constructed…Bill Toban contracted to build the grades… Toban had camps on … the Mitchell place across Mill Creek (Lang, Ellis, 1961 interview)."

This land was originally the Shurts homestead, but became known as the Mitchell place after 1912. At that time, "Wash" sold his homestead quarter to his neighbour Wm. Barclay. Charlie and his wife, "Sis" Buchanan, were now living on Charlie's homestead, so Wash and Aravella were free to move to the Shurts quarter. They lived there lived until Aravella's death in 1919.

By 1918 Wash Mitchell owned NE ¼ -35-5-2-W5. He no doubt purchased this quarter with the idea that Charlie would someday have at least two quarter sections of land, one across the road from the other. (See Map 2 *Quarter Section Homesteads in Beaver (Mines) Creek and Gladstone Valley, circa 1910.*)

Bessie Mitchell Truitt with Ruby and Sarah, two of her four children who were born in Idaho in 1900 and 1904 respectively, about 1906, soon after the family arrived in Canada. They are standing beside an unknown/unidentified family's chinked, square-log cabin. The inscription on the reverse reads: "Dear old log cabin"

Harry and Bessie's two young daughters, Ruby and Sarah, born in Idaho in 1900 and 1904, respectively (Friesen, 1974), also made the covered wagon trek from Idaho to Gladstone Valley along with their grandparents and uncle and aunt.

Bessie and Harry's next three children, Charles, Lenora and Vera, were born in Pincher Creek. Their eighth child, David, was born in Gilby, AB, and a ninth, Arvella, was born in Pincher Creek (Friesen, 1974).

In August 2004, Adam Truitt said this was not the homestead cabin of Harry and Bessie Mitchell Truitt. Moreover, this is not Gladstone Valley.

However, the above cabin does look like the one where Harry and Bessie Mitchell Truitt lived when I was a child and which was located about two miles south of Harold and Ruby's ranch in Beaver Mines Creek Valley. By then their family was grown up and had left home. In 1906 Harry and Bessie may have been visiting the people who lived in the above house with an eye to selling their Gladstone Valley place and moving to Beaver Mines Creek Valley, which they did in 1928 after living at Gilby, AB, since 1918 (Friesen. 1974).

Friesen, 1974, states: "Harry took out homestead rights (SE ¼-/4-22-5-2-W5) in Gladstone Valley district ... in that same year (1905). He built their home from logs and put on a sod roof. The family followed to the homestead at a later date (1906). A few years later the family had a big log house built on the homestead quarter." (Note: As of 2003 this latter log house, a two-storey structure, is still standing in Gladstone Valley).
Courtesy Ruby Jaggernath

When Charlie Mitchell married "Sis" Buchanan in 1914, the young couple lived on Charlie's homestead in the house that was first used as the Archie Vroom School. Their only child,

Jack, born 1920 in Pincher Creek, was six years old when Charlie sold this quarter to Ralph and Mollie Vroom, who raised their family of four children - Donald, Bessie, Bill and Marion - there.

Jack Mitchell told Ruby Jaggernath in 2000 that he had been born in a square box house that had bedrooms upstairs and that poplar saplings near the front porch had grown through the house by then. Jack as a baby and young child enjoyed standing, sitting and playing in the long grass beside that house.

After the death of his wife, Aravella "Belle" Piper, in 1919 Wash Mitchell sold the Shurts quarter to Charles Brown. Subsequently, Wash rented houses or lived with his son Charlie and his wife "Sis" Buchanan Mitchell or with his daughter, Ruby Mitchell (Mrs. Harold) Vroom.

Charlie sold his homestead quarter to Ralph and Mollie Vroom in 1926. He and "Sis" and their son, Jack, moved to the Shurts place east of Beaver Creek and west of Mountain Mill, which Brown had had to leave due to poor health. Charlie and "Sis" lived there until they moved to the West Coast in the early 1930s. I remember the Charlie and "Sis" Mitchell living on the Shurts place when my brother Donald and I attended Coalfields School in grades one and two in 1933-1934 and 1934-1935. Jack Mitchell was in about grade 7 and 8 at Coalfields School at the time.

Ruby Mitchell Vroom was very fond of her friend Edythe, who was left behind in Meridian, Idaho, when Ruby moved with her family to Gladstone Valley southwest of Pincher Creek, Alberta. Lovingly saved first by Ruby Mitchell Vroom, then by Ruby's daughter, Mae Vroom Peters, and now by her granddaughter, Ruby Peters Jaggernath, two of the postcards that Edythe wrote to Ruby have survived for more than 100 years. Edythe missed Ruby so much that she even considered an idea to follow Ruby to Canada. There is no record of Edythe coming to Canada.

Addressed to Miss Ruby Mitchell, Mountain Mill, Alberta, and postmarked April 29, 1907, in Meridian, Idaho, this postcard was received by Ruby from a friend, Edythe, who taught school in Meridian and who obviously missed Ruby a great deal when the latter left Meridian to come to Canada with her parents in the spring of 1906.

The postcard shows a prim young lady wearing a voluptuous gown and a very large, elaborately styled, hat. Mountain Mill was the address of all the homesteaders in Gladstone Valley and in Beaver Mines Creek Valley until Beaver Mines Post Office was opened December 15, 1911.

Edythe could not fathom the idea that her friend Ruby was now living on a very remote homestead that was nearly 15 miles from Mountain Mill where the post office was located in a private residence. The inscription around the picture reads: "Why don't you write? Don't forget me just because Mrs. Lehman is going to leave the country. I may make up my mind and follow there. Edythe" Courtesy Ruby Jaggernath

Ruby Mitchell's friend Edythe (surname unknown), dressed in a long white dress fashionable at that time, 1907, picking roses beside their vine-covered porch. As indicated by her message on the reverse of this postcard, Edythe was a schoolteacher in Idaho

Though the postmark date is ineligible on the reverse side of this photo it was probably written in October 1907, more than a year after Ruby had left Meridian, Idaho, for Canada. The handwriting, which was written using pen and ink on the reverse of the postcard noted above, reads: "Dear Ruby, Can you recognize the lady picking roses at the west end of the porch? The picture is a fright. Oral took it. Am busy as can be with 40 scholars - having lots of good times but am not very strong this winter. Write me. Edythe." Courtesy Ruby Jaggernath

(Above left) *The two Mitchell sisters, Ruby, born 1885, and Bessie Mitchell Truitt, born 1880, lovingly pose for a portrait together, about 1908. The young women are wearing high-collared, full-length, puffed sleeve blouses with dark skirts that were fitted to emphasize their small waistlines*

(Above right) *Dave Mitchell, 1908, youngest child of Wash and Belle Mitchell, specially decked out in cowboy regalia to have his picture taken to send to his mother*

The inscription on the reverse of this postcard reads: "Lethbridge 4/25/08 Dear Mother: I will drop you a card and will let you guess who it is. Will write soon and send a card to the rest of you. Your loving son Dave" The card was addressed to: "Mrs. Belle Mitchell, Mountain Mill, Alberta, Canada." There was no stamp on this postcard, so it may have been hand-delivered by someone travelling from Lethbridge to Mountain Mill, AB, or a stamp collector may have removed the stamp. Courtesy Ruby Jaggernath

Washington Mitchell holding his prize stallion, a beautiful snow-white animal, 1908. Comparing Wash's height with that of the stallion one can see that this was a tall horse, since Wash was over six feet tall

In describing Wash Mitchell, Friesen (1974) page 272 states, (Wash) was a good horseman and horse trader. He loved to tell yarns and was a good entertainer."

On the reverse side this post card was postmarked August 8, 1908, with some indistinguishable printing, somewhere in B.C. This postcard was addressed to: "Mr. W. J. Mitchell, Mt (sic) Mill, Alberta, Canada." The stamp is still on this postcard showing that in 1908, only a one-cent stamp was required on a postcard. Courtesy Ruby Jaggernath

A number of early settlers had film-developing and printing equipment at home. Making favourite pictures into postcards to give or send to friends was common practice in the early 1900s. This is an example of a homemade postcard.

"Sis" Buchanan Mitchell is on the left, some time after she married Charlie Mitchell in 1914. Coming to Canada from Glasgow, Scotland, in 1910, Sis Buchanan worked in the Pincher Creek post office until she married Charlie Mitchell. In addition to her work at the post office, Sis took an interest in other newcomers to the district and met many of the people who had come earlier. Sis soon became accustomed to western living and at ease in many different situations.

Here Sis is standing with two unidentified people in front of a team of fine horses hitched to a democrat standing beside a log house. Sis, standing directly in front of the team, is holding onto one rein of one horse rather gingerly. The unidentified woman, for added security, has a firm grip on the chinstrap of the other horse. Adam Truitt said these people are not his parents. The log house is probably their home. Sis and her friends are dressed in their "best" clothes as if they have just returned from an event or are just going somewhere. Maybe they are dressed up because they knew "Sis" was coming to drive them somewhere to visit another family.

A handwritten note on the reverse side of the postcard says, "Dear Mother, Don't write till I send you my address. What do you think of me now, mother? Love to all, Ada." Perhaps "Ada" was her mother's pet name for "Sis." Charlie Mitchell may have taken the picture. Ruby Jaggernath still has this postcard in her possession. Courtesy Ruby Jaggernath

"Sis" probably stopped working outside the home when she married Charlie Mitchell - women did that in those days - and that is why she was available and acceptable to take over the Beaver Mines Post Office while the Ballantynes went down East in 1934. Sis may have run the Beaver Mines post office a second time when the Ballantynes went down East in 1936. They were on the same train as Mollie when she went to Dr. Locke's clinic in Oshawa for treatments for her arthritis in 1936.

Charlie Mitchell (left) and an unknown man (right), about 1910, sitting astride their saddle horses at the McLaren Ranch at Mountain Mill

The McLaren Ranch buildings were near the "neat little cottage" built by Harold Vroom for himself and his bride, Ruby Mitchell, to live in after their marriage on July 5, 1910. The white house with two chimneys in the distant background of this picture is the McLaren ranch house. Several photos taken at Mountain Mill during this era show this same white house with two chimneys.

Charlie and his friend could have been at Mountain Mill checking on Harold and Ruby's cottage, or they could have been dressed in their "Sunday best" to attend Harold and Ruby's wedding that day. Charlie might have been Harold's best man. Charlie was a brother of Ruby Mitchell Vroom and Bessie Mitchell Truitt. Charlie came to Canada from near Meridian, Idaho, along with his parents and siblings in 1906. Courtesy Ruby Jaggernath

The windows on Harold and Ruby Mitchell Vroom's first cottage on the next page have the trim on them, but the siding is not yet on the cottage. The tarpaper covering the first layer of boards of the "neat little cottage" is held in place boards nailed vertically. A democrat is pulled up beside the cottage and there are other buildings in the background.

The group might have been at Mountain Mill checking that all was in readiness for the young couple when they returned from their honeymoon. At that time they would also pick up their mail while at Mountain Mill. Until the Beaver Mines Post Office opened all the homesteaders in that area of Alberta had the address "Mountain Mill," even though they lived up to 12 miles away from the post office as did the Wash Mitchell family.

Shown left to right are Harry Truitt, Harold Vroom and Bessie Mitchell Truitt at Mountain Mill, AB

The three people are standing beside their saddle horses in front of a partly finished cottage. This was the neat little cottage that Harold built for himself and Ruby to live in following their marriage on July 5, 1910, as reported in the Pincher Creek Echo *of July 21, 1910.*

This cottage was not the one that Ralph and Mollie Tyson Vroom lived in when they were first married. Courtesy Ruby Jaggernath

The inscription on the reverse of the above photograph reads, "Will & Colts, Mountain Mill". William Benedict Tourond, who was also known as "Will" or "Bill," when he was 20 years old, 1910. Born in Saskatchewan on January 17, 1890, Bill "worked at Mountain Mill and married Helen Borze in 1911. They had ten children." (Friesen, 1974) *Courtesy Ruby Jaggernath*

The 100th Anniversary Mountain Mill Church Commemorative Album quotes Bob Tourond, Will and Helen's second oldest son, as saying, "My father (Bob Tourond's father), William Benedict Tourond, worked at Mountain Mill in 1910 and lived in the Beauvais Lake area for a time."

When I was attending grade eight at St. Michael's School in Pincher Creek in the late 1930s, I knew the Tourond family, who were by then living in Pincher Creek. Elmira and Zilda Tourond were near my age. Years later, when I lived at Waterton Park and I was writing the "Wonderful Waterton" column for the *Lethbridge Herald*, I interviewed Robert Lang, who, it turned out, was a neighbour of Will and Helen when they lived at Beauvais Lake and Will worked for Fred

Link at Mountain Milll. In this interview Mr. Lang told one of his memories of Will: "Bill Tourond came to the house about five in the morning – his wife was expecting an increase in the family - to see if I could take her to town. It was about 30 below zero and about ten inches of snow on the road. I got to town and went for the doctor. I told him not to wait to dress, as it was a rush case. When he got into the car, he forgot his string of beads and had to go back for the beads. When we got to the house, the baby was born - a close call. It was a boy, and was killed in the Second War. After that trip I was called Doctor Lang for several years."

The baby, who was named George, was Will and Helen's third son. George Tourond "was killed overseas in World War II." (Friesen, 1974) Fred and Anne Harley Link's own children were young at the time (Friesen, 1974), so Fred hired Will to help with the ranch work. It was not uncommon in those days for men to work some distance from where their families were living, even though doing so placed a great burden of care and survival and their wives.

The two-storey, white house with two chimneys in the background of the picture on page 132 was the McLaren ranch house. It identifies the location of this picture as being Mountain Mill. When I was a child Mr. and Mrs. Fred Link (Fred and Anne Harley Link) and their family lived in the McLaren ranch house, which they were renting at the time. They purchased the land in 1936 (Friesen, 1974). One of Fred Link's outbuildings, the style of which I remember from my childhood in the 1930s, shows in the near background above.

Outbuildings similar to the one that Will Tourond stands beside in the photo, with the boards used as siding nailed on horizontally, show in other pictures of the same era that were identified as being at the McLaren Ranch at Mountain Mill. The uniquely styled white house with two chimneys also shows in other pictures that were taken at Mountain Mill. In 2005, Bill Link, a son of Fred and Helen Link, and his family still lived near the site of the old family ranch house at Mountain Mill.

Wash Mitchell with his first two grandchildren, 1915. His young grandchildren were the pride and joy of Mr. Mitchell. This was taken at the Harry Truitt homestead in Gladstone Valley.

Wash holds Vera Truitt, born 1914 in Pincher Creek, on his lap, while Lenora Truitt, born in 1911 in Pincher Creek, stands beside him. Vera and Lenora were daughters of Harry and Bessie Mitchell Truitt and granddaughters of Wash and Aravella.

This was taken when Harry and Bessie lived on Harry's homestead in Gladstone Valley. They lived there until 1918 when they moved to Gilby (Friesen, 1974). The two-storey log cabin that Harry Truitt built on his homestead does not show here. However, on the hillside behind Wash's head can be seen the grade that runs along the hillside below the John Truitt place and leads to what is currently the George Hagglund place. Courtesy Ruby Jaggernath

1906 Harold Palmer Vroom

1914 Ruby Mitchell Vroom (Mrs. HP)

1915 Washington J. A. Mitchell

1921 Charles "Charlie" V. Mitchell

Pre 1907 Thomas "T. B." Tyson

1915 George "Joe" Annand

T. B. TYSON: SCION OF AN ADVENTUROUS FAMILY

The oldest member of my mother's family that I knew was my great-uncle Thomas Banks Tyson. "Old uncle Tom," as we children called him - to differentiate him from my mother's brother, Uncle Tommy - was often called "T. B." by his friends. "T. B." was born in the goldfields town of Hokitika, Westland County, NZ, on April 12, 1869. He was the fifth child of Thomas II and Margaret Banks Tyson, who became the patriarch and matriarch of an adventurous family.

The Tyson family story begins in 1861 when Thomas II, son of Thomas I and Hannah Stable Tyson, married Margaret Banks in Ambleside, England. Within a year of their marriage, Thomas II and Margaret immigrated to Melbourne, Victoria, intending to search for gold in the Australian interior. The young couple started raising a family immediately. On February 10, 1862, Joseph was born at home in "Glen", Victoria, Australia.

In 1864 Hannah was born, also at "Glen" in Victoria, Australia. Tragically, tiny Hannah lived for barely a year. She died in 1865 in the town of Coghills Creek where her uncle Wilson Tyson was later buried.

In Australia in 1868, my great-grandparents Thomas II and Margaret Tyson are holding Joseph and Willam Dawes, their only surviving children at the time. Thomas is holding Joseph; Margaret holds William Dawes.

This photo was taken by "Flintoff, Photographer and portrait painter Sturt Street, opposite the Star Office, Ballarat, Australia." Author's Collection

In 1865 Mary was born in a moving wagon on the way to the goldfields at Ballarat. The early death of children was a fact of life in pioneer times.

Mary died at only three weeks old. Her parents buried Mary by the roadside in a homemade coffin and the family travelled on. Mary's birth was registered as being in "Newt", Victoria.

Mary's cousin Elizabeth, only child of Wilson and Jane Barbour Tyson had been born earlier in "Newt" in 1862. Elizabeth died as a child in "Geel", Victoria, at the age of 12 years in 1875.

On November 14, 1866, William Dawes Tyson was born at Smeaton Plains, Victoria. His birth was registered on February 23, 1867, at Kingston, Victoria.

Thomas II and Margaret Tyson, 1879, holding their two last children, who were born in Ambleside, England, after the family returned there from New Zealand in 1874.

Margaret is holding Annie, born in 1878. Thomas II is holding Jack Powley, born in 1876. Both Margaret and Jack Powley were born at "Glenthorne", Ambleside.

The photographer was M. Bowness, Ambleside. Author's Collection

Even though Margaret had two babies to care for under primitive conditions, in May 1867 Thomas II left Australia and headed for the gold fields of New Zealand. In May 1868, Thomas sent for Margaret and their children, Joseph and William Dawes (by now 18 months old), and they sailed to New Zealand.

The next year, Thomas Banks "T. B." Tyson was born in the goldfields town of Hokitika, Westland County, NZ.

In 1874, unbeknown to Margaret, her uncle William Dawes died leaving his home "Glenthorne" in Ambleside to her for her lifetime. Margaret was the only child of William's sister, Elizabeth Dawes Banks, who died five weeks after giving birth to Margaret.

The Dawes of "Groves Farm" raised Margaret from an infant. When Margaret's aunt and two uncles retired from the farm, they had "Glenthorne" built.

By the time "Glenthorne" was completed, only Margaret and her Uncle William were left. William was very fond of his niece, Margaret, who had been his housekeeper after his sister died.

Wm. Dawes' great anger when Thomas II took his niece Margaret far away to Australia resulted in him changing his Will in 1869. William left "Glenthorne" to Margaret in trust for her lifetime, then to her son, William Dawes Tyson (father of Ruth Tyson Brandes.) Margaret's husband, Thomas II, was allowed to live in "Glenthorne" only as long as Margaret was alive.

However, because of the slow pace of communications in the mid-1800s, Margaret was unaware of her uncle's death. Thomas kept on searching for gold and Margaret continued having babies. On July 18, 1871, Margaret Elizabeth "Maggie" was born in Westland Co, NZ.

My grandfather George Wilson Tyson was born in the goldfields town of Stafford, Westland County, NZ, on September 17, 1872. He was the seventh, and fifth surviving, child, of Margaret and Thomas II.

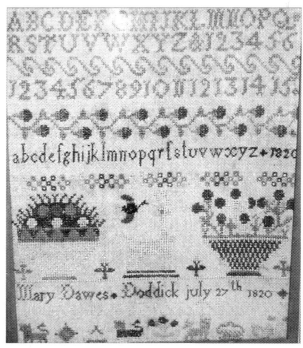

(Above left) *William Dawes was the dour uncle of Margaret Banks Tyson. He was the original owner of "Glenthorne" in Ambleside. William Dawes Tyson was the second son of Thomas II and Margaret Banks. He was named after his great-uncle.* Author's Collection

(Above right) *Mary Dawes Bodick made this intricately stitched sampler in 1920. Mary was a sister of William Dawes. My mother's cousin, Ruth Tyson Brandes, daughter of William Dawes Tyson, inherited the sampler and passed it on to her daughter, Mary Brandes.* Author's Collection

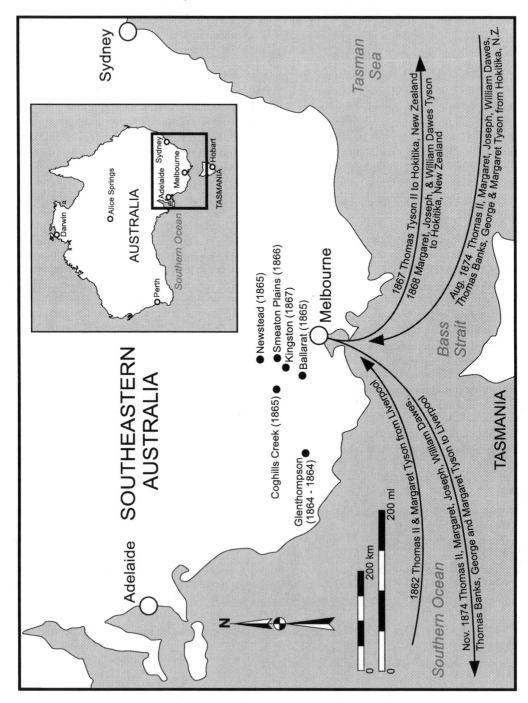

MAP 6 1862-1867, TYSON FAMILY – GOLD MINING in AUSTRALIA

MAP 6 1862-1867, Tyson Family - Gold Mining in Australia (see page 138)

    My great-grandparents Thomas II and Margaret Banks Tyson spent the first years of their married life, 1862-1874, living in the Ballarat gold fields in Victoria, Australia, and the Westlands gold fields of New Zealand. In 1862, the Thomas II and Margaret sailed from Liverpool, England, to Melbourne, Victoria, Australia, via Cape of Good Hope, South Africa. Upon landing in Australia the Tysons went straight to the Ballarat gold fields. They suffered from the extreme heat and scarcity of food and water as they travelled from place to place by covered wagon. Illustration by Edi-May Smithies, Cartography by Shelley McConnell

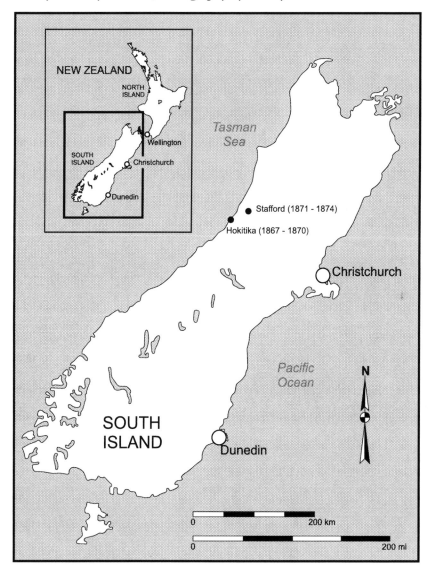

MAP 7 1867-1874, TYSON FAMILY – GOLD MINING in NEW ZEALAND

MAP 7 1867-1874, Tyson Family - Gold Mining in New Zealand (see page 139)

In 1867 Thomas Tyson II left his family behind and travelled on ahead to Hokitika, Westland County, NZ, to work in the gold fields there. In May 1868, Margaret, and their two young sons, Joseph and William Dawes, joined Thomas in Hokitika, Westland County, NZ. In New Zealand the Tysons, again travelling by covered wagon, lived in the gold mining towns of Hokitika, Westland County, 1867-1870, and Stafford, Westland County, 1871-1874.

In 1874, someone in Ambleside wrote to Margaret telling telling her that she had inherited a life interest in "Glenthorne" along with a few acres of land, a cow and some chickens. Margaret immediately borrowed 200 pounds from her brother-in-law Wilson Tyson (brother of Thomas II, Myles, Isaac, and Joseph), who was living in Victoria, Australia. With the money she booked passage home to England for herself and her five children.

In August 1874 Margaret Banks Tyson and her children, Joseph and William Dawes, Thomas Banks, Margaret Elizabeth "Maggie", and George Wilson, left New Zealand. They sailed first to Australia. There they visited friends and relatives before sailing to Ambleside. Illustration by Edi-May Smithies, Cartography by Shelley McConnell

The older children found the voyage from Australia to England very exciting. They remembered vivid details years later. When talking to the high school class of his granddaughter, Mary Brandes, in Iowa, William Dawes Tyson recalled his eighth birthday in November 1874. He celebrated it aboard a sailing ship en route to England.

This was several years before the opening of the Suez Canal. William remembered the storm-tossed passage as the crowded vessel rounded Cape Horn, through the Strait of Magellan. In the Torrid Zone, the extreme heat caused the tar to ooze out of the ship's planks. Their ship avoided becoming becalmed because it had both sail and steam. William counted at least 34 becalmed sailing vessels as they passed through the Torrid Zone.

The captain aboard the Tysons' ship provided all passengers with fresh fish each day, William recalled. Margaret cooked her family's meals in the ship's galley. Fresh bread, baked daily by the ships's chef, was doled out to all passengers. The family survived the tedious trip without any of them becoming ill with seasickness.

With their sea voyage ended, and themselves released from their restricted quarters, the children joyously romped and played on the hills around Ambleside.

Thomas II's return to England in 1875 meant more pregnancies for Margaret. The following year she became pregnant for the eighth time. Their youngest son, John "Jack" Powley Tyson, was born May 5, 1876, at "Glenthorne" in Ambleside, England. Jack eventurally moved to Liverpool as a young man and then to Durban, South Africa. He died in South Africa on November 28, 1922.

In 1877 Margaret became pregnant again. This was Margaret's ninth pregnancy with what was to be her last baby. On May 29, 1878, Annie was born at "Glenthorne" in Ambleside. This made a total of nine children born to Thomas and Margaret with seven surviving. That would be a large family by today's standards, but in those days the number of children was as many as 16 and 18, or even more. Parents needed many sons and daughters to be helping hands on their farms and there was a need to populate new countries.

Thomas II and Margaret Tyson took in summer visitors at "Glenthorne" for extra income. Although Margaret had only one cow, she supplied milk to some other families as well. She was a dear soul. Everyone spoke well of her. Her nephews loved to walk 4-5 miles to see her - she always gave them a lump of cake and a glass of fresh milk before they started home.

In 1881, Margaret Elizabeth "Maggie" stayed at "Glenthorne" to help her mother with boarding summer visitors. She was only 10 years old. I remember Granny Mary Tyson speaking of Aunt Maggie.

This is my great-grandfather, Thomas II at "Glenthorne" after the family moved back to England from New Zealand. He was the assistant overseer and county court bailiff at Ambleside until his retirement. He died at Pull Wyke Cottage in Ambleside on November 29, 1921 and was buried on December 2, 1921. Author's Collection

Four brothers—Joseph I, Wilson, Isaac, and Myles Tyson—were born in England in 1832, 1827, 1830, and 1840, respectively. The year 1855 was very significant for them. Myles, Wilson and Isaac heeded the call to help populate the British Empire. Wilson and Isaac went to Australia hoping to make their fortunes in the gold fields. Myles Tyson came to Canada.

The fourth brother, Joseph, married Ann Fleming and the young couple immigrated to the United States in 1855. Joseph died July 2, 1887, in Mound City, Mo., at 55 years of age. Over the years, Thomas Banks "T. B." Tyson corresponded with their son, John, writing him a letter soon after he arrived in Canada.

In 1858, Wilson Tyson married Jane Barbour in Australia. Shortly thereafter, his brother Isaac, who had accompanied Wilson to Australia, moved to Brisbane, Australia. Wilson and Jane Barbour Tyson had only one child, Elizabeth. Wilson (1827-1911) died in Ballarat, Victoria, Australia, at the age of 84 years.

Seen here about 1900, Myles Tyson and his wife, Catherine Solomon Tyson, were well-known residents of Killarney, ON, having cleared a farm there in about 1874.

Myles (1840-1928) and Catherine (1851-1931) were married in June 1874. They had seven children, who were all born in Killarney. Their four sons were Thomas W., born 1875, John "Jack", born 1878, William "Bill" birth year unknown, Edward 'Ned', born 1914. Three daughters were Margaret, Hannah and Kate. Courtesy Marlene Anderson

This is Myles and Catherine Tyson with four of their five oldest children circa 1877. Left to right are Margaret and Thomas W., with Hannah and Kate in front. Myles, who was born July 26, 1840, in Westmoreland, England, was a brother of Thomas Tyson II, husband of Margaret Banks.

Although Myles was only 15 years of age when he immigrated to Canada, this was not unusual for Tysons. A generation later, my great-uncle T. B. Tyson immigrated to Canada in 1885 when he, too, was only 15 years old, arriving about a month before his 16th birthday.

Myles and Catherine Solomon Tyson became "characters" in the Killarney area of Ontario. A Killarney Provincial Park brochure states: "Myles, a blue-eyed son of an English family journeyed to Killarney, where he met and married a short, dark-haired Canadian girl, Catherine Solomon. Everyone called them "Mammy & Pappy." One map of Killarney Park, showing park trails notes the wagon and sleigh trail made by the Tysons to the nearby village of Killarney. There is also a Tyson Lake, ON, named after Myles and Catherine Tyson.

This photographic treasure was given to T. B. Tyson, as a remembrance of loved ones left behind when he moved west. Author's Collection

In July 1885, eighteen-year-old William Dawes Tyson had a sudden urge to follow his brother, "T. B." and immigrated to Canada. At the time William Dawes was employed as a plowman on a farm near Penrith, England. He had no qualms about pulling up stakes and travelling to a far-off land.

Arriving in Quebec Cityon a Sunday, William sailed immediately to Hamilton via the St. Lawrence River. For the next three years he lived near Hamilton. He also worked near Caledonia, which is east of Brantford, halfway between Hamilton and Lake Erie. While in the vicinity, William visited his father's brother Myles Tyson and his wife, Catherine, in "the big woods," which became the town of Killarney, near Manitoulin Island.

T. B. Tyson then prevailed upon Willaim to try to get my grandfather, and their brother, George, to immigrate to Canada. This photo was takin in 1888 before William Dawes Tyson left Hamilton, ON, and went to England spending seven weeks there, some of which time he spent trying to convince George of the merits of immigrating to Canada.

Upon leaving England, William Dawes Tyson immigrated to United States settling near the town of Galena, Jo Davies County, Ill. In the summer of 1894, on a pre-marital excursion, William visited his brother "T. B." at Fishburn, NWT, returning to Galena, Ill., and area in the fall of 1894. On November 13, 1895, William Dawes Tyson married Lida Jane Ivey. Author's collection

(Left above) *In 1884 Joseph Tyson returned to England from his home in Australia to serve his apprenticeship as a printer in Ambleside. He is seen here in 1884 as a dapper curly-haired young man with a Clark Gable-type mustache. When he finished his apprenticeship, Joseph returned to Australia in the winter of 1884-85. Sadly, however, Joseph was not a strong man. He took ill, dying in 1890 in Warragul, Victoria, at the age of 27 years.* Author's collection

(Right above) *The children of Thomas II and Margaret Tyson were born in the following order: Joseph, William Dawes, Thomas Banks, Margaret Elizabeth, George Wilson, John Powley and Ann. Two other Tyson children -- Hannah and Mary, both died in Australia as infants.*

Just as Thomas and Margaret expected, after the family returned to England from Australia and New Zealand, wanderlust struck their sons. Their father's brother, Myles Tyson, and his wife Catherine, were already raising a family in Killarney, ON, Canada.

Here, in 1881, before the older boys left home for distant parts of the British Empire, Thomas and Margaret had this photo taken of their seven children. They are framed by the front door of "Glenthorne," the family home in Ambleside. When far away, this photo would remind each of them of their loved ones and help them remember the happy days of their childhood.

Back row (left to right), all standing: Margaret Elizabeth "Maggie" born 1871 in New Zealand, 10 years; Joseph born 1862 in Australia, 19 years; Thomas Banks, born 1869 in New Zealand, 12 years, and William Dawes, born 1866 in Australia, 15 yearss.

Front row (left to right): Thomas II (father), Ann "Annie" Tyson born 1878 at "Glenthorne," 3 years; my grandfather, George Wilson born 1872 in Staffordtown, NZ, 9 years; Margaret (mother); John "Jack" Powley Tyson born 1876 at "Glenthorne," 5 years. Author's Collection

Born in the gold fields town of Hokitika, Westland County, NZ, on April 12, 1869, my great-uncle Thomas Banks "T. B." Tyson, attended school in Ambleside. T. B. and his siblings returned to Ambleside from New Zealand with their mother in 1874.

In March 1885, after a fond farewell to his mother and a promise to return to visit her, Tom, left his home and set sail for Canada from Liverpool. He travelled in steerage, the cheapest class, being unable to afford anything else. The immigrants slept 20 to a room for the duration of the five-week voyage. Johanne Larson Schoening (Friesen, 1974), tells briefly to her parents' crossing the Atlantic Ocean to the United States: "in 1886 during the days of sailing vessels, taking four to five weeks to cross. They had a lot of bad weather, the crossing must have been quite an experience…they ran out of fresh drinking water making it necessary to boil ocean water to remove the salt."

In April 1885 at 15 years of age, T. B. Tyson landed in Canada. "T. B." worked initially as a farm labourer near Glenford, ON. As noted in a letter dated April 6, 1885, from his father to his father's cousin John Tyson, son of Joseph, "T. B." hoped to earn enough to repay his mother the money she lent him for his fare from England, and to buy a suit of clothes. Eventually, "T. B." was able to do this.

This photo, taken by Farmer Brothers, 810 King St. W., Hamilton, ON, shows Tom at 17 years of age. A note written by May Mann on the reverse side of the picture, says, "He joined the Canadian Army and went overseas to serve in France in World War I." Much to his sadness, "T. B." never did get back to England to see his mother. Although she was sick and dying, the Army would not grant him a leave of absense from the fighting in France to visit her. Author's Collection

Shown here, lleft to right, are three Tyson brothers - William Dawes, Thomas Banks "T. B.," and George Wilson - in an 1888 Photo taken by Farmer Brothers, Photographers, 810 King St. West, Hamilton, ON. The same photographer took the picture immediately above of "T. B."

George, born September 17, 1872, turned 16 years old in September 1888. The brothers had a reunion of sorts with this picture taken to commemorate the occasion. After this visit to Canada, George had some idea what living in Canada would entail when he moved his family to Fishburn, AB in 1914.

The cities Hamilton and Toronto, ON, where the Tyson brothers had pictures taken together and separately, are located in the general area of Glenford, ON, where Thomas B. Tyson was employed as a farm labourer from 1885 to 1889 while learning how to farm in Canada. Author's Collection

Thomas B. "T. B." Tyson (left) and Tom Newton (right) were school chums in Ambleside, England, and lifelong friends. In 1890, Thomas Newton, drawn by reports of Canada from his old schoolmate "T. B.", came with another man from Ambleshide to Manitoba. He moved to Fishburn, NWT, in 1891, again following the lead of T. B. Tyson (Friesen, 1974).

In 1889, "T. B." pulled up stakes and moved from Ontario to the Fishburn District east of Pincher Creek in the Northwest Territories. Train accommodation was available to Lethbridge, AB. However, "T. B." travelled by Red River wagon from Manitoba because that was cheaper than by train.

In Friesen (1974), Sophia Spark (Mrs. Tom Newton), gives some details of stagecoach travel from Lethbridge to Fishburn in 1897.

T. B. located on a quarter section adjoining Tom Newton in the Fishburn district. In 1892, T. B. Tyson received his Letters Patent for the SW ¼-22-5-28-W4th. When he had proved up on this quarter, "T. B" sold it to Tom Newton and bought two other quarters closer to the Waterton River (Friesen, 1974). The names and locations of a number of other early homesteaders in the Fishburn district are also shown on a map in Friesen of quarter sections in the Fishburn district. Photo by K. W. Snider; corner King and St. John Sts., Hamilton. Author's Collection

George Hole, father of Mildred Hole Clark and her brother Fred, came to Canada in 1896. A handwritten memoir by Mildred, originally from Twin Butte, AB, contains part of her dad's description of what life was like for a 16-year-old immigrant to Canada in the late 19th century.

His ship crossed the Atlantic in two weeks, which was much faster than 11 years earlier when Thomas "T. B." Tyson came to Canada. In all that time the passengers had no fresh meat. The first thing that George did upon reaching Montreal was to have a big steak dinner with all the trimmings. George, like many other young immigrants, did not settle down right away when he first came to Canada, but had several jobs before he took out a homestead near Twin Butte, AB.

Before coming to southern Alberta Mr. Hole worked as a commercial fisherman on Lake Winnipeg for a spell, then on a sheep ranch in Oregon. Still later, George got a job on the railway and for a few years travelled back and forth across Canada. Eventually, he homesteaded land in the Twin Butte area, married and raised a family there.

Mildred Hole Clark remembers her mother carding sheep's wool to make yarn with which to knit sweaters, mitts, toques and other warm clothing for her family. They lived so far from a school that Mrs. Hole, in addition to all her homemaking chores, taught her family at home using correspondence lesssons.

To put events occurring in southwest Alberta into the timeline of Tyson family, A. L. Freebairn, in his book *Pincher Creek Memories. Old Timers Souvenir Album* (revised), said that in 1879 the Dominion Government began operations on the Government or Indian Farm on Chipman Creek, southeast of Pincher Creek. Mr. Clark, the father of Mrs. Duthie and Mrs. Lauchie Bell, was in charge of the Farm. By 1882, as noted by Freebairn, Gus Newman was working on the Indian Farm on Chipman Creek.

In the 1880s Methodist missionaries from Ontario came to the Northwest Territories and "Services were held regularly...in Mounted Police Barracks at Pincher Creek, at the Indian experimental Farm, and the Mountain Mill in the foothills, on the first Sunday of every month"...continuing until 1886... (T)he other Sundays and weekdays were filled with services at Fort Mcleod, and the Peigan and Blood Indian camps," according to a letter written by Rev. John McLean, a Methodist missionary (George, 1996).

By 1889 (Freebairn, undated), the Indian Department had decided that the Indian Farm was a failure. The department also closed the ill-fated Mountain Mill sawmill in 1881. William Berry bought the Indian Farm for $1.00 per acre turning it back to the Government after making one payment. About 1891 A. L. "Scotty" Freebairn homesteaded the Old Indian Farm on Chipman Creek, NW ¼ -34-5-29-W4. John Freebairn homesteaded the adjoining quarter section, NE ¼ 34-5-29-W4 (Freebairn, undated, and National Archives of Canada, Western Land Grants website).

This is a view of land near the Waterton River in the Fishburn district. It was once owned by "T. B." Tyson. This field has a gently sloping south exposure making it a piece of excellent farmland that still produces fine crops. My great-uncle Tom's land had a small lake on it that provided ample water for livestock.

"T. B." took up homesteading in 1892. He filed on NW ¼ 22-5-28-W4 adjacent to Tom Newton's homestead. "T. B." received his letters patent for this land in 1904. He then sold his homestead quarter to Tom Newton in 1906 so that Mr. Newton would have a half-section block. Next T. B. purchased the homestead quarters of James "Jim" William Smith (SW ¼-14-5-28-W4) and Charles "Charlie" Christoper Irvine (SE ¼-14-5-28-W4) so that "T. B." also had one-half section of farmland (Friesen, 1974)

"T. B." was a member of the Fishburn United Church, which was built in 1904. The church is still in operation more than 100 years later, being lovingly cared for by members of the Fishburn district, many of whom are descendants of Fishburn homesteaders. I, along with some of my children, attended the 100th anniversary celebration of the Fishburn United Church in 2004. Courtesy Edi-May Annand Smithies

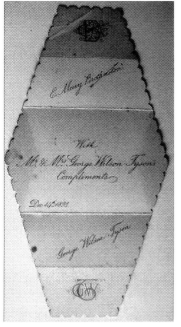

On December 14, 1898, George Wilson Tyson, who was a mail driver resident at "Glenthorne," married Elizabeth Mary Brotherston. At the time Ms Brotherston was a nanny/governess resident at "Jiffy Knots." She and my grandfather were married at Brathay, Lancaster.

In 1894 my grandfather George, at age 22, started a new career, working as a mail carrier between Ambleside and Coniston, England. George carried on with this work for the next 20 years, leaving it only when he, along with his family, immigrated to Canada.

By 1911, George was making only 110 pounds per year. Out of that meagre salary he had to pay the expenses of keeping his horse, harness and mail cart, having two stables, one in Coniston and one in Ambleside, keeping his house in Ambleside—including upkeep on the house, taxes, heat and light and food and clothing for his family.

A letter from John P. "Jack" Tyson to his sister-in-law, Lida (Mrs. Wm. Dawes) Tyson, dated April 15, 1905, suggests that Elizabeth Mary Brotherston Tyson was not entirely happy living so close to her in-laws, having some kind of friction with her sister-in-law Annie. That situation probably helped George and Elizabeth Mary to make the decision to come to Canada. Author's collection

One of the artistic people that T. B. Tyson knew was photographer Marietta "Etta" Irwin McRae, who especially loved the grandeur of the mountains in the main range of the Rocky Mountain as seen while looking westward from south of Twin Butte. Pictures taken by Ms McRae are still treasured by her grandniece Kay McRae (Mrs. Art) Leigh. Mrs. McRae's photograhic work is described earlier in this volume.

On the occasional summer Sunday, "T. B." joined in with the McRae family he was working for at the time and went with them as they travelled, first by team and wagon and later by early-model car, to Waterton Lakes National Park for a daylong picnic. Taken from #6 highway near Spread Eagle School in 2003, this is the same view of the Rocky Mountains that "T. B." and his friends saw as early as 1889 when they arrived in the Fishburn district.

In the Waterton Lakes National Park area of southwestern Alberta there are no foothills. The undulating prairies roll right up to the foot of the Rocky Mountains. Gently curving in the above photo, the highway emphansizes the contours of the terrain. Courtesy Edi-May Smithies

T. B. Tyson developed into a sociable bachelor getting out into the community and taking part in whatever was going on. He was interested in drama and debating. In 1894 T. B. Tyson's hearing began to deteriorate, a condition that plagued him the rest of his life. Then, in a freak accident in 1898 "T. B." fractured a bone in the metatarsus of his right foot, also fracturing a bone in the lower tibia. The breaks healed improperly leaving T. B. with malformed bones. By 1918, when T. B. Tyson joined the Canadian army, the examining physician reported that his physical "condition is that of one of his age, who has engaged in physical labour for years."

Shown in this 1905 picture are 11 members of the Pincher Creek Citizens' Band 1905 (also known as the Oddfellows' Band), identified as Left to Right, Back row: Tom (T. B.) Tyson, Jim Watson, Hec(tor) McGlenning, and George Allison; Middle row: F. W. Lindsay, Billie Taylor, Joe Whittaker, J. E. (Ed) Upton, Lorne Dobbie and John Whittaker; Front row, sitting: Alex R. Dempster, Bert McKenzie, Watson's son (first name unknown). The Archives of the Pincher Creek and District Historical Society Accession Number 994.24.17

(Opposite page) *"T. B." knew Kootenai Brown, who is seen here astride his fine saddle horse. Kootenai is gazing off into the mountains that cradle Upper Waterton Lake. This picture was taken on a bright summer day looking northward from somewhere in the present location of Waterton Park Townsite campgrounds.. A part of the hill where the Prince of Wales Hotel now stands is in the background. The bottom part of Mount Crandell also shows in the background.*

Kootenai's Park Warden badges, symbols of his authority in that area of southwestern Alberta, are pinned to the front of his vest. Kootenai has saddle bags for carrying food to eat on his outing and a few small personal items slung across the pommel of his saddle, while his slicker is tied firmly behind the cantle as insurance against any inclement weather he might run into during his daylong or weeklong ride, as the case may be.

Kootenai has his high-topped boots thrust into his stirrup which are covered with long Spanish-style, heavy leather tapaderoes. These saddle features are designed to keep the rider's foot from slipping through the stirrup in the event he is thrown from his horse for some reason. Tapaderoes also protect the rider's boots from low shrub bush often traversed by riders in those days.

    Kootenai's expert horsemanship is evident in the way he holds his bridle reins; the reins are held lightly in his left hand and well above the saddle pommel. Short sections of light chain are used to attach the reins to the bridle bit, a mild, curbed type used by experienced riders to control well-trained saddle horses. The horse stands quietly patiently awaiting Kootenai's command to move on. Courtesy Edith Jack Hochstein

Teenagers Frances Dennis (Mrs. Jim) McWhirter and her brother, Jack, about 1934, riding their saddle horses, "Midnight" and "Fly", respectively. Frances was the babe in arms being held by her mother, Ida Dennis, in a previous (1917) photo. When they were taking elementary grades classes at their local country school, the Dennises rode horseback to Robert Kerr School every day. When they became teenagers Frances and Jack thought nothing

heading off on horseback to attend a dance at the Twin Butte Community Hall or to visit friends who lived up to 30 miles away. "T. B." Tyson often rode or walked over to visit the Dennis family.

In May – June 1921, the Bruce family lived briefly in the Chipman Creek district, southeast of Pincher Creek, and the three Bruce boys, who were teenagers by then, attended either Chipman Creek or Robert Kerr School for a short time. Ronnie and Michael Bruce were about the same age as Margaret and Jack Dennis, who attended Robert Kerr School. Frances and Jack Dennis became good friends of the Bruce boys at that time.

I remember Jack Dennis attending the Saturday night dances in Pincher Creek when I was a young teenager in the early 1940s. Courtesy Frances Dennis McWhirter

More than 10 years later, in the early 1930s, when Bruce family moved to Beaver Mines after living at various other places, Frances and Jack Dennis rode on horseback to visit them.

Shown left to right are Michael Bruce, Jack Dennis, Frances Dennis (Mrs. Jim McWhirter), Anthony Bruce, and Ronald Bruce at the Bruce home. Courtesy Frances Dennis McWhirter

Once when Frances and Jack Dennis went to visit the Bruces, Frances took her autograph album. These were a popular item with teenagers in the 1930s and 1940s. She hoped Mrs. Bruce would write in it.

Not only did Mabel Bruce write a bit of sage advice for Frances - "Love many. Trust few. Always paddle your own canoe" - she painted a watercolour picture that Frances cherishes to this day.

The miniature painting is of three majestic buck deer standing proudly beside a calm pool of water in the woods, making a perfect reflection in the mirror-like surface of the water. The painting is dated: April 26, 1934. Courtesy Frances Dennis McWhirter

MOLLIE TYSON: "I'M GOING TO MARRY A COWBOY"

My mother's life changed dramatically when she immigrated to Canada with her parents and brother in 1914. Her family lived a well-ordered, relatively comfortable life in Ambleside, England. During the 10-year period preceding WWI, her family was quite content. Ambleside is set amid the gently rolling hills of northwestern England in the heart of the Lake District. My grandfather, George, had a steady job driving the mail wagon daily between Coniston and Ambleside, a distance of about seven miles.

Since no railway runs through Ambleside the mail had to be picked up in Coniston. My grandfather Tyson was employed driving the mail wagon between Coniston and Ambleside, a distance of seven miles

George Wilson Tyson sits in the driver's seat of his two-wheeled mail cart ready to make his last trip to Amblesside. He holds the reins of his bob-tailed gelding horse which stands in the cart shafts ready for his return trip to Ambleside. Three of George's colleagues, one on a bicycle and one with a hook in place of his left hand that was lost, perhaps, in an industrial accident, pose with George and his cart taken in front of the Coniston Post Office.
Author's collection

Shown circa 1912, Granny Tyson stands with her neatly dressed children a few years before they left for Canada in 1914.

Mollie had naturally curly hair like her father. Granny encouraged Mollie's hair to hang in tidy ringlets during the day by wrapping Mollie's long hair around rags each night.

Like many other young women of her day, Elizabeth Mary Brotherston was a nanny for an English family in Ambleside when she met her future husband, my grandfather, George Wilson Tyson. They were married in the nearby village of Brathay, Lancaster in 1898. Granny, a gentle Scotswoman, who was born in Kelso, Scotland, adored children.

My grandfather George was busy with his mail delivery job, which entailed feeding, grooming and stabling his driving horse. Granny, in the meantime, was busy doing the housewifely chores of the day--keeping their house on Rydal Road spotlessly clean, keeping her children neatly and appropriately dressed, and engaging in various social activities and family festive occasions. In the summertime, the family crowded into fewer rooms and Elizabeth ran a bed and breakfast catering to the tourists, who even then came to picturesque Ambleshide for their vacations. Courtesy George and Shirley Tyson

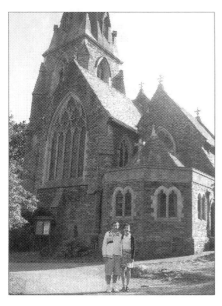

Left, Warren Smithies, right, Edi-May Annand Smithies, standing in front of St. Mary's Anglican Church in Ambleside, England, 2007

Edi-May and Warren are the great-granddaughter, and great-great grandson of George W. and E. Mary Brotherston Tyson. George and E. Mary, and their children Tommy and Mollie, attended St. Mary's Anglican Church regularly before immigrating to Canada in 1914.

The church, built in the mid-1800s, is constructed in Early Gothic style. Its tall, tapered spire was built of soft-hued sandstone, not the local slate. After more than 150 years, the spire continues to awe visitors to the Lake District in Cumbria in northwestern England. Another beautiful stone church in the Lake District is the Grasmere Church in the town of Grasmere, only a few miles from Ambleside. The Grasmere Church has a square steeple, while St. Mary's Anglican Church in Ambleside has a spectacular pointed steeple.

Edi-May was so intrigued by the story of her grandparents' lives before they immigrated to Canada in 1914 that she took several trips to England to see the locale of these stories. On one occasion she took this striking picture of the church silhouetted against a dull grey sky.

At his new home in Fishburn Grandpa Tyson continued his regular church attendance at the Fishburn Church along with his brother "T. B." and their neighbours. Granny gave up attending church in Canada due to her hearing loss. Courtesy Wayne & Edi-May Smithies

1905, Tommy Tyson's grade 1 class in Ambleside, taken about nine years before Tommy immigrated to Canada. The boys are wearing their school uniform.

Two are identified: Front row 1st on right, Tommy Tyson, grade 1; Second row 2nd from right, Percy Mason, Tommy's best friend. Handwriting on the reverse notes: "To Tom Tyson with Percy Mason's compliments Jan. 1905." Photo by Chas. G. Mason, Lake Rd, Ambleside, possibly Percy's father." Author's collection

The Tyson family's plan to immigrate to Canada necessitated many hard decisions. The saddest realization was that many loved ones—relatives and good friends--had to be left behind. This 1907 picture of Mollie's public school class, which was given to Mollie before she left Ambleside with her parents in 1914, provided her a lasting memory of her classmates in England. The person that my mother missed the most was her best friend, Winnie, a girl her own age who had been Mollie's friend since Kindergarten. They played together daily, often venturing beyond the narrow confines of the street where they lived. Mollie led a carefree life in Ambleside. Always an active child, she and Winnie often played beside Stock Gill Force, the stream that ran through the village of Ambleside. By the time the family immigrated to Canada in 1914 Mollie and Winnie were climbing and playing on the beautiful green hills of the Cumbrian Mountains, which surrounded Ambleside in the Lake District of England. This area of England was also the home to some of England's most famous poets. Author's collection

Life in other parts of the world was not so peaceful and idyllic as Ambleside. Along with his friends in faraway southern Alberta, my great-uncle Tom "T. B." Tyson heard by radio and newspaper that the storm clouds of the Great War were gathering over Europe. In addition, T. B.'s brother Wm. Dawes, now living in Galena, Ill., USA, who had visited George during a seven-week visit to England in 1888, wrote to T. B. suggesting that their younger brother George's prospects as mail driver between Coniston and Ambleside were not very good and stated further that he thought George could do better at earning a living for his family if he, too, immigrated to Canada.

William Dawes' assessment of George's financial outlook was accurate, it seems. George Wilson Tyson began work as a mail carrier between Ambleside and Coniston, England, in 1894, a job he held for nearly 20 years, until he immigrated to Canada. George's salary increased very slowly and his expenses climbed, so financially he was making little headway.

That information, added to Tom's conviction that war in Europe was inevitable, was too much to bear. Uncle Tom wrote to George urging him to bring his family to Fishburn to start a new and better life in this young country.

Two very happy occasions were the marriage of George's sister Margaret Elizabeth "Maggie" to John (Jack) Satterthwaite (sitting center front in this photo) and the subsequent birth of George's nephew Ted Satterthwaite.

Ted married Miss Emma Pearson. Ted and Emma's daughter, Margaret, married Dennis Dodd. My mother, who often spoke fondly of her cousin Ted, who was near her age, corresponded with Ted and his wife, Emma Pearson Tyson, every year at Christmastime. This meant that when I went to visit them in 1977, nearly 10 years after my mother's death, they already "knew" me. They were real family. Author's collection

Once Grandpa Tyson made the decision to immigrate to Canada, he lost no time in making preparations for the move. First he booked passage for the four of them on the luxury liner, *Lusitania*, a modern steamship that took less that a week to cross the Atlantic. The *Lusitania* was a far cry from the sailing ships on which earlier generations of Tysons crossed the Atlantic to emigate to Canada. Then Grandpa made all the other arrangements necessary when moving one's family from one country to another.

When my mother, Mollie Tyson, only 12 years old, heard her parents' plans she promptly swam across Windermere, a distance of about one-half mile. By the time Mollie came home that evening she had made up her mind what going to Canada meant to her. "I'm going to marry a cowboy," she declared determinedly. My mother got her heart's desire; she married the "cowboy of her dreams," my dad, Ralph Vroom, on January 4, 1921, when she was 19 years of age.

Finally, in April 1914 George and E. Mary Tyson immigrated to Canada, intially working for Hector McGlenning so that George could learn Canadian farming methods. Alberta became a province of the Dominion of Canada in 1905, so their address was Mr. and Mrs. G. W. Tyson, Fishburn, AB.

My mother's brother, Tommy, was sixteen years old by then so went out to work right away when the family arrived in Canada. Mollie went to school at Utopia School right away. Even though Mollie was ahead in literature and grammar she was not strong in mathematics so the teacher, Mr. William Cameron, put her in grade 5, recalled Rosamund Blackburn. Rosamund and Mollie were in grade five and six together. Mollie continued her studies at Utopia School until 1919, when she left school and went to work for a neighbour family.

(Above left) *Thomas Tyson II (1838-1921), father of George and T. B. Tyson, photographed by Herbert Bell, Ambleside. Interestingly, this photo was found underneath one of Bill Vroom riding a jumping horse owned by C. C. Cross in a 1950 horse show in Regina. At that time Mr. Cross, a Calgary oilman, owned the Buckhorn Ranch in the Beaver Mines district.* Courtesy Moe Vroom

(Above right) *Circa 1890, is Margaret Banks Tyson (1834 —ca 1915), photographed by Herbert Bell, Ambleside. Grandpa Tyson sorely missed his parents when he moved to Canada. He never saw them again.* Courtesy Moe Vroom

The two people most missed by my grandmother were two of her sisters, Meg Brotherston Hogarth and Vi Brotherston, whom she left behind in Kelso, Scotland, when she moved to Ambleside. I remember Granny Tyson having an enlargement of a photograph of her sister Meg Brotherston Hogarth in a light brown wooden frame that hung in Granny Tyson's home on their farm at Fishburn.

My great-aunt Meg and my grandmother E. Mary Brotherston and her sister Meg Brotherston Hogarth were very fond of each other. Aunt Meg lived in Galashiels, Scotland, and she and Granny Tyson wrote letters back and forth regularly over the years. Aunt Meg periodically sent us bundles of warm clothing, particularly hand-knitted sweaters for winter. She once sent my mother an ankle-length mink fur coat when we lived at Beaver Mines. Mom wore her very practical fur coat for warmth during winter trips by team and sleigh for a number of years on journeys taking anywhere from one to four hours each way.

My grandfather Tyson was well liked and respected by his colleagues at the post office. Here a group of 11 men pose for photographer Dair of Middom, England, so George could remember the camaraderie they shared while he lived in Ambleside and worked as a mail driver there. Another of George's friends gave him a postcard with a coloured photo of the town of Coniston where George picked up the mail each day. The postcard gives an idea of the exceptionally beautiful scenery in the Lake District of England.

A postcard written by George's friend, E. Edwards, was received by mail before George left for Canada the next day. Grandpa kept it as a remembrance all of his life. The note on the back of the postcards reads: "Dear George, I presume you are leaving Ambleside tomorrow. Sorry I have not seen you. I am sending you this card to wish you good-bye with a pleasant journey and success in your new undertaking. You will recognize this picture without any explanation. Signed: E. Edwards." The card is addressed to "Mr. George Tyson, Late Mail Driver, Ambleside" Author's collection

Hand-drawn pen and ink sketch of the profile of my great-grandfather Andrew Brotherson. Andrew Brotherston was the beloved father of my grandmother, E. Mary Tyson. He died in 1891, at the age of 56 years, in the Parish of Kelso, County of Roxbourgh, Scotland. Granny missed him for the rest of her life.

Andrew Brotherston was a noted naturalist in the Galashiels area of Scotland. The caption under this photo reaads: "The portrait, which is from a photograph by Mssrs. Mackintosh & Co., Kelso, is that of the late Mr. Andrew Brotherston, Kelso, a well-known Border taxidermist, botanist and scientist. His attainments secured him more than local fame and brought the acquaintence, and even friendship, of some eminent men." This picture was printed in a newspaper in Scotland. Courtesy Ralph Tyson

In the summer of 1959, when she was 10 years old, Edi-May Annand (Smithies) spent the summer with her grandparents, Ralph and Mollie Vroom, in Creston, BC.

Her grandmother recounted to her the story of how Tom "T. B." Tyson brought this pine hutch from Ontario when he moved to the Fishburn district of the Northwest Territories (now Alberta) in 1889.

To save money T. B. travelled by Red River wagon from Manitoba to Fishburn carrying all his belongings with him. The CPR went to Medicine Hat, AB, and the local "Turkey train" went as far as Lethbridge. However, T. B. chose a slow, noisy, laborious Red River wagon train because it was a cheaper mode of travel. Thomas knew that he needed every spare penny that he had earned as a farm laborer in Ontario to start up a home on his western homestead and get a farming operation in production.

Some years ago Edi-May Smithies and her husband, Wayne, lovingly restored this hutch to its former beauty. The hutch was in "really bad shape," Ms. Smithies recalled, so they cleaned it up, replaced missing knobs and applied several coats of shellac, so that the luster of the original pine was preserved.
Courtesy Wayne & Edi-May Smithies

A large grandfather clock, which may have been a wedding present from family, was the most valuable personal treasure that my grandparents George and Mary Tyson brought to Canada in 1914 from their home in Ambleside. On the inside of the clock, as noted in a 1947 letter from Jacques Jewellers in Calgary, "there are repair dates on the movement, dating to May 25th, 1875, Oct 16th, 1858, one very faint which looks like Sept 17th, 1837." The clock towered over me as a child. I would stand gazing at it trying to read the strange numbers - Roman numerals - on its face.
Courtesy Shirley and George Tyson

For safe travel Granny and Grandpa wrapped the clock in blankets and packed it in the middle of the blanket box in which they brought all their bedding for their new home in Canada. The clock made the long journey across Canada by CPR passenger train to Brocket, AB, finally making the last few miles of its journey to the farm of Hector McGlenning in Fishburn by team and wagon.

After a few years of working for Mr. McGlenning to learn Canadian farming methods, Granny and Grandpa bought their own farm. The grandfather clock was again loaded in a wagon for its journey to Granny's new house.

Granny Tyson sold her farm to Aylmer Stuckey in 1944. She lived with my mother and us four children in Pincher Creek until WWII ended, and Dad came home from Overseas. After the War, Granny went to live with her son Tommy and his family in Kimberley, BC, taking her treasured grandfather clock with her. In the 1950s Granny lived with her grandson, my brother Donald and his family at the Kimberley Airport.

Granny Tyson continued her loving care of her grandfather clock until the day she died. While she lived with Tommy and Mary, Granny sent the clock to Jacques Jewellers in Calgary to be repaired. The oldest piece of correspondence showing how Granny Tyson continued to treasure her grandfather clock is a letter postmarked October 22, 1947, and was sent by Harry Jacques Jewellers in Calgary to Mrs. M. Tyson, Kimberley, BC. The letter, dated Oct. 23, 1947, states:

"Dear Mrs. Tyson: We are sending your grandfather clock by CPR Express collect today. The larger weight goes to the time card, smaller weight to the striking side. These weights seem to be the correct ones. For your information there are repair dates on the movement, dating to May 25th, 1875, Oct 16th, 1858, one very faint, which looks like Sept 17th, 1837. To time this clock to run faster turn (the) burr on the bottom of the pendulum to shorten (the) pendulum. To make the clock run slower, turn to lengthen pendulum. Yours very truly, HARRY JACQUES JEWELER. Signed, Per (Signature) HJ/KD"

When Granny Tyson died in December 31, 1957, her grandfather clock took its final journey, to the home of her grandson George and his wife, Shirley. George is the oldest son of Tommy and Mary Laidlaw Tyson. Shirley says "The grandfather clock stands 7 feet in height and George thinks it's made from walnut and oak but he's not certain." Shirley has a bill from Ernest Yolander, European Clock Repair, Calgary, AB, dated December 26, 1991, gives what appears to be the following information: "Clock Type: Grandfather; Clock Make, Dundee."

This adorable 1906 photo of my mother, Mollie Tyson, and her brother, Tommy, was one of my grandmother's treasured possessions. It hung in its wooden frame in Granny's living room at Firsburn for as long as I can remember, reminding Granny of the quiet, peaceful life that she and her children were living in the picturesque village of Ambleside before immigrating to Canada.

A very large, framed, charcoal-pencil drawing of this photo is now proudly displayed in the home of Edi-May and Wayne Smithies.

In 2008, the Tyson family home on Rydal Road still stands unchanged from when Tommy & Mollie lived there as children. As with other buildings in Ambleside, their home is protected as part of the Lake District National Trust. Author's collection

Shown above are a matching porcelaine sugar bowl and cream jug and a lone creamer with a hunting scene reminiscent of the song "John Peel" brought from Ambleside by E. Mary Tyson. The items are decorated with gold leaf. Many women brought tangible items with them when they immigrated to help them remember their homeland. Wrapped amongst the blankets that my grandmother packed around her grandfather clock were these pieces of delicate china, probably part of a larger set at the time. Author's collection

When Granny and Grandpa moved to their own farm in about 1915 Granny's first move was to start a vegetable garden with a small patch of old-fashioned flowers, such as bachelor's buttons, cosmos, and marguerite daisies, in one corner. My grandmother inherited her father's love of gardening and ability to grow beautiful flowers in a hostile environment. As well as describing the location of rare plants in his home district of Kelso, her father, Andrew Brotherston studied and wrote, in Latin, a number of scientific papers describing and naming plants found in the vicinity of Tweedside, Scotland.

I now understand why in my younger years I was an avid gardener and why I still love all flowers and plants.

While I lived in Waterton Lakes National Park I nursed my flower garden along under hostile conditions that included a short growing season, a windy exposure, relatively poor soil, plus the added hazard of deer nipping off my pansy blossoms every morning. However, I perservered and finally cultivated a bright, colourful flower garden that lasted from June until the first snowfall that sometimes came as early as the first week in September.

When Granny and Grandpa Tyson and their children, Tommy and Mollie, emigrated from England to Canada Granny was able to bring only a few family treasures with her. One of these treasures was a lady's silver pocket watch, a fashion accessory of the time.

Granny Tyson's watch has scrolled designs engraved on its case; tiny emerald and ruby gems are embedded in the face of this beautiful old watch. A chain, to be attached to a buttonhole in the blouse or jacket of the wearer, ensures the safety and convenience of the watch and then hangs down as a decoration. An 1859 British coin is attached to one end of this decorative three-stranded chain. On one side of the coin, which is worn very thin, are the words "... (Ineligible) Gracia Britanniar (sic): H.E.G. ... (Ineligible) The head of the monarch of the time, Queen Victoria, who reigned from 1837 to 1901 (nearly 64 years), is in the centre of this side of the coin. A wreathe of what appears to be oak and laurel leaves is imprinted on the other side of the well-worn coin. The only eligible printing on this side is the year '1859.' The coin's value would be lessened by the fact that a hole was drilled in it so that it could be attached to the chain.

A tiny key, which was used to wind the watch, is attached to the other end of this decorative chain. On one side of the head of the key are the words: "Wm. Greenwood 92 Brigdate Leeds." On the other side of the key are the words: "Watch Maker and Jeweler"

At one time it kept perfect time. It could be repaired, but because certain parts would have to be specially made the repairs would be expensive

My husband, George Annand of Waterton Park and I are dancing an old-time waltz at the 83rd Annual Old-Timer's Ball, December 1968, organized by the Lethbridge and District Pemmican Club in Lethbridge, AB. Music was by Reg Romiuk and his Westerners. At the time it was the oldest, continuous year-end ball in Canada.

I am wearing a rich-brown velvet dress that my grandmother Tyson brought from England in her limited luggage space when she immigrated in 1914. My Aunt Marion Vroom Cyr, a skilled dressmaker living in Pincher Creek, made necessary repairs and altered it to fit me. The bodice of the dress is a fitted style with a modified sweetheart neckline. A pleated fold of the luxurious material, with golden brown hand-embroidered French knots, frames the neckline. The long, gored, princess-style skirt is finished with a similar piece of material, which is also adorned with golden brown hand-embroidered French knots.

Before my grandmother Tyson emigrated she paid a dressmaker in Ambleside, England, to make the dress for her for a special occasion. Though sewing machines were coming into common use at the time, finishing details were hand-sewn with tiny, even stitches. Zippers were not in common use when this dress was made so the back of the bodice is closed with hooks and eyes.

A piece of velvet material, hand-sewn to one side of the bodice and attached unobtrusively with small hooks and eyes to the other side conceals the hooks and eyes. The wide pleated, French knot decorated collar extends around the back of the neck as well, further concealing the bodice closure. A matching piece of embroidered velvet forms a sort of small cape at the top of the long sleeves, which are finished at the wrists with the same fine, light brown net that that fills in the sweetheart neckline.

The sleeve cuffs, like the high collar, are finished with a row of pleated, cream-coloured net. The dress is still beautiful and I felt very special wearing it on that occasion. To the surprise of my husband and me the above picture, taken at the ball by a staff photographer for the Lethbridge Herald, *appeared in the next day's paper to be a reminder forever of that wonderful evening. Courtesy* Lethbridge Herald, *Lethbridge, AB. Author's collection*

When Granny and Grandpa Tyson emigrated they left behind the rolling, emerald green mountains that surrounded the peaceful village of Ambleside. These hills are above the home of a friend of Margaret Dodd, widow of Dennis. This view is typical of the Westmoreland area. The farmland is divided into neat, rectangular fields separated by wide hedges. Groves of trees here and there emphasize the contours of the land. By contrast the land that Tysons bought at Fishburn, AB was barren and dry. Courtesy George and Shirley Tyson

Granny and Grandpa Tyson's farm at Fishburn was situated about a half mile west the Waterton River across from the community of Glenwood in southwest Alberta. It was the original homestead quarter of Fred Thomas.

The gently undulating land extends west and south and borders on land to the south that was owned by Aylmer and Gracie Stuckey. This view looks eastward to the Waterton River Valley and the community of Glenwood across the river.

Needless to say, Granny Tyson was somewhat dismayed when they arrived in Canada and found that the land stretched unobstructed to the horizon. Compared with Ambleside, which is surrounded by high hills something like the foothills of the Rockies in southern Alberta, the prairie seems to go on forever. There was some consolation, however. By looking westward, instead of eastward, Tysons could see the main range of the Rockies, albeit some 40 miles in the distance. Courtesy Edi-May Smithies

For a map of the neighbours of the Tysons in the Fishburn district, the reader is referred to the map *"Forty Miles on a Load of Poles"* in Volume 1 The *VROOMS of the FOOTHILLS: Adventures of My Childhood* (Ellis, 2006 and 2003)

When the mountains are snow-clad, they are absolutely glorious at sunrise and sunset. Shining through the densest part of the earth's atmosphere, the sun's rays turn the mountains a fiery red. The brilliant colour lasts for only a few minutes, but anyone who sees the scene never forgets it. Marietta "Etta" Irwin McRae took this photo in the fall of 1908 from the site of Malcolm and Etta McRae's homestead ranch in the Cyr district on Highway 6 from Pincher Creek to Waterton Park. It captures the beauty of the mountains in a very dramatic way. Spread Eagle Mountain is to the left of center. On the far right is Victoria Peak. Etta developed this photo on her homestead using the same method as Connie Warburton Holroyd described earlier in this book.

This is the view my mother saw, but from further away, the winter of 1914-15, her first winter in Canada. "When I first came to Fishburn," my mother used to tell me, "the mountains looked so close that I thought I could walk to them before breakfast." The mountains seem even closer on a clear, cold southern Alberta day. Courtesy Kathleen "Kay" McRae Leigh

Securing food for the family was part of homesteaders', ranchers' and farmers' wives' duties. Some women became excellent marksmen. My grandmother E. Mary Tyson, shown here in 1937, was an excellent fisherman and caught many a string of fish in the Waterton River.

Granny regularly walked to the Waterton River, which was just ½ mile east of their farm at Fishburn. She never caught more than her limit, which was ample to feed her family for one or two meals. Here Granny holds a string of five pan-size fish. Her fishing rod and the rest of her catch lie on the ground at her feet. Courtesy George and Shirley Tyson

Granny caught both trout and other fish, some of which she called "graylings". Graylings are correctly called Rocky Mountain whitefish, said George R. "Geordie" Annand. He was the son of homesteaders George and Betsy Annand. Geordie fished in the Waterton River and other streams in the area from the time he was able to cast a fly or a baited hook until he died. Geordie, too, often caught a string of whitefish just a few miles further up the Waterton River from where Granny Tyson fished, and brought them home for dinner in Waterton Park.

Taken in 1914, here are four people with Scottish roots. Three of them were born in Scotland. Identified by information in Friesen (1974) and other sources, shown here are: Standing, left to right: Mrs. Cameron and William Cameron, teacher at Gladstone Valley school. Seated, left to right: E. Mary Tyson (Mrs. George W.) and Hector "Hec" McGlenning. The photo was taken in the McGlenning home.

Hector McGlenning travelled west from Ontario to the Fishburn district of Alberta by covered wagon along with his parents, Mr. and Mrs. John McGlenning, in 1897 (Friesen, 1974). When they first arrived in Canada, George and E. Mary Tyson worked for Hector McGlenning, who was established on his own farm in the Fishburn district.

My mother, who attended Utopia School for about four years, often talked about her teacher, Mr. William Cameron, and how he took a great interest in all of his students, encouraging them to stay in school as long as possible.

Mr. and Mrs. William Cameron came to Canada from Scotland in 1907 (Friesen, 1974). They homesteaded SW ¼-16-5-2-W5 in Gladstone Valley and lived just west of the William Barclay family. William Cameron taught at Gladstone Valley School in 1913-1914 and 1914-1915 (Unfolding the Pages, 1992). In September 1915, he went to teach at Utopia School and boarded at Hector McGlenning's place where the Tysons were also living. To give moral support to their fellow countrymen Mr. and Mrs. Cameron drove to McGlennings for a visit one day in 1914. This picture was taken to commemorate the occasion. Glenbow Archives NA-184-60

George and E. Mary Tyson soon made friends with their neighbours, some of whom had also emigrated from England. Taken in the summer of 1917, all are dressed in their "Sunday Best", likely for church or a special occasion, but maybe just for a visit to a dear neighbour's home for tea.

Left to right: Frederick John "Jack" Dennis (four years old) holding his mother's hand, Ida (Mrs. Fred) Dennis holding one-year-old Frances Dennis (Mrs. Jim McWhirter), Isabella "Bella" McRae (Mrs. Ed) Joyce, E. Mary (Mrs. George) Tyson, and Mollie Tyson. In the front row (left to right) are: Norma Joyce (daughter of Bella and Ed) and Margaret Dennis (Mrs. Jack Finlay). Both girls are six years old. The Dennis and Joyce families homesteaded in the Robert Kerr district.

Mollie, 16 years old, is wearing her long brown, naturally curly hair in ringlets. The wide, three-quarter length sleeves of Mollie's dress are trimmed with lace, which she crocheted herself. On January 4, 1921 Mollie Tyson married her cowboy, Ralph Vroom, the love of her life.

Bella Joyce was one sister of Malcolm McRae, who was the father of Kay McRae Leigh. Bella was the wife of Ed Joyce who came west from Ontario with the MacRaes and homesteaded on the quarter section that abutted Malcolm McRae's to the north. As with many homesteaders' wives who had been raised in a life of privilege, Ida Dennis found life on the ranch very isolated and difficult. She missed England greatly, and enjoyed the company of Mary and Mollie because they, too, came from England and could talk about "home."

Behind the groups is a 3-strand page wire fence. Homesteades found these fences useful for keeping their livestock contained. The cattlemen who drove large herds of cattle north from Texas to the railway that ran east and west through Montana hated these fences. The situation where a large herd of cattle regularly got hung up in a page wire fence was not a Canadian phenomenon, but occasionally horses or cattle would get caught in a barbed-wire fence. This resulted in torn skin and ripped flesh that might become infected and cause serious pain and suffering for the afflicted animal (Friesen, 1974). Used with the kind permission of the Archives of the Pincher Creek & District Historical Society, from "Prairie Grass to Mountain Pass", page 605.

EPILOGUE

Writing Volume 2 *The VROOMS of the FOOTHILLS: Cowboys & Homesteaders* enhanced my awareness of the richness of the history of my native land, Canada. There are over 220 photographs in this book, courtesy the generosity and good will of the descendants of people who came west to homestead in the Pincher Creek district of Alberta about the time that my grandparents and their family came. To these descendants I owe a debt of gratitude.

The first chapter tells how my grandfather Oscar Vroom, a descendant of United Empire Loyalists and living as a young man in Clementsport, Nova Scotia, became enthralled with idea of travelling to western Canada. He saved up enough money to pay his rail fare on the newly built Canadian Pacific Railway (CPR) as far as Medicine Hat, NWT, which at that time, 1886, was the end of the line. Oscar worked as a blacksmith with crews building the rail line as far as Macleod, NWT.

Anxious to get to Pincher Creek, Oscar purchased a saddle horse and headed west. There he rode around the Pincher Creek area, being particularly enthralled by the Rocky Mountains as viewed from the Beaver Mines Creek Valley southwest of Pincher Creek. He made up his mind that Beaver Creek Valley was where he would make his home, tentatively settling on a quarter section homestead there. After a year in the West, Oscar returned to Nova Scotia and married Alena Blanche Munro, living in Clementsport for 10 years and raising a three sons and a daughter.

Oscar came west for a second time in 1897 this time, accompanied by three of his brothers and a brother-in-law, and travelling by train to Macleod, NWT. In Macleod, the Vrooms, who were skilled as blacksmiths and carpenters joined CPR work crews and worked laying CPR tracks through the Crowsnest Pass to Cranbrook, BC. There the Vroom brothers dispersed, one staying in Cranbrook as a businessman, one travelling further west, and one moving to Saskatchewan to set up a business. Oscar, fulfilling his dream of ranching near Table Mountain, homesteaded a quarter section south of Beaver Mines.

When my dad heard that the family was moving west, he declared, "I'm going to be a cowboy!" Dad became a cowboy in the truest sense of the word. And the wives and families of homesteaders transformed the homesteaders' log shacks into cozy homes.

The Klondike gold rush affected all people of that era. One of our family friends went up the Yukon River to Dawson City by boat; one of my great-uncles drove cattle to the Klondike in 1897 to feed the gold rushers.

As soon as the Gold Rush to the Yukon ended, the rush of homesteaders to western Canada started. One family who settled in Gladstone Valley near my childhood home came by covered wagon from meridian, Idaho. My great-uncle T. B. Tyson came to Canada in 1855 to work as a farm labourer. After a few years he came west, travelling part way by ox team and cart, to homestead at Fishburn, NWT.

There was an inrush of immigrants from Great Britain and continental Europe. When my mother, Mollie Tyson, daughter of George Tyson and E. Mary Brotherston Tyson heard that the family was moving to Canada, she declared: "I'm going to marry a cowboy!" and she did.

Several more books in the series, *The VROOMS of the FOOTHILLS*, are planned and partly written.

MAPS

MAP 1 Trails/Creeks/Rivers of Extreme SW Alberta, circa 1910   9

MAP 2 Homesteads, Beaver Mines Creek and Gladstone Valley, circa 1910   45

MAP 3 Village of Beaver Mines, circa 1910 - 1950   83

MAP 4 Village of Mountain Mill,circa 1880 - 1976   95

MAP 5 1906, Mitchell Family - by covered wagon from Idaho to Alberta   125

MAP 6 1862-1867, Tyson Family - gold mining in Australia   138

MAP 7 1867-1874, Tyson Family - gold mining in New Zealand   139

REFERENCES AND SOURCES OF INFORMATION

Official publications and records
Land Office, Municipal District of Pincher Creek, Pincher Creek, Alberta, 1934 and 1950 maps.

Museums and Archives
Glenbow Museum, Calgary, AB
National Archives of Canada, Ottawa, ON

Newspapers
Cranbrook Courier. Cranbrook, BC
Cranbrook Herald. Cranbrook, BC
Pincher Creek Echo. Pincher Creek, Alberta.
Shell Waterton News. D. Brestler, publisher

Books
1907-1913 Alberta Brands Books, Alberta Department of Agriculture, Edmonton, Alberta
Berton, Pierre. KLONDIKE: The Last Great Gold Rush 1896-1899. McClelland and Stewart Limited, Toronto, Ontario. Revised Edition by Pierre Berton Enterprises, 1972
Cashman, Anthony "Tony." *Singing Wires: The Telephone in Alberta*, Edmonton: Alberta Government Telephone Commission, 1972
Crowsnest and Its People. Published by Crowsnest Pass Historical Society, Coleman, AB 1979
Complete Atlas of the World. Bramley Books. Copyright 1989. Colour Library Books Ltd. Goldaming, Surrey, England, pages 119 and 123.
Decoux, Vern. *History of the Crowsnest Pass*, or some such name, ca 1960
Dempsey, Hugh A. *The Gentle Persuader: A Biography of James Gladstone, Indian Senator*, 1986.
Dent's Canadian School Atlas, Published by The Aldine Press, Letchworth, Herts, Great Britain For J. M. Dent & Sons (Canada) Ltd. 1970 revision
Department of the Secretary of State, *The Canadian Style: A Guide to Writing and Editing*. Dundurn Press Limited, Toronto, Ontario, 1985
Elder, Bruce. *Presenting Australia – The Making of a Nation*. New Holland Publishers Pty Ltd., 2000.
Friesen, D. W. & Sons Ltd., printers. *"Prairie grass to mountain pass": History of the Pioneers of Pincher Creek and District*. Published by Pincher Creek Historical Society, Pincher Creek, Alberta, 1974
Freebairn, A. L. *Pincher Creek Memories: Old Timers Souvenir Album* (revised)
George, James L. *There's a Church in the Valley: A history of Mountain Mill Church*. Published by the Women's Institute of Canada, ca 1996
George, Jim. "Fishburn United Church – A History." In *Journal "United Church."* (Date of publication is unknown at this time).
Guralnik, David B., Editor in Chief. *Webster's New World Dictionary, Second College Edition*, The World Publishing Company. New York and Cleveland. 1970.
Hacker, Diana. *A Canadian Writer's Reference*. Nelson, Canada, 1989.
Huddlestun, F. A. (Fred). *A History of the Settlement and Building Up of the Area in S.W. Alberta Bordering Waterton Park on the North From 1889*. Privately published, undated (circa 1969).
Lynch-Staunton, Mrs. C. *A History of the Early Days of Pincher Creek*: and *of the District and of the Southern Mountains*. Published by the Members of the Women's Institute of Alberta. Undated (Circa 1920)

Pincher Creek and District School Division #29. *Unfolding the Pages*. Pincher Creek: Gorman & Gorman Ltd., 1992.

Primeau, Anne (Sikina). *Frenchy Riviere (Henri A. Riviere 1868-1956)*

Rodney, William. *Kootenai Brown: his life and times*. The Morriss Printing Company Ltd. Victoria, British Columbia. 1969.

Russell, Andy. *The Canadian Cowboy Stories of Cows, Cowboys and Cayuses*. Toronto: McClelland & Stewart, 1993

Webster's New World Dictionary, Second College Edition. The World Publishing Company, 1970.

Articles

Liddell, Ken., Furrows & Foothills column, "Homestead Plans Excite Old Couple."
The Calgary gHerald, November 5, 1952

"UP THE YUKON TO DAWSON" Reprinted from the *Cheltenham Examiner* of Wednesday, November 23rd, 1898

"JOURNEY FROM DAWSON TO DYEA" Reprinted from the *Cheltenham Examiner* (December 1898)

On-line material

"1835 Shire Map of WESTMORLAND Cumbria England Kendal." The Internet.

http://www.historylearningsite.co.uk/lusitania. World War I. *The Lusitania*.

"Last Voyage of the Lusitania" in "The Lusitania Essays" at Essays.com The Internet

"Retire2 Lake District – The South" The Internet

The *1901 Census of Canada* (from http://automatedgenealogy.com/census/index.html)

"The St. Mary's River Crossing and the High Level Bridge at Lethbridge, Alberta." Crowsnest Railway Construction 12/15. Internet Explorer

www.collectionscanada.ca Library and Archives Canada, *ArchiviaNet: On-line Research Tool, Western Land Grants (1870-1930)* website.

The Willow Tree website

Unpublished material

Brooks, Alessina Bruce, *Dad's Memories - Happy 80th Birthday Dad*, unpublished memoirs of Anthony Bruce, undated (circa 1994)

Bruce, Anthony, 'For Nigel and Carolyn," undated (circa 1994)

Ellis, Bessie Vroom, Ralph Vroom Timeline, 1977

_____. "A Sequence of Ralph and Mollie Vroom Family History and Some Related Information." Revised, 1992, 1994(Revised) and 1996 (Revised)

Fooks, Georgia. Fort Whoop-Up, Historical Society of Alberta, Lethbridge Chapter, 1983.

Lang, Robert. *Memories of Bob Lang*. Crestview Lodge, February 6, 1961. Interview by Bessie Vroom Annand (Ellis).

MacFarlane, Winnifred. *An incomplete genealogy of first known VROOMS in Holland*. Ottawa, Undated (Circa 1970) Based on the date of the most recent entry, which was the date of death of Ralph Ernst Vroom in Pincher Creek, Alberta, July 26, 1969.

Appendix I

INDEX

"Cake Walk", 88

"Clutche", 88

"Glenthorne", 136, 137, 140, 141, 147

"Jocke", 88

"Peter", 88

"Stranger", 88

"Battleaxe", 114

"Fly", 149

"Fox", 31

"Funeral Wagon", 32

"Midnight", 149

"Pedro", 113

100th Anniversary Mountain Mill Church, 132

Alberta Ranch, 29, 90, 96

Allison, George, 148

Ambleside, Eng., 136, 140, 143, 145, 147, 151, 152, 153, 154, 155, 156, 157, 158, 159, 160, 161

American Revolution, 5

Annand, David and/or Gerry Hoff, 32

Annand, George and/or Bessie Vroom, 8, 160

Annand, George and/or Betsy Penny, 98, 163

Annand, Jim and/or Shelley McConnell, 9, 44, 82, 95, 125

Annapolis Valley, NS, 5

Ashcroft, BC, 106, 107, 116

autograph album, 150

Avion Ridge, 32

Babin, John, 77

Baker, Betty Annand (Mrs. George), 8

Baker, I. G., 96

Baker, Mabel, 38

Ballantyne, David, 51

Ballantyne, George, homesteader, and/or Sarah McJanet, 11, 51, 62, 82, 115, 116, 131

Ballarat, Australia, 135

Banks, Elizabeth Dawes, 136

Barclay, Agnes, 50, 81

Barclay, Alexander and/or Margaret Martin, 50, 81

Barclay, James "Charlie" and/or Sonia Chiesa, 50

Barclay, Lillian, 50

Barclay, Minnie, 81

Barclay, Nellie, 81

Barclay, William and/or Jane Rae, 43, 50, 126

Barclay, William Jr., 50

Bay of Fundy, 47, 48, 53

Beauvais Lake, 89, 96, 132

Beaver Mines, 5, 8, 19, 20, 21, 22, 24, 26, 33, 35, 39, 42, 49, 52, 53, 60, 63, 65, 66, 68, 77, 85, 91, 92, 94, 106, 114, 116, 119, 150, 165

Beaver Mines Creek, 11, 59, 82

Beaver Mines Creek Valley, 11, 19, 22, 41, 42, 44, 47, 49, 56, 60, 65, 66, 68, 72, 75, 76, 91, 124, 126, 127, 128, 165

Beaver Mines Hotel, 82

Beaver Mines Lake, 19

Beaver Mines Livery Stable, 79

Beaver Mines Post Office, 11, 72, 128, 131

Beaver Mines Tennis Club, 82, 94

Beaver Mines Women's Institute, 72, 77, 81

Beaver Mines-Gladstone Valley, 16, 75

Bell, Donald, 96

Bell, Lachlan and/or Mrs. Bell, 96, 101, 145

Bellevue, AB, 67

Bennett, Marguerite Link, 74

Berton, Pierre, 107

Big Bear, Angelique, 97

Big Bear, Cree Chief, 97

Big Snake, Chief, 109

Bird, Bill and/or Elizabeth "Liz", 50

Blackburn, Rosamund, 155

Blackfoot Indian Reserve, Gleichen, AB, 107

blacksmith, 7, 24, 33, 37, 39, 42, 50, 68, 165

Blairmore, AB, 35

Blood Indian Reserve, 14, 29

Bodick, Mary Dawes, 137

Boise, ID, 122, 123, 124

Boston, Mass., 37

Bow River, NWT, 97

brand, Annand, George and/or Betsy Penny, 134

brand, Brown, Kootenai and/or Nichemoos, 86

brand, Cyr, Dominic and/or Marion Vroom, 86

brand, Mitchell, Charles and/or Mary Ellen Buchanan, 134

brand, Mitchell, W.J.A. and/or Aravella Piper, 134

brand, Tyson, Thomas Banks, 134

brand, Vroom, Alfred and/or Margaret Coulter, 86

brand, Vroom, Claude and/or Mary McLaren, 86

brand, Vroom, Harold and/or Ruby Mitchell, 134

brand, Vroom, Oscar and/or Alena Munro, 71

brand, Vroom, Ralph and/or Mollie Tyson, 71

Brandes, Elmer and/or Ruth Tyson, 137

Brandes, Mary, 137, 140

Brantford, ON, 142

Bremner, Bill, 82

Brooke, Lionel, 15, 16, 17, 96

Brotherston, Andrew, 156, 159

Bruce, Alan Cameron, 105

Bruce, Anthony, 105, 106

Bruce, Edward and/or Mabel Elliott Noyes, 81, 82, 85, 92, 105, 106, 107, 109, 111, 112, 113, 115, 116, 150

Bruce, Michael, 77, 114

Buchanan, Ed and/or Mary Gamache, 94

Buckhorn Ranch, 155

buffalo bulls, 112

bull team, 96

Butcher shop, Cyr, Dominic & Cyr, Theodule, 82

Butte Ranch, 17

Caledonia, ON, 142

Calgary Exhibition and Stampede, 31, 32

Calgary, AB, 107

California, USA, 66

Cameron, Wm. and/or Mrs., 155, 163

Canadian Bucking Horse Championship, 32

Canadian Expeditionary Force (CEF), 19

Canadian Rodeo (Association) Hall of Fame, 30

Cape Horn, South America, 140

Cape of Good Hope, S. Africa, 139

Cariboo-Chilcotin, BC, 106, 116

Carpenter, Dave and/or Madeleine Gladstone, 98

Castle Mountain, 21, 31, 33, 89

Castle River, 54

Castle River Cattle Association, 32

Castle River Stampede, 54, 78

chaps, leather, 115

chaps, white woolly, 87, 93, 103

christening gown, 80, 112

Christie Ridge, 89

Christmas Day, 1902, 41

Church of England, Macleod, 103

Clementsport, NS, 6, 12, 23, 24, 25, 39, 47, 48, 53, 69, 116, 165

Cluny, AB, 10, 107

coal mine, #1, 82

coal mine, Christie, 89

coal mine, Frank Holmes, 82

coal mine, Good, 89

coal mine, Link, 57

Coal mines, Beaver Mines, 94

Coghills Creek, Australia, 135

Coleman, NWT/AB, 36

Coniston, England, 151

Conrad, Martin, 17

Cote, Hector, 90

Cranbrook, BC, 12, 23, 25, 28, 35, 37, 40, 47, 61, 116, 165

creamer with a hunting scene, 159

Creston, BC, 157

Cross, Clifford C., 155

Crowsnest Pass, AB/BC, 12, 23, 24, 25, 26, 28, 29, 34, 35, 36, 39, 91, 97, 165

Crowsnest River, 28, 34

Cumbrian Mountains, Eng., 153

Currie, Colin and/or Mrs., 57, 82

Cyr, Dominic and/or Marion Vroom, ii, 12, 37, 48, 72, 79, 80, 82, 90, 93, 94, 160

Damon, Art, 14

Damon, Bill, 14

Dawes, William, 137

Dawson City, Yukon, 106, 107

Dawson Creek, BC, 116

death teepee, 110

Decoux, Vern, 35

Dempster, Alex R., 148

Dennis, Fred and/or Ida, 164
Dennis, Jack, 150, 164
Dobbie, Lorne, 148
Dobbie, William, iron mine, 8
Dodge, C. C. and/or Elizabeth Munro, 5, 12
Drywood Creek, AB, 103
Drywood Mountain, 90
Durban, South Africa, 140
Dutch Creek, BC, 88
Dyea, Alaska, 106, 107
East Kootenays, BC, 37, 88
Ellis, Bessie Vroom, 78
fall snowstorm, 89
Father Lacombe, A., O.M.I., 97
Finlay, Jack and/or Margaret Dennis, 164
Fish Lake, 79
Fishburn United Church, 146, 152
Fishburn, NWT/AB, 142, 145, 154, 155, 157, 161, 162, 163
Fooks, Georgia, 124
Fort Benton, MT,-Whoop-Up, NWT, Trail, 124
Fort Pitt, SK, 99
Fort Steele, BC, 38
Frank Slide, 35
Frank, AB, 35
Freebairn, A. L., 145
Gamache, Edward and/or Elizabeth Pope, 94
Gamache, Ken and Jessie, 94
Gavalin, Fred and/or Anna Lund, 81
gentling a colt, 88
gentling a wild horse, 102
Gingras, Homer and/or Vera Cyr, 25, 93
Gladstone Creek, 100
Gladstone Valley, NWT/AB, 66, 67, 72, 75, 122, 123, 128
Gladstone, George and/or Marion Johnson, 97, 98
Gladstone, Leonard and/or Anna de Geest, 18, 62, 99
Gladstone, William II and/or Mary Samat Vandal Johnson, 18, 98, 102, 103
Gladstone, William III and/or Louise Spence, 18, 99
Gladstone, William IV, 62
Gladstone, Wm. Shanks (Wm. I) and/or Harriet LeBlanc, 15, 18, 80, 94, 100, 102
Glasgow, Scotland, 123

Glenbow Museum, 18
Glenford, ON, 144
Goble, Frank and/or Linnea Hagglund, 67, 81
gold fields, Ballarat, Aus., 139, 141
gold fields, Hokitika, NZ, 135
gold fields, Kingston, Aus., 136
gold fields, Smeaton Plains, Aus., 136
gold fields, Yukon, 116
gold rush, 116
Good, Andy and Kate, 36
Gould, Dr. Clark and/or Amanda Vroom, 37
grandfather clock, 158
Grasmere Church, 152
Grechman, Marion Vroom, 88
Hagglund, Erik and/or Olga Lund, 67, 81
Hagglund, George, 133
Hagglund, Hilding, 67, 81
Hagglund, Swan, 81
Hamilton, Gordon, 68
Hamilton, ON, 142, 144
Hamilton, Rev. Gavin and/or Jessie Willigar, 57, 61
happy hunting grounds, the, 110
Helena, MT, 124
High Level Bridge, Lethbridge, AB, 27
Hokitika, NZ, 135, 136, 140, 143
Hole, Fred, 145
Hole, George, 145
Holmes, Frank and/or Louise Riley, 82, 94
Holroyd, Bo and/or Constance Warburton, 84, 162
Holroyd, Jack, 162
Homestead, Brooke, Lionel, W ½ -25-6-2- W5th, 17
Homestead, Cameron, William and Mrs., SW ¼-16-5-2-W5, 163
Homestead, Freebairn, A. L., NW ¼ -34-5- 29-W4, 146
Homestead, Freebairn, John, NE ¼ 34-5-29- W4, 146
Homestead, Gladstone, Steve, SE ¼ -1-4-30- W4th, 99
Homestead, Gladstone, William Shanks, William I, NW ¼-7-6-1-W5, 94
Homestead, Irvine, Charles, SE ¼-14-5-28- W4, 146
Homestead, Mitchell, Charles, NW ¼-35-5- 2-W5th, 44

Homestead, Mitchell, W. J. A., NE ¼ -6-5-2-
W5th, 126
Homestead, Newton, Thomas, NW ¼-22-5-
28-W4th, 145
Homestead, Prentice, NE ¼ -33-5-2-W5th,
44
Homestead, Shurts, NW ¼-12-6-2-W5, 126
Homestead, Smith, William, SW ¼-14-5-28-
W4, 146
Homestead, Spence, Margarette, NW ¼-1-4-
30-W4, 99
Homestead, Truitt, Harry, SE ¼-/4-22-5-2-
W5, 127
Homestead, Tyson, Thomas Banks (T. B.),
SW ¼ -22-5-28-W4th, 145
Homestead, Vroom, Claude, NE ¼ -34-5-2-
W5th, 26
Homestead, Vroom, Harold, SE ¼ -32-5-2-
W5th, 66
Homestead, Vroom, Oscar, NE ¼ 29-5-2-
W5th, 11
Homestead, Vroom, Ralph, SW ¼ -28-5-2-
W5th, 44
Homestead, White, Alex, NE ¼ -12-6-2-
W5th, 94
Homesteads, McLaren, Peter, SE ¼ -13-6-2-
W5th and SW ¼ -18-6-1-W5th, 94
Hovis, Fern, 15
Hovis, Shirley, 15
Huddlestun, Billy, 17, 88, 99
Hughes, Tommy, 94, 116
Hunter, Rev. J. F., 76
Indian Farm, AB, 145, 146
Jaggernath, Ruby Peters, 66, 76
Jenkins, Bud, 8
Jenkins, Tom and/or Frankie, 8
Jenks family, 82
Johnson, Mary Samat Vandal, 98
Joyce, Ed and/or Isabella McRae, 164
Joyce, Edward and/or Elsie Belle Crosbie,
72, 82, 94
Joyce, Norma, 164
Jughandle Ranch, 14
Keeping's Store, Beaver Miines, 82
Kelso, Scotland, 152, 156
Kemp, (Unknown) and/or Ann Barclay, 50
Kenya, Africa,, 32
Killarney Park, ON, 142

Killarney, ON, 141, 142
Kimberley, BC, 104
Klondike, the, 105, 106, 116
Kootenay & Alberta Railway, 82, 92, 94, 115
Kootenay Region Metis Association Pedigree
Chart, 97
LaGrandeur, Emery, 30, 31
LaGrandeur, Mose and/or Julia Livermore,
28, 29, 30
LaGrandeur, Pete and/or Edith Vliet, 30, 31,
32
LaGrandeur, Robin, 31
LaGrandeurs Crossing, 28
Lailey, Michael and/or Evelyn Annand, 61
Lake District of England, 153
Lang, Robert, 15, 16, 23, 132
Leigh, Kay McRae, 82, 164
Leskosky family, 82
Liddell, Hern, 82
Lindsay, W., 148
Link, Albert, 62
Link, Dave and/or Marjorie Clemens, 94
Link, Fred and/or Anne Harley, 94, 133
Link, William, 92, 94, 133
Liverpool, Eng., 139
Livingstone Range, 21
Lone Man, 97
Lund, Fred and/or Anna Hagblad, 81
Lund, Gunnar, 81
Lund, Indgred, 81
Lundbreck Falls, 34
Macleod, NWT/AB, 12, 24, 28, 29, 98, 165
Manitoulin Island, ON, 142
MAP 1 Trails/Creeks/Rivers of Extreme
Southwest Corner Alberta circa 1910, 9
MAP 2 Quarter Section Homesteads in
Beaver (Mines) Creek Valley and
Gladstone Valley, circa 1910, 45
MAP 3 Village of Beaver Mines, circa, 1910-
1950, 83
MAP 4 Village of Mountain Mill, circa 1870
to 1976, 95
MAP 5 1906, Route of Mitchell Family by
covered wagon from Idaho to Gladstone
Valley, AB, 125
MAP 6 1862-1867, Tyson Family Gold
Mining in Australia, 138

MAP 7 1867-1874, Tyson Family-Gold Mining in New Zealand, 139
McClelland, Douglas and/or Leona Gingras, 93
McClelland, Elva Ballantyne, 60
McDonald, Malcolm and Edna Mitchell, 94
McDowall, Archie, 19, 77, 78
McDowall, Douglas, 77
McDowall, Elsie, 19, 77
McDowall, Hector and/or Lenora Truitt, 77, 133
McDowall, Ken and/or Ina Kokkila, 77, 78, 82
McDowall, Leslie, 19, 77
McDowall, Malcolm, 77
McDowall, Marjorie, 19, 77
McDowall, Mary Lou, 77, 78
McDowall, Neil, 77
McDowall, Roy, 77
McDowall, W. D. and/or Emma Price, 57, 76, 77, 78
McGlenning, Hector, 155, 157, 163
McGlenning, John and Mrs., 163
McKenzie, Bert, 148
McLaren Ranch, 94, 131
McLaughlin, Judge and/or Rosalie Biron, 91
McLean, Rev. John, 146
McRae, Malcolm and/or Marietta Irwin, 82, 84, 147, 162, 164
McVicar, Samuel and/or Gertrude, 94
McWhirter, Bill and/or Frances Riviere, 98, 99, 101, 102, 103, 104
McWhirter, Jim and/or Frances Dennis, 164
Medicine Hat, NWT/AB, 157, 165
medicine man, 108, 109
Melbourne, Australia, 139, 141
Meridian, ID, 119, 121, 122, 123
Methodist missionaries, 146
Mill Creek Valley, 94
Mitchell, Charles and/or Mary Ellen Buchanan, 19, 44, 122, 123, 130, 131
Mitchell, Dave and/or Glendora, 19, 66
Mitchell, Jack, 118, 122, 123, 128
Mitchell, W. J. A. and/or Aravella Piper, 52, 81, 118, 119, 121, 122, 123, 124, 126, 128, 133
Montana, USA, 124
Morrison, Mr. and/or Mrs., 94
Mount Gladstone, 100

Mount Kilimanjaro, 32
Mount McAlpine, 21
Mountain Mill, 88, 133
Mountain Mill Church, 61, 77, 94, 115
Mountain Mill post office, 123
Mountain Mill Trestle, 94
Mowat, A. N., 17
Moyie City, BC, 38
Munro, Brent, 5
Newman, Gus, 146
Newton, Thomas and/or Sophia Spark, 145, 146
North Saskatchewan River, 99
Northwest Mounted Police, 98, 100, 102
O'Neill, Archbishop Michael, 25
O'Neill, Peter and/or Maude Vroom, 6, 23, 24, 25
packhorse, 91
packtrain, mules, 118
Pattons Lake, BC, 40
Peigan Indian Reserve (Piikani Nation), 15, 32, 52
Peters, Miles and/or Mae Vroom, 19, 66
Picard & Gamache Blacksmith Shop, 57, 82
Pincher Creek cemetery, 37
Pincher Creek Citizens' (Oddfellow's) Band, 148
Pincher Creek Echo, 16, 30, 75, 76, 96, 132
Pincher Creek livery stable, 55
Pincher Creek Ranch, 14
Pincher Creek, NWT/AB, 165
Pincher Station, AB, 33, 34
pine hutch, Canadiana, 157
Pleasant Valley, AB, 67, 68
poke bonnet, 123
Pommier, Lorraine, 100
Prozak, Mike, 82
Pull Wyke Cottage, 141
Quebec City, PQ, 142
railway trestle, wooden, 27, 34, 69, 74, 92, 94, 115
railway trestle, wooden, bronc on a, 92
Red River wagon, 145
Richardson, Charles, 126
Riviere, Bob and/or Mary Burns, 16, 100, 103
Riviere, Emilie (Mimi), 100
Riviere, George and/or Maggie Clark, 16, 102, 103, 104

Riviere, Henri and/or Nellie Gladstone, 13, 16, 17, 51, 93, 96, 98, 100, 101, 102, 103
Riviere, Henry, 16, 98, 100
Riviere, James and/or Gaye, 98, 103
Riviere, Jessey Nellie "Babe", 80, 98, 100
Riviere, John, 16
Riviere, Mary, 16, 100
Robbins, Gerald and/or Adeline Cyr, 66
Rocky Mountains, the, 11, 15, 21, 24, 33, 34, 35, 67, 82, 90, 121, 126, 147, 165
Rodeo Hall of Fame, 31
Roodee Ranch, 94, 113, 115, 116
Round Mountain, 21
Ruby Creek, 11, 66, 91
Russell, Harold and/or Lorenda, 84
Satterthwaite, Jack and/or Margaret Elizabeth Tyson, 140, 141, 143
Satterthwaite, Ted and/or Emma Pearson, 154
Schoening, Johanna Larson, 144
School, Archie Vroom, 43, 53, 60, 69, 126, 127
School, Archie Vroom, quarter, NW ¼-35-5-2-W5th, 44
School, Beaver Mines, 82, 94
School, Chicken Coop, 82
School, Coalfields, 18, 74, 77, 82, 94, 123, 128
School, Fishburn, 13, 62
School, Gladstone Valley, 43, 61, 163
School, Robert Kerr, 13
School, Spread Eagle, 147
School, Utopia, 13, 155, 163
Scobie, Andrew and/or Mrs., 57, 82
sewing machine, 62, 63
Sheffield, ON, 144
Shell Waterton News, 96
Siksika (Blackfoot) Indian Reserve, 107, 108, 109, 110
Smith, Babe and/or Iona Truitt, 81
Smith, George, 123, 126
Smithies, Warren, 152
Smithies, Wayne and/or Edi-May Annand, 61, 152, 157
Snake River, ID, 124
Spence, Gerry, 99
Spence, Joe, 99
Spence, Mrs. Margarette Louise, 18, 99

Spread Eagle Mountain, 33, 162
St Michael's, Alaska,, 107
St. Anthony's Catholic Church, 82
St. Edwards Anglican Church, 48
St. Mary's Anglican Church, Ambleside, Eng., 152
St. Michael's School, 132
St. Michael's, Alaska, 106
Stuckey, Aylmer and Gracie, 161
Summit Hotel, 36
Sun Dance, 10, 108, 110
Sunny Vale Ranche, 5, 8, 42, 49, 65, 72, 73, 74, 91
Table Mountain, 18, 21, 42, 65, 165
Targhee Pass, ID/MT, 124
Taylor, Billie, 148
Telegraph Creek, BC, 106, 116
Thomas, Bob, 13, 15
Toronto, ON, 144
Torrid Zone, 140
Tourond, Bob and/or Hazel Truitt, 132
Tourond, Elmira, 132
Tourond, George, 133
Tourond, William and/or Helen Borze, 132, 133
Tourond, Zilda, 132
tricycles, 113
Truit, Dewey, 68
Truitt, Adam and/or Hazel Anderson, 43, 52, 67, 81, 92, 127
Truitt, Alice, 124
Truitt, Dewey, 81
Truitt, Doc, 81
Truitt, Harry and/or Bessie Mitchell, 19, 43, 81, 119, 121, 123, 124, 126, 127, 129, 131, 132, 133
Truitt, John and/or Melcina Newton, 43, 67, 68, 81, 133
Truitt, John Jr., 124
Truitt, Lawrence, 19, 67, 68, 81
Truitt, Ruby, 124
Truitt, Sarah, 124
Truitt, Vera, 133
turkey train, 7, 157
Turtle Mountain, 35
Twin Butte Community Hall, 150
Twin Butte, AB, 13, 17, 21, 79, 96, 102, 145, 147

two-storey log cabin, 42, 48, 56, 68, 72, 133
Tyson Lake, ON, 142
Tyson, Annie, 136, 143, 147
Tyson, Edward, Killarney, ON, 141
Tyson, Elizabeth, 136
Tyson, Elizabeth, dau. Wilson and Jane, 141
Tyson, George and/or E. Mary Brotherston, 140, 143, 144, 147, 151, 152, 156, 158, 159, 162
Tyson, George and/or Shirley, 158
Tyson, Isaac, 141
Tyson, John Powley, 136, 140, 143
Tyson, John, Killarney, ON, 141
Tyson, John, USA, 141
Tyson, Joseph, Ambleside, 143
Tyson, Joseph, born, Australia, 135, 140, 143
Tyson, Joseph, born, Australia, 136
Tyson, Myles and/or Catherine Solomon, 141
Tyson, Ralph and/or Linda, 104
Tyson, Thomas Banks, 136, 140, 142, 143, 144, 145, 147, 148
Tyson, Thomas I and/or Hannah Stables, 135
Tyson, Thomas II and/or Margaret Banks, 135, 139, 140, 143
Tyson, Thomas W., 141
Tyson, Tommy and/or Mary Laidlaw, 153, 158
Tyson, William, Killarney, ON, 141
Tyson, Wilson and/or Jane Barbour, 136, 141
Tyson, Wm. Dawes and/or Lida Jane Ivey, 135, 137, 140, 144
United Empire Loyalists (UELs), 5, 48, 165
Upton, J. E. (Ed), 148
Upton, Phil and/or Mary "Dot" Lucas, 13
Victoria Peak, 67, 162
Vroom, Alfred and/or Margaret Coulter, 12, 19, 55, 76, 90
Vroom, Anna May, 6
Vroom, Archie and/or Alberta Butler, 6, 25, 41, 43, 51, 52, 53, 63, 64, 70, 74, 165
Vroom, Claude and/or Mary McLaren, 6, 25, 42, 165

Vroom, Harold and/or Ruby Mitchell, 19, 66, 118, 122, 123, 124, 126, 132
Vroom, Herbert, 6, 26, 42, 50, 106, 107, 116
Vroom, Isaac, 6
Vroom, Jennie Louise, 6
Vroom, Minnie, 6
Vroom, Nat, 64
Vroom, Oscar and/or Alena Munro, 5, 6, 8, 10, 11, 12, 13, 15, 18, 19, 20, 22, 23, 25, 26, 28, 39, 40, 47, 48, 49, 50, 61, 66, 68, 70, 77, 78, 79, 94, 165
Vroom, Oscar Jr., 19
Vroom, Ralph and/or Mollie Tyson, 12, 61, 88, 90, 93, 94, 96, 126, 132, 152, 154, 157, 158, 164, 165
Vroom, Ralph Voorhees and/or Bessie Newcombe, 6, 23, 24, 26, 37, 41
Vroom, Ralph Voorhees and/or Marie Blanshard, 37
Vroom, Ron, 64
Vroom, Ross, 6, 24, 26
Vroom, Sarah, 6
Vroom, William "Bill", 155
Vroom, William Voorhees and/or Sara Ann Woodman, 5, 6, 24, 26, 48
Wallace, Adam and/or Helen "Nellie" Barclay, 50
Waterton Lakes National Park, AB, 14, 18, 32, 84, 147, 160
Waterton River, AB, 162, 163
Watson, Jim, 148
Watson, SK, 64
Western Coke & Coal Co., 82
White, Alex, 94
Whittaker, Joe, 148
Whittaker, John, 148
wild horses, East Kootenays, BC, 88
Windymere Ranch, 78
Wojtula, Andy, 82
World Champion Bronco Rider, 31
WWI, 19, 75, 76, 116, 151
WWII, 79, 87, 133
Yarrow Creek, AB, 99

ABOUT THE AUTHOR

The VROOMS of the FOOTHILLS: Cowboys & Homesteaders is the second volume of several in a social history series written by Bessie Vroom Ellis. She published her first book, Volume 1 *The VROOMS of the FOOTHILLS: Adventures of My Childhood*, in 2003, and a second revised edition in 2006.

In Volume 1, Bessie Vroom Ellis, herself the daughter and granddaughter of homesteaders, told the story of her happy, adventurous childhood on her parents' ranch in the foothills of southwestern Alberta.

In Volume 2, using over 200 photographs from the treasured albums of the children and grandchildren of homesteaders in the Northwest Territories in the area of Canada that in 1905 became the province of Alberta, Bessie recounts the stories of old time cowboys in the 1880s and 1890s and of the homesteaders who followed the cowboys in the early part of the twentieth century.

Bessie attended one-room country schools for her elementary grades, riding on horseback for a round trip of nearly nine miles each day. She graduated from Pincher Creek High School and attended Calgary Normal School. Bessie taught in a country school near Drumheller, AB, and at Waterton Park School. In Waterton, she met and married a local resident, George Annand Jr. They raised a family of four children, Edith, Evelyn, David and James.

During her more than 20 years in Waterton Park, Bessie wrote feature articles and the column "Wonderful Waterton" for *The Lethbridge Herald*. She also contributed news items to CJOC Radio and CJLH-TV in Lethbridge, and to *The Calgary Herald* and *Calgary Albertan* in Calgary and the *Hungry Horse News in* Columbia Falls, Montana, being active, as well, in the Girl Guides of Canada and the Anglican Church.

After 15 years at home, Bessie returned to her teaching career. She updated her qualifications, through night extension classes, Summer School and day classes. Bessie was awarded a Bachelor of Education degree by the University of Lethbridge and a Master of Education degree by University of Alberta. She then taught in Lethbridge. After her remarriage in 1975, Bessie moved to Regina, SK, and taught there for another 15 years, for a total of over 29 years of service in the teaching profession. At the University of Regina, she earned a post-graduate Diploma in Educational Administration.

During her years in Regina, Bessie travelled extensively in Canada, Europe, Mexico, and the United States. Active in politics, she ran for political office herself and worked to promote the election of more women at the provincial and federal levels. In the early 1980s, the Saskatchewan New Democratic Women (SNDW) established the Bessie Ellis Fund, to assist women running for nomination.

In 1992 Bessie was awarded the Commemorative Medal for the 125 [th] Anniversary of the Confederation Canada, 1867 – 1992, "in recognition of significant contribution to compatriots, community and to Canada." Upon retirement, Bessie returned to her writing.

Printed in the United States
By Bookmasters